Guides to Collection Development for Children and Young Adults

Guides to Collection Development for Children and Young Adults

John T. Gillespie

Ralph J. Folcarelli

1998
Libraries Unlimited, Inc.
Englewood, Colorado

To
Jessica, Carol, and Christopher

Libraries Unlimited, Inc.
P.O. Box 6633
Englewood, CO 80155-6633
1-800-237-6124
www.lu.com

Production Editor: Kevin W. Perizzolo
Copy Editor: D. Aviva Rothschild
Proofreader: Sebastian C. Hayman
Typesetter: Kay Minnis

Library of Congress Cataloging-in-Publication Data

Gillespie, John Thomas, 1928–
    Guides to collection development for children and young adults /
  by John T. Gillespie, Ralph J. Folcarelli.
      x, 191 p. 19x26 cm.
      Includes indexes.
      ISBN 1-56308-532-1
      1. Children--United States--Books and reading--Bibliography.
    2. Teenagers--United States--Books and reading--Bibliography.
    3. Bibliography--Bibliography--Children's literature. 4. Children's
    literature--Bibliography. 5. Bibliography--Bibliography--Young
    adult literature. 6. Young adult literature--Bibliography.
    7. Bibliography--Bibliography--Children's literature, English.
    8. Children's literature, English--Bibliography. 9. Bibliography--
    Bibliography--Young adult literature, English. 10. Young adult
    literature, English--Bibliography. I. Folcarelli, Ralph J.
    II. Title.
Z1037.G495   1998
011.62--dc21   98-12944
                                                              CIP

Contents

Introduction

The expansion of interlibrary loan systems, the development of library networks that share materials, and the increased use of electronic technology (e.g., databases, fax transmission of documents) has brought new meaning to the phrase "library collection development." As a result of these developments, even the smallest elementary school library is able to give its users access to a tremendous number of resources hitherto unavailable. In order to identify and make accessible these resources, bibliographies have become increasingly important in the collections of today's libraries serving children and young adults.

The purpose of this book is to supply information on these bibliographic sources to librarians, other educators, and parents who work with children and young adults. Using these bibliographies will not only help in the process of selecting and acquiring materials for the library collection but will also aid in locating additional items for readers' advisory and interlibrary loan purposes. Additionally, these bibliographies can be used for collection evaluation.

This work is based in part on sections of the authors' *Guides to Library Collection Development* (Libraries Unlimited, 1994). That work cited bibliographies published and reviewed from 1986 through late 1993. In some cases exceptions were made to accommodate useful publications from 1985. The titles in this parent volume that were suitable for inclusion in the present volume because of their scope, content, and recentness were reviewed and updated when necessary. The annotations were revised to reflect the needs of the new audience. To these entries, approximately 300 new entries have been added, reflecting recommended titles published from 1994 through the beginning of 1997 and making a total of over 600 entries. Most of the works included are completely bibliographic in nature. Others had sufficiently valuable and extensive bibliographic content to warrant their inclusion, even though part of their contents was nonbibliographical. This criterion accounts for the inclusion of titles that are not normally classified as bibliographies, such as curriculum guides, teaching manuals, handbooks, subject encyclopedias, and biographical dictionaries.

Guides to Collection Development for Children and Young Adults was written to cover both current titles as well as classic works most often consulted in children's libraries. Purchase availability information is shown (whenever known to the authors) in order to facilitate collection development. As this book is released some titles will be going out-of-print or into newer editions, and the reader is advised to check availability with one of the popular bibliographic databases such as Bowker's *Books in Print*, or Amazon.com, which can often locate out-of-print or hard-to find titles.

The bibliographies were identified by consulting a number of selection and reviewing sources. The most important of these were the periodicals *Booklist*, *Horn Book*, *School Library Journal*, *Library Journal*, *Book Report*, *Voice of Youth Advocates* (VOYA), and *Curriculum Review*. Among the many retrospective sources consulted was the H. W. Wilson Standard Catalog series. Only recommended titles from these sources were considered for inclusion.

This book is organized into five main sections: Periodicals, Sources for Both Children and Young Adults, Sources for Children, Sources for Young Adults, and Sources for Professionals. The Children's and Young Adult Sources sections have many subdivisions by content.

Included in the Young Adult section are bibliographies of adult materials if they contain a substantial number of entries suitable for young adult collections. The Professional Materials section includes bibliographies of materials that would be found in professional collections in libraries and curriculum centers for use by educators and other adults.

The annotations were prepared by consulting and adapting reviews, by using other secondary sources (e.g., publishers' catalogs), or in many cases by personal examination of the titles. Bibliographic material was verified in publishers' catalogs and *Books in Print Plus*. Only titles currently in print were included, with the exception of a few important works that are still readily accessible in library collections.

The annotations are intended to give the reader an indication of the scope of the work, size (often actual number of entries), kinds of material included, purpose, arrangement, nature of entries, indexes, special features, and a recommendation statement. In the interests of brevity, sometimes only the most salient aspects of a work are cited, particularly in very specialized sources.

Preceding each entry is an indication of audience and type of library level:

C: Works containing materials suitable for children's collections (i.e., preschool through grade 6).

Y: Works containing materials suitable for young adult collections (i.e., grades 7 through 12).

A: Material for adults from college age on up.

After each entry subject headings are included for ease of reference to the subject index.

Readers should be aware that titles are listed only once in the text. Books that contain material suitable for more than one age group have been placed in the areas most appropriate to the books' contents. It is essential, therefore, that all sections of this directory, including the subject index, be consulted to obtain complete coverage of materials for a specific age group.

The length of the annotation is not an indication of the importance of the work. However, an asterisk (*) after an audience code signifies a highly recommended title. This recommendation refers only to its use in collection development and not its general importance.

Works cited within annotations are of two types. Those without bibliographic information have individual entries, while those with bibliographic information are cited only for informational purposes. Major series are given separate descriptive entries, but individual titles in these series might have separate entries if they are considered to be of great importance. To facilitate access to the citation, there are two indexes: author-title, and subject.

This guide was intended to be comprehensive. However, to make it a practical one, esoteric and specialized works have been excluded. It is our sincere hope that this volume will be found of value in developing library collections and providing library services that will enrich and enhance the lives of our children and young adults.

I

Periodicals

General

Y*
1. **The ALAN Review**. 1972. 3/yr. $15. Assembly on Literature for Adolescents, National Council of Teachers of English, 1111 Kenyon Rd., Urbana, IL 61801.

This periodical is devoted to an examination of literature for young adults. In each issue there are articles that focus on particular topics explored in YA literature (e.g., divorce, historical novels) as well as many profiles of individual authors and specific aspects of their work. In the center are four pages of pull-out signed reviews of both hardcover and paperback books suitable for readers in junior and senior high grades. Features include "The Library Connection," in which librarian-teacher cooperation is often discussed; "The Publisher Connection"; and "The Membership Connection," in which there is current news about ALAN activities. *YOUNG ADULT LITERATURE (GENERAL)*

C*; Y
2. **Appraisal: Science Books for Young People**. 1967. 4/yr. $44. ($56 Canada). Children's Science Book Review Committee, School of Education, 605 Commonwealth Ave., Boston, MA 02215.

This journal reviews trade books in science and mathematics for children from preschool to high school. There are approximately 90 books reviewed per issue arranged alphabetically by author. For each book there are two reviews of about 15 lines each: one by a librarian and the other by a subject specialist. Each review also contains a rating (E = excellent; VG = very good; G = good; F = fair; U = unsatisfactory; * = qualifications) and an age suitability indication. Each issue also contains a section that updates series by indicating and annotating new books that have been added. There are about 40 of these reviews per issue. The index is cumulated for each year by author, title, and subject. *SCIENCE*

C
3. **Bayviews**. 1990. 13/yr. $30. Association of Children's Librarians of Northern California, Box 12471, Berkeley, CA 94701.

This association of librarians issues this review journal with a Western perspective 13 times a year. Reviews are signed by the participating librarians, and the total number of reviews printed per year now averages about 1,200. There is also an annual selection of the best books of the year printed in a separate list, *The ACL Distinguished Book List*. A single copy is available for $0.75 from the above address. *CHILDREN'S LITERATURE (GENERAL)*

C*; Y
4. **Book Links: Connecting Books, Libraries, and Classrooms**. 1991. 6/yr. $16.95 (U.S. and Canada). American Library Association, 50 E. Huron St., Chicago, IL 60611.

This new magazine offers ideas for stimulating reading and integrating children's books into the school curriculum. Each issue has annotated lists of books on various subjects, places, events, or people plus profiles on individual authors. There are also essays that link together books on similar themes. A two-month calendar at the back lists occasions to use specific types of books. This most attractive, colorful periodical averages 40 pages per issue and is intended for librarians working with children from preschool through the eighth grade. *CHILDREN'S LITERATURE (GENERAL)*

Y*

5. **The Book Report: The Journal for Junior and Senior High School Librarians**. 1982. 5/yr. $39. ($49 Canada). Linworth Publishing, 480 E. Wilson Bridge Rd., Ste. L, Worthington, OH 43085-3963.

This lively periodical is a combination of reviewing journal and a manual on how to bring students and books together. Before the review section are many features that include a section on tips and other bright ideas from readers, material on how to motivate readers and how to teach library skills, a section on the use of computers in libraries, and "Books and Other Things," which gives news on professional books, government documents, pamphlets, and bibliographies. The review section is divided into fiction and nonfiction with many subdivisions by genres and subjects. There are about 120 reviews per issue. Each is about 15 to 20 lines in length and indicates grade levels and if the book is recommended or not. Books specifically for young adults as well as adult books suitable for young adults are included. Reviews are written by practicing librarians. Some software, videos, CD-ROM products, and paperbacks are also included. Black-and-white reproductions of dust jackets are used extensively in the review section. This is an excellent, highly recommended reviewing journal for all librarians working with young adults. It will be particularly useful in high schools.   *YOUNG ADULT LITERATURE (GENERAL)*

C

6. **Bookbird**. 1962. 4/yr. $30. International Board on Books for Young People (IBBY) and the International Institute for Children's Literature and Reading Research, Box 807, Highland Park, IL 60035-0807.

This publication originates in Denmark. In addition to giving news about IBBY and its affiliates, it has numerous articles on children's books. For example, the section on "Books of International Interest" highlights important books in a country-by-country arrangement. Each issue contains profiles of a specific author and illustrator and lists international prize winners. This is a fascinating worldwide view of children's literature.   *CHILDREN'S LITERATURE (GENERAL)*

C*; Y*; A*

7. **Booklist**. 1905. 22/yr $65. ($80 Canada). American Library Association, 50 E. Huron St., Chicago, IL 60611.

One of the oldest and best reviewing journals in America, *Booklist* has received an editorial facelift in recent years that has improved both its appearance and content and made it an even more valuable selection aid for all level of public and school libraries. After the section "Upfront: Advance Reviews," which gives prepublication reviews of important new adult fiction and nonfiction books that are anticipated to be in demand in libraries, there is a section of reviews of adult books, many of which are also recommended for young adults (these are indicated by YA followed by critical comments). In the section "Adult Books for Young Adults," these books are again cited with specific recommendations for YA audiences. There follow sections on books for older readers (grade 7 and up), middle readers (grades 4 through 6), and the young (preschool through grade 3). Each book included has passed a preliminary review for quality before inclusion; those of exceptional value are starred. Reviews are staff-written and are noted for perceptive, incisive comments. The frequent retrospective bibliographies on specific topics are an added bonus. A nonprint review section evaluates videos, filmstrips, audiobooks, and the like at all levels. A closing section, "Reference Books Bulletin," gives thorough, perceptive reviews of reference books and materials. Semiannual and annual indexes are included in the February 15 and August issues respectively. A must for all libraries.   *CHILDREN'S LITERATURE (GENERAL);*
YOUNG ADULT LITERATURE (GENERAL);
ADULT BOOKS AND READING

C

8. **Books for All Kids**. 1990. 4/yr. Books for All Kids, 3336 Aldrich Ave. South, Minneapolis, MN 55408.

This book reviewing journal evaluates children's literature from the standard criteria with special attention paid to racial and ethnic minorities, disabled characters, male and female roles, characters of various ages, gay and lesbian characters, and families of various types. Send a stamped self-addressed envelope and $1 to *Books for All Kids* for more information and sample reviews.
    CHILDREN'S LITERATURE (GENERAL)

C

9. **Canadian Children's Literature**. 1975. 4/yr. $28. University of Guelph, Dept. of English, Guelph, ON N1G 2W1.

This journal is devoted "to the literary analysis, criticism and review of books written for Canadian children." Each of the four quarterly issues has a particular theme or topic covered in a series of bibliographic essays. A book reviewing section follows. Most of the articles are in English, although some are in French. This periodical will be of primary interest in Canadian libraries.

CHILDREN'S LITERATURE (GENERAL); CHILDREN'S LITERATURE, CANADIAN

A

10. **Current Index to Journals in Education, CIJE**. Gale, monthly. $225/yr. ISSN 0011-3565.

This monthly index provides access to the contents of articles appearing in more than 700 periodicals. Available separately are the semiannual cumulations, also priced at $225/yr. There is a special combination subscription price of $430. This index is a valuable extension of the basic material found in Wilson's *Education Index*; however, its price will restrict its purchase to large libraries or district-wide curriculum centers.

EDUCATION

C*; Y

11. **Center for Children's Books. Bulletin**. 1947. 11/yr. $40. University of Illinois at Urbana-Champaign, Graduate Library School, 501 E. Daniel St., Champaign, IL 61820-6211.

This is one of the most respected reviewing sources of books for children and young adults (preschool through junior high). There are approximately 60 reviews per issue. They are usually written by members of the editorial staff, although some are contributed by the specialists that make up the advisory committee. Books are arranged in one alphabet by author's last name. Each review is about 10–15 lines in length and contains a rating: * = special distinction; R = recommended; Ad = additional purchase; M = marginal; NR = not recommended. The reviews are astute and perceptive. At the end of each review are subjects listed that indicate curricular use and developmental values. The last page is an unannotated bibliography of new books, articles, and pamphlets of interest to professionals. There is a combined author and title annual index in the July/August issue. This selection aid is highly recommended, particularly for elementary schools and children's rooms in public libraries.

CHILDREN'S LITERATURE (GENERAL); YOUNG ADULT LITERATURE (GENERAL)

C

12. **Children's Book News**. 1978. 4/yr. $40. Children's Book Centre, 35 Spandina Rd., Toronto, ON M5R 2S9.

Each issue of this quarterly publication contains book announcements of children's books for preschoolers through the ninth grade. Annotations are about 50 words each. Though noncritical in nature, this publication informs librarians about new children's books, particularly those originating in Canada. There is also a news section with material on developments in the field of children's literature in Canada.

CHILDREN'S LITERATURE, CANADIAN; CHILDREN'S LITERATURE (GENERAL)

C

13. **Children's Book Review Service**. 1972. 14/yr. $40. Children's Book Review Service, 220 Berkeley Pl., No. 1D, Brooklyn, NY 11217.

Each of the monthly issues of this reviewing service contains about 60 to 80 reviews written by librarians and teachers. An issue is divided into three parts: one for picture books, one for young readers, and another for older readers (ages 10 to 14). Each review is 50 to 100 words in length. This will be of value in elementary schools and children's rooms in public libraries.

CHILDREN'S LITERATURE (GENERAL)

C*

14. **Children's Magazine Guide**. 1948. 10/yr. $55. ($43 Canada). R. R. Bowker, 121 Chanlon Rd., New Providence, NJ 07974.

This would more accurately be called "Children's Magazine Index" because it supplies an index to the nonfiction contents of about 40 magazines suitable for children from ages 6 through 14, such as

Boy's Life and *Highlights for Children*. Entries are arranged by subject, and there is a separate index to articles in nine professional magazines like *School Library Journal* and *Horn Book*. The August issue contains the annual cumulation. These annual issues, covering 1987 on, are available for $20 each. Though not intended as a buying guide, this guide will nevertheless be helpful in choosing magazines for elementary schools and children's rooms in public libraries. There is a videocassette available for $49 called *How to Use Children's Magazine Guide*.   *PERIODICALS*

Y; A*

15. **Choice: Current Reviews for Academic Libraries**. 1964. 11/yr. $185. Choice, 100 Riverview Center, Middletown, CT 06457.

     In its almost 30 years of existence, this journal has become the premier current book selection aid for college libraries. In its pages are about 6,600 reviews per year arranged into four main sections: reference, the humanities, science and technology, and social and behavioral sciences. Each section contains many subdivisions by subject. Reviews are signed and are usually written by academic subject specialists. Each review is numbered by volume and a consecutive digit within each volume. Some nonprint items are included. Each review is about 15 to 20 lines or about 150 words in length. There is an index in each issue and an annual cumulative index for each volume by author, title, and nonprint item. This is an essential purchase for all academic libraries and large public libraries. Some large high school libraries with advanced courses will find it of value.   *ADULT BOOKS AND READING*

C; Y

16. **Curriculum Review**. 1960. 6/yr. $35. Curriculum Advisory Service, 517 S. Jefferson St., Chicago, IL 60607.

     Each issue begins with several feature articles on a timely curricular topic. Some of these articles also contain useful retrospective bibliographies. There are columns devoted to mentioning new resources and materials for schools and libraries. Some of these columns highlight materials that can be of value in developing library collections, but this periodical is primarily a news magazine of current trends and developments in schools.   *INSTRUCTIONAL MATERIALS*

C*; Y*

17. **Emergency Librarian**. 1973. 5/yr. $49. Dyad Services, Dept. 284, Box 34069, Seattle, WA 98124-1069.

     This Canadian publication offers practical tips on management and many evaluations of materials for school librarians. Each issue has a section on professional reading that contains about 15 reviews. There are also reviews of new paperbacks and recordings for children and young adults, software reviews, a video file, and a feature called "Footnotes" that often lists pamphlets, bibliographies, and useful books. Other features found in most issues are bestseller lists (one for Canada, one for the United States); a section called "Outstanding New Books, K–12," (about 20 books are noted with annotations); and a profile of an outstanding Canadian author or illustrator. This periodical contains many useful hints for successful school library management plus many practical suggestions for effective collection development.   *CHILDREN'S LITERATURE (GENERAL); YOUNG ADULT LITERATURE (GENERAL)*

Y

18. **English Journal**. 1912. 8/yr. $40. National Council of Teachers of English, 1111 Kenyon Rd., Urbana, IL 61801.

     This is essentially a professional journal that discusses issues, trends, and practices in the teaching of English in junior and senior high schools. Although it is not primarily a reviewing journal, there are sections that review professional books, media, and computer software regularly. As well, there are frequent bibliographic articles that survey young adult literature from the perspective of a particular concern, subject, or author.   *YOUNG ADULT LITERATURE (GENERAL)*

C

19. **The Five Owls**. 1986. 6/yr. $20. ($26 Canada). Hawline University, Crossroads Center, 1536 Hewitt Ave., St. Paul, MN 55104.

The purpose of this attractive publication is "to encourage reading and literacy among young people by advocating children's books with integrity: those that can be judged intelligent, beautiful, well-made and worthwhile in relation to books and literature in general." Each issue is 16 pages. In addition to articles about children's literature, an issue contains about 10 to 15 book reviews, tips on collection building, interviews with authors, and ideas on how to use books with young people. This distinguished publication will be of value in children's rooms and large elementary schools.

CHILDREN'S LITERATURE (GENERAL)

C; Y

20. **Free Materials for Schools and Libraries**. 1979. 5/yr. $20. Connaught Education Service, Dept. 349, Box 34069, Seattle, WA 98124.

This publication contains listings of completely free materials available for libraries. Each piece of material has been reviewed professionally for accuracy, suitability, and quality, and each is annotated with descriptive information. Full ordering instructions are given. This title is very helpful in developing vertical files in libraries serving children and young adults.

FREE MATERIALS; VERTICAL FILE MATERIALS

C; Y; A

21. **Freebies**. 1978. 5/yr. $8.95. Freebies Publishing, 1135 Eugenia Pl., Box 5025, Carpinteria, CA 93014.

This bibliography lists approved free and inexpensive material for both children and adults. Included are newsletters, pamphlets, pictures, maps, and catalogs and some nonprint material. All are arranged by subject. Each item is annotated and includes ordering directions. This is a useful tool for building vertical file material.

VERTICAL FILE MATERIALS; FREE MATERIALS

C*; Y

22. **The Horn Book Magazine: About Books for Children and Young Adults**. 1924. 6/yr. $36. Horn Book Magazine, Park Square Bldg., 31 James Ave., Boston, MA 02116.

This is one of the oldest and most prestigious reviewing sources in the field of children's literature. Each issue contains articles about individual authors or illustrators and scholarly essays on topics related to children, their reading and education. The review section is divided by age group. Most of the books are favorably reviewed because they have been screened for quality in advance. A spinoff, *The Horn Book Guide to Children's and Young Adult Books* (2/yr. $35), reviews virtually every trade book published in hardcover for children in the United States. The reviews in *Horn Book* delve into perceptive details that might escape reviewers in other journals. In addition to the regular reviews there are sections on professional news and publications, paperbacks, new editions and reprints, and outstanding paperbacks. Both of these stimulating periodicals are extremely important in children's rooms and elementary school libraries for assuring quality book selection. Because of the highly selective nature of the reviews of young adult books in *Horn Book*, it is of lesser importance in junior high schools.

CHILDREN'S LITERATURE (GENERAL); YOUNG ADULT LITERATURE (GENERAL)

C; Y

23. **Interracial Books for Children Bulletin**. 1966. 8/yr. (four double issues). $18. Council on Interracial Books for Children, 1841 Broadway, New York, NY 10023.

This interesting periodical contains articles on multicultural coverage in children's and young adult books past and present, educational services to these minority groups, and pertinent issues such as bilingual education. An important part of each issue is "Bookshelf," which reviews "books that relate to minority themes." Books are evaluated by members of the minority group depicted. This stimulating periodical should be available in elementary schools and children's collections in public libraries.

MULTICULTURALISM

Y; A

24. **Journal of Adolescent and Adult Literacy**. 1957. 8/yr. $38. International Reading Association, 800 Barksdale Rd., Box 8139, Newark, DE 19714-8139.

This companion to *The Reading Teacher* is a journal for professionals working with adolescent and adult learners. In addition to information on concerns in this area and teaching strategies, the journal has reviews of instructional materials, professional books, books for young adults, tests, and software. There are also sections on current research and on reading supervisors and their interests.

YOUNG ADULT LITERATURE (GENERAL); LITERACY

C; Y

25. **Journal of Youth Services in Libraries**. 1987. 4/yr. $40. ($50 Canada). American Library Association, 50 E. Huron St., Chicago, IL 60611.

This quarterly is the official publication of two divisions of the American Library Association: the Association for Library Service to Children and the Young Adult Services Division. It began in 1942 as *Top of the News* and in 1987 took its present name. Although it contains information on activities and programs of these ALA divisions, it also has articles on working with children and YAs as well as on content analyses of books for these groups and on individual authors and illustrators. Although the journal does not review juvenile books, these articles are often useful in book selection. There are sections on current research, technology, and new professional books.

CHILDREN'S LITERATURE (GENERAL); YOUNG ADULT LITERATURE (GENERAL)

C; Y; A*

26. **Kirkus Reviews**. 1933. 24/yr. $255. Kirkus Service, 200 Park Ave. South, New York, NY 10013.

Noted for its realistic, straightforward reviews, this publication evaluates books months before their actual publishing dates, which allows libraries time to anticipate demand and order in advance accordingly. A loose-leaf format is used for easy filing in binders. Each issue is divided into two parts, one dealing with adult books (there are sections for fiction and nonfiction, each arranged alphabetically by author), and the other arranged the same way for children's and young adult books. Books of unusual merit are given a pointer. These books are highlighted at the beginning of each section. The price will probably restrict this useful selection tool to purchase in medium-sized public libraries and up.

CHILDREN'S LITERATURE (GENERAL);
YOUNG ADULT LITERATURE (GENERAL); ADULT BOOKS AND READING

Y*

27. **KLIATT: Reviews of Selected Current Paperbacks, Audiobooks, and Educational Software**. 1966. 6/yr. $36. KLIATT, 33 Bay State Rd., Wellesley, MA 02181.

This periodical is issued six times a year; each issue contains about 300 to 400 reviews of paperbacks. All types of paperbacks are reviewed: trade and mass market as well as young adult titles and adult titles suitable for young adults. Some of the subject divisions are fiction, literature, biography, education and guidance, social studies, history and geography, science, arts, and recreation. Symbols used in the reviews indicate the suitability of the work from advanced to low reading ability; M means mature contents, and a * signifies a publication of exceptional merit. The reviews are short but give a good indication of both content and quality. There are also reviews of new audiobooks and selected software. This selection aid is highly recommended for both junior and senior high schools and young adult collections in public libraries.

YOUNG ADULT LITERATURE (GENERAL); COMPUTER SOFTWARE; AUDIOBOOKS

C; A

28. **Language Arts**. 1924. 8/yr. $40. National Council of Teachers of English, 1111 Kenyon Rd., Urbana, IL 61801.

This authoritative periodical deals with the teaching of English primarily in the elementary grades (although some of the articles are also pertinent for junior high teachers). The articles deal with composition skills, language, and literature. In the latter area are occasional articles on themes and authors in children's literature. As well, there are selective reviews of children's books and other professional materials. This is a basic title for elementary schools that will also be of some help in collection building. *CHILDREN'S LITERATURE (GENERAL)*

Y*; A*
29. **Library Journal**. 1876. 20/yr. $94.50. Cahners, Box 59690, Boulder, CO 80322.

This is one of the most read and consulted journals in the library world for its articles and special columns as well as its reviews. In the former area, each issue (semimonthly except for January, July, August, and December) has articles on current library conditions and concerns at the public, college, and special library levels. The February 15 and September 15 issues respectively deal with spring and fall book announcements, and the January issue highlights the best books of the year. There are also an annual roundup of the best in science and technology and a buying guide issue. In the regular review section, books are arranged by broad subjects (e.g., arts and humanities), with many subdivisions (e.g., poetry). Reviews are written and signed by practitioners or subject specialists. There are also departments that review magazines, videos, audiocassettes, reference materials, and professional reading. This is a must for all libraries serving an adult population. Also, all but the smallest of senior high schools will find it extremely valuable. *ADULT BOOKS AND READING*

C*
30. **Library Talk: The Magazine for Elementary School Librarians**. 1988. 5/yr. $39. Linworth Publishing, 480 E. Wilson Bridge Rd., Ste. L, Worthington, OH 43085-3963.

This companion to *The Book Report* is aimed at librarians in elementary schools. Each issue contains articles on how to bring children and books together as well as news items and reports on new bibliographies, media, and professional publications. The reviews are grouped under headings like poetry, arts and crafts, nonfiction, reference books and general series books, mysteries (including science fiction and fantasy), general fiction (divided by grade level), easy readers, and folk tales. The reviews in each section are by a single individual. There is a separate annotated section on paperbacks. This attractive magazine is illustrated with many black-and-white dust jacket reproductions. It is of great value in selecting materials in elementary schools and children's rooms in public libraries.

CHILDREN'S LITERATURE (GENERAL)

Y; A
31. **Locus: The Newspaper of the Science Fiction Field**. 1968. 12/yr. $43. Locus Publications, Box 13305, Oakland, CA 94661.

This hugely entertaining magazine for science fiction buffs begins with news items about the world of science fiction publishing, its authors, awards, groups, conventions, and meetings. There is also a series of reviewing columns (usually about six), each by a different reviewer and containing chatty reviews of about six books each. Other sections include short reviews, an article on science fiction around the world, lists of forthcoming books in the United States and Great Britain, an annotated catalog of books and magazines received, and a chart of the month's best sellers. Children's and young adult books are included for review. This is a fine guide to fantasy and science fiction for both acquisition librarians and patrons. *SCIENCE FICTION; FANTASY*

C*; Y*
32. **Media and Methods: Educational Products, Technologies, and Programs for Schools and Universities**. 1964. 5/yr. $29. American Society of Education, 1429 Walnut St., Philadelphia, PA 19102.

This periodical covers various forms of nonprint media and their use in education. Each issue has five or six articles on media projects and products and their management in the classroom and library. As well, there are a department on new products and a review section that includes material on videocassettes, filmstrips, books, databases, software, and videodiscs. There are also lists of catalogs to send for and directories of equipment manufacturers. This journal has proven to be a great asset in libraries from elementary school through junior college levels.

AUDIOVISUAL MATERIALS; INSTRUCTIONAL MATERIALS

C; Y; A

33. **MultiCultural Review** 1992. 4/yr. $59. MultiCultural Review, Greenwood Publishing, 88 Post Rd. West, Box 5007, Westport, CT 06881-5007.

This acquisition journal evaluates multicultural print and nonprint materials suitable for children, young adults, and adults. In addition to penetrating reviews of material associated with American ethnic, racial, and religious experiences, there are several articles per issue that give overviews on various facets of these subjects. The reviews, which are organized by subject areas, cover new books, magazines, and audio/video materials. An effort is made to include material from both mainstream and alternative publishers. In school, public, and academic libraries where this coverage is needed, this is an excellent selection aid. *MULTICULTURALISM*

C; Y; A*

34. **The New York Times Book Review**. 1890. 52/yr. $52. New York Times, 229 W. 43 St., New York, NY 10036.

This standard book reviewing source can be purchased as part of the Sunday edition of *The New York Times* or separately by subscription. The latter method assures the purchaser of receiving it at least a week before it is released generally. This 50- to 60-page publication reviews fiction and nonfiction of general appeal to the American reader. The reviews vary in length from two pages to about 15 to 20 lines in the "In Short" section. The reviewers are identified by name. There are special sections on mystery and detective fiction and on new paperbacks. The bestseller lists (for both hardcover and paperback books) are determined by nationwide surveys of bookstores. Five or six children's books are reviewed per issue, and there are two supplements per year on children's books. Other annual supplements include ones on business books, science and technology, and university press books. This is an essential purchase for libraries at the senior high school level and up. Other noteworthy weekly newspaper book reviewing supplements are *The Los Angeles Times Book Review* (ISSN 0458-3035) and *The Washington Post Book World* (ISSN 0006-7369). *ADULT BOOKS AND READING; CHILDREN'S LITERATURE (GENERAL); YOUNG ADULT LITERATURE (GENERAL)*

C*

35. **Parent's Choice: A Review of Children's Media**. 1978. 4/yr. $20. Parent's Choice Foundation, Box 185, Waban, MA 02168.

This tabloid-sized newspaper reviews books, television, movies, home videos, recordings, toys, games, computer programs, and rock 'n' roll for children up to about age 12. The articles are both informative and entertaining. They try to represent a child's point of view and interests. Of particular value is the once-per-year Awards Issue, which lists and annotates the best in toys, picture books, movies, story books, rock 'n' roll, audio recordings, videos, television, magazines, computer programs, paperbacks, and video games. This is an excellent selection aid for librarians as well as parents. *INSTRUCTIONAL MATERIALS; CHILDREN'S LITERATURE (GENERAL)*

C

36. **Perspectives: Choosing and Using Books for the Classroom**. 1990. 5/yr. $24.95. Christopher Gorden Publishers, 480 Washington St., Norwood, MA 02062.

This is a relatively new addition to the growing number of reviewing sources for children's literature. Written from the standpoint of the classroom teacher, this periodical stresses literary values in books for children and how these books can be used creatively in the classroom. Included are fiction, nonfiction, and general works of literature including books of poetry. *CHILDREN'S LITERATURE (GENERAL)*

C

37. **The Reading Teacher**. 1947. 9/yr. $41. International Reading Association, 800 Barksdale Rd., Box 8137, Newark, DE 19714.

This periodical deals with various aspects of reading instruction at the elementary school level. Many of the articles deal with trends and issues affecting the teaching of reading; others focus on a particular theme or genre in children's literature. The latter articles often contain good bibliographies for collection development. A regular feature is "Children's Books," a bibliographic essay on a special theme that can cite as many as 50 to 60 individual titles. There are also reviews of professional books. This useful tool for elementary school teachers can also be used by librarians for background information on children's literature.   *CHILDREN'S LITERATURE (GENERAL)*

C*; Y*
38. **School Library Journal**. 1954. 12/yr. $79.50. School Library Journal, Box 57619, Boulder, CO 80322.

This is an excellent all-purpose magazine for school librarians and public librarians who work with children and young adults. The first sections are devoted to features and articles that deal with various aspects of school and public services to young people. There are also departments on recent news, a calendar of events, and similar updates. The sections devoted to reviews represent about two-thirds of the text. First are audiovisual reviews that cover such media as films and videos, filmstrips, and recordings with a separate section on computer software. The book reviews are divided into four areas: preschool and primary, grades 3–6, junior high and up, and adult books for young adults. These reviews total about 4,200 items per year (3,200 are books) and are written chiefly by practitioners. Both recommended and not recommended titles are included. Reviews are signed and indicate grade level suitability. Books of unusual merit are starred. Each December issue contains a list of the best books of the year as chosen by the editors. This issue also contains the annual index by author and title and an annual list of the best reference books of the year. This publication is a must for all library collections involved with children and young adults.
CHILDREN'S LITERATURE (GENERAL); YOUNG ADULT LITERATURE (GENERAL)

C; A
39. **Science and Children**. 1963. 8/yr. $52. National Science Teachers Association, 1840 Wilson Blvd., Arlington, VA 22201.

This is a magazine about the teaching of science in elementary school with some material for junior high grades. Articles deal with concerns and problems in instruction in science classrooms, with many ideas for new approaches and improvements. Although this is not primarily a selection tool, there are some reviews of books, curriculum materials, and software for collection building.   *SCIENCE*

C*; Y*; A*
40. **Science Books and Films**. 1965. 5/yr. $20. American Association for the Advancement of Science, 1333 H St., NW, Washington, DC 20005.

This excellent reviewing source for science materials for students from the elementary grades through college gives coverage to books, films, and filmstrips on the life sciences, physical sciences, social sciences, and mathematics. College texts are included but not texts for grades K through 12. The reviews are arranged by Dewey Decimal Class numbers with author, title, and subject indexes. The reviews are astute, practical, and from the scientist's point of view. Levels of difficulty are noted, and each book is given one of four possible overall ratings from "not recommended" to "highly recommended." This is an excellent reviewing source for work with all levels of students. The latest compilation of reviews excerpted from this publication is *Science Books and Films' Best Books for Children, 1992-95* (1996).   *SCIENCE; AUDIOVISUAL MATERIALS*

Y; A
41. **Science Teacher**. 1934. 9/yr. $52. National Science Teachers Association, 1840 Wilson Blvd., Arlington, VA 22201.

Like its companion periodical, *Science and Children*, this is an official publication of the National Science Teachers Association and therefore includes association news. The emphasis in the articles is on teaching science at the secondary school level. Although it is not intended as a major selection aid, the journal has some reviews of books, professional materials, and software.   *SCIENCE*

C; Y; A
42. **Social Education**. 1937. 7/yr. $59. National Council for the Social Studies, 3501 Newark St. NW, Washington, DC 20016.

This is the official publication of the National Council for the Social Studies. It concentrates on articles about teaching various topics in social studies. Many of these articles contain bibliographies for both students and teachers. Of particular importance is a feature of the May/June issue: the annual list of "Notable Children's Trade Books in the Field of Social Studies" (see separate entry). The section called "Resources" also includes articles, many of which are bibliographies of educational materials on specific subjects. Most of the material in this periodical is directed to elementary and junior high schools.
SOCIAL STUDIES

Y; A
43. **U.S. Government Subscriptions**. 4/yr. Free. Superintendent of Documents, U.S. Government Printing Office, Washington, DC 20402.

This extremely valuable work is one of the *Subject Bibliographies* available free from the Superintendent of Documents. It lists, with annotations and ordering information, key periodicals published by various government agencies. The items are arranged by title, and there is an agency index with a list under each entry of the periodicals currently available. This is a very useful buying guide for secondary school and public libraries. *PERIODICALS; UNITED STATES—GOVERNMENT DOCUMENTS*

Y*; A*
44. **Vertical File Index**. 1932. 11/yr. $50. H. W. Wilson, 950 University Ave., Bronx, NY 10452.

Through the years, this publication has become a mainstay for building vertical files. It is a subject index to inexpensive pamphlets and paperbacks that covers selected government publications, charts, posters and maps, art exhibition catalogs, and selected university publications. Examples of the topics covered are energy, taxes, hobbies, consumer issues, and nutrition. Entries give prices and ordering information. Each issue contains a title index, and there is a semiannual cumulated subject index.
VERTICAL FILE MATERIALS; FREE MATERIALS

C; Y*
45. **VOYA: Voice of Youth Advocates**. 1978. 6/yr. $38.50. VOYA, 4720 Boston Way, Ste. A., Latham, MD 20706.

No other publication for teachers and librarians so accurately conveys the needs, concerns, and attitudes of young adults as VOYA. Each issue has four or five interesting, sometimes controversial articles on young adult reading and recreational interests, important authors, techniques for bringing adolescents and books together, or bibliographies on specific topics. The reviews section (more than two-thirds of each issue) is divided into various topics: audiovisual (mostly films and videocassettes), fiction, science fiction/fantasy/horror (a particularly strong area), nonfiction, professional, reference, and reprints. Book reviews are written and signed by practicing librarians and are uniquely coded for the book's quality (one to five Qs) and potential popularity (one to five Ps). Although the emphasis is on material for junior and senior high schools, there also are reviews of books aimed at a middle school audience. Each issue has a title index. This lively, provocative publication deserves a place in all junior and senior high schools and young adult departments in public libraries, where it will be an excellent aid for collection building. *YOUNG ADULT LITERATURE (GENERAL); INSTRUCTIONAL MATERIALS*

Nonprint

C
46. **Children's Video Report**. 1985. 8/yr. $60. 370 Court St., No. 76, Brooklyn, NY 11231.

This is a comprehensive guide to videos for children. An average issue is about eight pages in length and contains several short reviews and five or six major reviews of about 250 words each. The reviewers are professionals in child development and media evaluation. Issues also contain ideas for video programming and related activities for young people. This title will be of value for parents and for librarians in medium to large public libraries and school district professional collections.
VIDEOCASSETTES

A

47. **Database: The Magazine of Database Reference and Review**. 1978. 6/yr. $110. Online, Inc., 462 Danbury Rd., Wilton CT 06897.

This quality journal, a companion to *Online*, reviews databases and has review articles on various subjects as they are handled in different databases. For example, an August 1991 article surveyed environmental information as covered in approximately 50 different databases. There is also news about new databases and services in each issue. This title will be of value chiefly in academic libraries or in very large curriculum centers. *DATABASES*

C; Y; A

48. **Electronic Learning**. 1981. 8/yr. $19.95. Scholastic, 555 Broadway, New York, NY 10012.

Intended for elementary, junior, and senior high school teachers, this periodical contains articles of interest to all teachers plus reviews of various software programs. A buyers' guide helps readers make decisions concerning software and other educational materials. Very practical and interesting. *INSTRUCTIONAL MATERIALS; COMPUTER SOFTWARE*

Y; A

49. **INFOWORLD: The PC News Weekly**. 1979. 52/yr. $145. INFOWORLD Publications, 155 Boret Rd., Ste. 800, San Mateo, CA 94402.

This weekly tabloid covers microcomputers and news about them. In addition to articles on trends, new products, and various applications of existing software, the periodical has reviews of new hardware and software. Another popular magazine that covers similar territory is *PC World* (12/yr. $29.90. PCW Communications, 501 Second St., Ste. 600, San Francisco, CA 94107). *COMPUTERS; COMPUTER SOFTWARE*

C; Y; A

50. **KIDSNET Media Guide**. 12/yr. $265. KIDSNET, 6856 Eastern Ave., NW, Ste. 208, Washington, DC 20012.

This newsletter covers all aspects of the mass media aimed at children. It is a guide to radio and television programs and material on other media. It also surveys media offerings in relation to school curricula and identifies prime-time family programming devoted to literature, social issues, history, and culture. A fascinating but unfortunately expensive publication, KIDSNET also prepares study guides that are available free. Send for a brochure. *RADIO; TELEVISION; MASS MEDIA*

C; Y; A

51. **Learning and Leading with Technology**. 1979. 8/yr. $61. International Society for Technology in Education, University of Oregon, 1787 Agate St., Eugene, OR 97403-9905.

Though this is not exclusively a reviewing journal, it does include lists of software useful in schools plus a few reviews. However, most of the articles deal with how to teach computer use and how to use computers in teaching. This periodical was formerly *The Computing Teacher*. Somewhat similar in scope and number of reviews included is *Computers in the Schools* (1984. 4/yr. $40. Haworth Press, 10 Alice St., Binghamton, NY 13904). These are important professional journals but of limited value in the selection process. See also *Technology and Learning*. *COMPUTERS; COMPUTER SOFTWARE*

A

52. **Library Software Review**. 1981. 6/yr. $170. Sage Publications, 2455 Teller Rd., Thousand Oaks, CA 91320.

This periodical was formerly named *Software Review*. Each issue usually contains two or three general articles on software and its use in libraries, and a section, "In the Literature," that consists of abstracts of articles on these subjects. The greater part of the magazine, however, is devoted to in-depth reviews of software products. There are eight to ten reviews per issue, each averaging three to six pages in length. In addition to many illustrations of Windows, the reviews include material on functions, features, content, ease of learning and use, documentation and support, and recommendations. There is also a book review section. This authoritative journal will be of value in large library systems and curriculum centers. *COMPUTER SOFTWARE*

Y; A

53. **Online: The Magazine of Online Information Systems**. 1977. 6/yr. $110. Online, Inc., 462 Danbury Rd., Wilton, CT 06897.

This practical magazine has articles on how to improve online searches, new technologies, microcomputer applications, and news of developments in the worlds of online and CD-ROM information. In addition to these general articles, each issue has a section called "Reviews/Product Tests" that reviews software, online sources, and books pertinent to the online industry and profession. This section always has a "Software Pick of the Month." This title will be of value in academic and large public libraries and very large curriculum centers.   *COMPUTER SOFTWARE; ONLINE DATABASES*

C; Y

54. **Software and Networks for Learning**. 1972. 9/yr. $65. Sterling Harbor Press, PO Box 3894, Santa Barbara, CA 93130.

This newsletter, formerly called *EPIEGRAM*, contains information related to curriculum and instruction, but primarily it evaluates educational products and equipment. It is a valuable asset to district-wide school collections that need guidance in buying expensive curriculum-related items.
INSTRUCTIONAL MATERIALS;
EDUCATION EQUIPMENT AND SUPPLIES; COMPUTER SOFTWARE

C*; Y*

55. **Technology and Learning**. 1980. 8/yr. $24. Peter Li, Inc., 330 Progress Rd., Dayton, OH 45449.

This periodical was formerly known as *Classroom Computer Learning* and before that as *Classroom Computer News*. As its old names would suggest, the emphasis in this periodical is on using computers in education, although other media like videodiscs are given coverage. There are many practical articles plus news items about new products, software developments, conferences, meetings, and other educational activities. There are four very thorough reviews of software products per issue plus other material on texts, catalogs, and periodicals. Of great importance to schools are the annual software awards in which the best educational software is highlighted. The top five titles are featured, and others are arranged by subject areas like science and social studies. About 50 titles are so honored each year. This periodical is valuable in both elementary and high schools.
COMPUTER SOFTWARE; INSTRUCTIONAL MATERIALS

C; Y; A

56. **Video Librarian**. 1986. 6/yr. $47 ($52 Canada). Video Librarian, Box 2725, Bremerton, WA 98310.

This 10-page magazine opens with introductory material on practical advice about videos, but its heart is the approximately 50 reviews per issue (written chiefly by the editor) of new videocassettes. The reviews are arranged into four sections: children's, documentaries, how-to, and miscellaneous. The annotations are both descriptive and critical. Each video is rated by a star system from one (poor) to four (excellent). Especially fine products also receive the Editor's Choice honor. Availability, addresses, length, price, and producers are given for each video. Libraries anxious to build quality video collections will find this publication useful.   *VIDEOCASSETTES*

Y; A

57. **Wired Librarian's Newsletter**. 1983. irregular. $15. Eric Anderson, 292 Hammerton Rd., Jackson, OH 45640.

This lively newsletter discusses the use of computer hardware and software in libraries and contains frank and perceptive reviews of these types of products. There are also book reviews of professional materials.   *COMPUTERS; COMPUTER SOFTWARE*

II

Sources for Both Children and Young Adults

General and Miscellaneous

C; Y*

58. **Best Books for Junior High Readers**. By John T. Gillespie. Bowker, 1991. 567p. $55. 0-8352-3020-1.

Gillespie, a former junior high school librarian, professor of library science, and noted authority on young adult literature, has edited this as well as *Best Books for Children* and *Best Books for Senior High Readers*. This important bibliography in his series lists almost 7,000 titles for young people, grades 7 through 9 (ages 12–15). Titles are arranged by broad subject areas—curriculum-oriented for nonfiction and interest categories for fiction. Each entry includes full bibliographic information and a brief descriptive annotation. All titles are recommended in at least two reviewing sources. Author, title, and subject/grade level indexes add to the value of this highly recommended tool. This is a basic reading guidance and collection development source for all libraries working with young people. Continued in *Best Books for Young Adult Readers* (Bowker, 1997). *YOUNG ADULT LITERATURE (GENERAL)*

C; A

59. **Books to Build On: A Grade-by-Grade Resources Guide for Parents and Teachers**. By John Holdren and E. D. Hirsch. Delta/Dell, 1996. 361p. $10.95 pap. 0-385-31640-2.

This useful bibliography will be helpful for teachers, librarians, and parents in giving reading guidance. In libraries it can also serve as a collection building aid. It is divided into six main curriculum areas: language arts, world history and geography, American history and geography, visual arts, music, and science and mathematics.

Each is subdivided by grade levels (K–12) and smaller subjects. Both print and nonprint materials, such as software and recordings, are included and briefly annotated. Highly recommended items are indicated; however, there is no specific indication of reading levels. There are a combined author, title, and subject index and introductory material on the application of the Core Knowledge concept to the school curriculum. *CHILDREN'S LITERATURE (GENERAL); YOUNG ADULT LITERATURE (GENERAL)*

C; Y

60. **Canadian Books for Young People. Livres Canadiens pour la Jeunesse**. 5th ed. By Andre Gagnon and Ann Gagnon. University of Toronto Press, 1995. 186p. $18.95 pap.

This update of the 1988 edition includes more than 2,500 titles in two sections, English and French. Each section is arranged by subjects, such as picture books, fiction, and science, and covers material from preschool through senior high school. Age levels are assigned and brief annotations are given. There are author, title, and illustrator indexes plus information on awards and prizes. This work will be extremely valuable in Canadian schools and libraries.

CHILDREN'S LITERATURE, CANADIAN; YOUNG ADULT LITERATURE, CANADIAN; CANADA

C; Y; A

61. **Censorship and Selection: Issues and Answers for Schools**. rev. ed. By Henry F. Reichman. American Library Association, 1993. 172p. OP. 0-8389-0620-6.

This is not a bibliography; however, it gives much important information about selection and censorship in school libraries. Issues surrounding challenged books are explored; selection policies and procedures are defined; and actual cases are outlined. Advice on how to handle censorship problems is given. Appendixes include important documents (e.g., School Library Bill of Rights), summaries of court cases, and an annotated bibliography. *CENSORSHIP*

C; Y

62. **Children's Books in Print**. Bowker, annual. $155 (1996 ed.). 0-8352-3687-0.

This annual spinoff from *Books in Print* lists by author, title, and illustrator the children's books in print for a given year in the United States. Entries now total more than 90,000 and deal with books for preschoolers through age 18. Full bibliographic information is given plus an indication of grade suitability. Introductory material contains a listing of children's literary awards and their winners for the previous 10 years. A companion annual volume is *Subject Guide to Children's Books in Print* ($155. 0-8352-3686-2 for 1996 volume). Though not collection building tools per se, these bibliographies help determine availability of candidates for purchase. *CHILDREN'S LITERATURE (GENERAL)*

C; Y

63. **The Collection Program in Schools: Concepts, Practices and Information Sources**. 2nd ed. By Phyllis J. Van Orden. Libraries Unlimited, 1995. 376p. $42.50; $32.50 pap. 1-56308-120-2; 1-56308-334-5 pap.

A revision of the 1990 title, this work is divided into three parts. The first discusses theoretical aspects of collection building in school libraries; the second is on general and specific criteria for evaluating various materials; and the third supplies details on administering the program. Of particular value is an appended 28-page annotated list of bibliographic and selection tools. There are also lists of associations and organizations plus reprints of key documents. This is a highly respected textbook on collection development and one that is particularly useful for the beginner. New to this edition are sections on students' intellectual rights, copyright, the impact of telecommunications, and such formats as CD-ROMs, interactive videodiscs, and online databases. *INSTRUCTIONAL MATERIALS*

C; Y

64. **Cooperative Children's Book Center Choices**. By Kathleen T. Horning and others. Cooperative Children's Book Center, annual. $4.65.

This publication lists and annotates about 250 quality books published during a given year as chosen by a group of specialists in the Cooperative Children's Book Center. Titles are grouped under such subjects as history, people and places, and fiction for young readers and for teenagers. Suggested age levels are given. Copies can be obtained by sending a 9x12 SASE and a check for $4.65 payable to Friends of the CCBC, Inc. to Publications, Friends of the CCBC, Box 5288, Madison, WI 53705. *CHILDREN'S LITERATURE (GENERAL); YOUNG ADULT LITERATURE (GENERAL)*

C; Y

65. **Distinguished Books [year]**. By the Association of Children's Librarians of Northern California. ACL. 32p. $2.50.

This annual list of approximately 100 titles is culled from the Association's reviewing journal *BayViews*. A few of the titles are suitable for middle and junior high schools. Back issues of this highly selective list are also available. Send inquiries to ACL, Box 12471, Berkeley, CA 94701. *CHILDREN'S LITERATURE (GENERAL)*

C; Y

66. **El-Hi Textbooks and Serials in Print 1997**. 125th ed. Bowker, 1997. 16,000p. $149. 0-8352-3915-2.

Though this is not an evaluative listing, it does indicate what textbooks and related material are currently in print in the United States. This annual publication (now more than 100 years old!) contains about 75,000 materials from almost 1,000 publishers. The materials are arranged under 21 basic subjects like art, business, and literature, with more than 300 subcategories. Citations include basic bibliographic information plus grade levels and an indication of additional teaching materials. There are author, title, and series indexes; sections on professional books and serials for the educator; and a directory of publishers. This is a valuable bibliographic guide in school libraries, but its price probably dictates that it can only be purchased for district-wide collections.   *TEXTBOOKS; PERIODICALS*

C; Y

67.   **Focus on Books**. Library Services Department, Los Angeles Unified School District, 1995. 3 vols. $35/vol.

Each year more than 7,000 books for children and young adults are evaluated by the Library Services Department of the Los Angeles Public Schools. Their cumulated reviews are published in three bibliographies: *Focus on Books, Elementary* (Grades K–6); *Focus on Books, Secondary* (Grades 6–12); and *Focus on Books, Spanish*. Books are designated as excellent, very good, or good. Each entry has an annotation and cataloging information. Indexes are by author, title, and subject. Copies can be ordered for $35 each from Ms. Bonnie O'Brian, Supervisor of Library Services, Los Angeles Unified School District, Library Services, Room 171, 1320 W. Third St., Los Angeles, CA 90017.
CHILDREN'S LITERATURE (GENERAL);
YOUNG ADULT LITERATURE (GENERAL); SPANISH LITERATURE

C; Y; A

68.   **Guides to Library Collection Development**. By John T. Gillespie and Ralph J. Folcarelli. Libraries Unlimited, 1994. 441p. $59. 1-56308-173-3.

Intended to enhance collection development in school, public, and college libraries, this volume lists more than 1,600 bibliographies that can be used in selecting materials for various kinds of libraries. It is divided into three major parts: "Periodicals and Serials," "Children's and Young Adult Sources," and "Adult Sources." In each section there are subdivisions by subject. Entries are confined to works published roughly from 1985 through 1995. Each entry contains symbols to indicate age level, complete bibliographic information, a descriptive annotation, and subject headings. There are author, title, and subject indexes. All the bibliographies suitable for use with children and young adults have been collected, edited, and updated for this spinoff volume, *Guides to Library Collection Development for Children and Young Adults*.   *BIBLIOGRAPHIES*

C

69.   **Hit List: Frequently Challenged Books for Children**. By Donna Reidy Pistolis. American Library Association, 1996. 61p. $22 pap. 0-8389-3458-7.

Y

70.   **Hit List: Frequently Challenged Books for Young Adults**. American Library Association, 1996. 63p. $22. 0-8389-3459-5.

These two paperbacks give background information on children's and young adult books that are frequently challenged by censors. The children's list centers on 23 books, like Maurice Sendak's *In the Night Kitchen* and Lois Lowry's *The Giver*. For each are given a lengthy annotation; examples of challenges; citations of reviews, articles, and awards; sources about the author; and where the book is recommended. Comparable information is found in the young adult volume, which deals with 26 titles, including John Steinbeck's *Of Mice and Men*, Robert Cormier's *The Chocolate War*, and Nancy Garden's *Annie on My Mind*. Both volumes supply good material on how to combat censorship.   *CENSORSHIP*

C*; Y*

71.   **Magazines for Young People: A Children's Magazine Guide Companion Volume**. 2nd ed. By Bill Katz and Linda Sternberg Katz. Bowker, 1991. $38. 0-8352-3009-0.

Formerly *Magazines for School Libraries*, this new and revised edition changed more than a title that denoted a narrower scope. Also as the subtitle indicates, an attempt was made to avoid a great deal of direct duplication—only about 100 of the 1,300 titles are for young children, preschool through age 14; the remainder include about 900 young adult titles, for 14–18 years of age, and about 200 indicated as professional titles. Magazine titles are arranged alphabetically under 74 specific subject areas that are further subdivided into three groups by level or audience. Typical entries might include founding date, frequency, price, editor, publisher and bibliographic data, other formats (e.g., microforms, online), where indexed, and book reviews. Annotations are both descriptive and evaluative and indicate a possible political leaning. Indexes by title, subject, and level complete this excellent resource. This work is highly recommended for all secondary school libraries and all but the smallest elementary school libraries; it is also an important purchase for all public libraries serving young people.   *PERIODICALS*

C; Y; A

72. **MatchMaker Basic**. Econ-Clad Books, annual. CD-ROM. IBM PC or compatibles. 386SX or higher. $99/yr. with manual.

    This CD-ROM contains thousands of titles of permanent bound paperbacks listed in the American Econ-Clad Service book catalog. An Introduction Guide aids in installing the program as well as in searching for titles by combining title, author, interest and reading level, and subject. The major limitation of this title is that it only contains works currently available through the Econ-Clad Service. Still, the service would be useful as a selection tool for those public or school district libraries building large collections of paperbacks.   *PAPERBACK BOOKS*

C*; Y*

73. **Middle and Junior High School Library Catalog**. 7th ed. Ed. by Juliette Yaakov. H. W. Wilson, 1995. 1,008p. (Standard Catalog Series). $175. 0-8242-0880-3.

    This catalog was begun 30 years ago as the *Junior High School Library Catalog* to provide a basic selection tool for libraries serving young people in grades 7, 8, and 9, or roughly ages 12 to 16. With this edition it was expanded to include materials for grades 5 through 9. It is considered a mainstay for building book collections, and it bridges the gap (with little overlapping) between the equally fine *Children's Catalog* and *Senior High School Library Catalog*. Like previous editions, this highly selective bibliography is divided into three parts. Part 1 is a "Classified Catalog," which is arranged by the Abridged Dewey Decimal Classification for nonfiction and alphabetically by author's or editor's name for fiction and short story titles. Each entry contains full bibliographic and cataloging information plus generous (usually two) excerpts from reviews. Part 2 is an extensive author, title, subject, and analytical index. Part 3 is a directory of publishers and distributors. There are more than 4,200 titles in this edition and about an equal number of analytical entries. Titles were chosen by committees of librarians and include listings of professional tools, like other bibliographies, as well as books for young adults. The purchase price includes four annual supplements (covering 1996-1999), each of which will contain approximately 600 new titles in the same arrangement. This work continues to be extremely useful for building a basic collection for this age group, for evaluating existing collections, and for the preparation of bibliographies.   *CHILDREN'S LITERATURE (GENERAL); YOUNG ADULT LITERATURE (GENERAL)*

C; Y

74. **Select Annual Database: A Computer-Based Selection and Acquisitions Tool**. Select School Library Materials, annual. $70/level.

    This compilation and summary of reviews of curriculum-related materials found in *Booklist, School Library Journal, Bulletin of the Center for Children's Books*, and *Book Report* is available for three different levels: elementary (K–6), middle/junior high (5–9), and senior high (9–12). Each contains records for more than 1,300 items and is available on either an Appleworks or dBase III+ diskette. Both print and nonprint materials are included, but those items not recommended by the reviewers are excluded. A manual accompanying the diskette explains how to generate consideration lists and orders. For each item, standard bibliographic information is given, plus a brief annotation, curriculum-based subjects, and identifiers. Each diskette covers one year of reviews, from the April 1 through the March 15 issues of these periodicals. This service began in 1990. For further information write: Select School Library Materials, Box 2386, Gaithersburg, MD 20886.   *INSTRUCTIONAL MATERIALS*

C; Y; A

75. **Using Government Documents: A How-to-Do-It Manual for School Librarians**. By Melody S. Kelly. Neal-Schuman, 1992. 176p. $32.50. 1-55570-106-X.

The first part of this handy little volume is chock-full of practical tips for ordering and using free and inexpensive U.S. government documents. The main part of the text consists of a listing of recommended documents organized into broad subject (curriculum) areas with recommended grade-level designations. The intended audience is elementary and middle schoolers; however, many of the ideas and manuals apply equally well for higher grade levels. Annotations are provided, as in Ekhaml and Wittig's *U.S. Government Publications for the School Media Center*. However, the clearly divided curriculum areas aid in accessing documents by subject. Also, the Kelly work focuses on a younger level. Most school media centers may want to consider both for beginning and developing a collection of documents.   *UNITED STATES—GOVERNMENT DOCUMENTS*

C; Y; A

76.   **Worth a Thousand Words: An Annotated Guide to Picture Books for Older Readers**. By Bette D. Ammon and Gale W. Sherman. Libraries Unlimited, 1996. 230p. $26.50. 1-56308-390-6.

Based on the premise that picture books aren't just for the very young, the authors have compiled a bibliography of almost 650 picture books deemed useful for older individuals from grade 4 to adulthood. They were selected for their literary as well as artistic quality and because they dealt with themes, issues, or concepts that affect or appeal to older students. The titles are listed alphabetically by author. Each entry has a brief annotation and a symbol designating whether the book is useful for math, history, art, etc. Subject headings are provided. Subject, author/illustrator, and title indexes complete the volume. This interesting bibliography is recommended for all school and public libraries.

PICTURE BOOKS

C; Y

77.   **The Young Reader's Companion**. By Gorton Carruth. Bowker, 1993. 681p. $44. 0-8352-2765-0.

Carruth, a noted reference editor, has produced a literary encyclopedia that does for young people what Benet's *The Reader's Encyclopedia* does for adults. The preface states the purpose very simply: This illustrated A to Z short-entry encyclopedia has as its chief purpose the promotion of reading. This important reference work is designed for teens and preteens from grades 5 through senior high school. There are more than 2,000 entries, including 800 on books, 750 on authors, 280 on historical persons, and 200 on mythological and legendary characters. The book entries cover classics and contemporary titles. Entries are about 200 words in length, and in addition to a summary of each title, they contain bibliographic information and an indication of level—MR for middle reader and YA for young adult. Along with the usual biographical information, the author entries summarize in detail the author's works. The detailed subject index (which is the most useful for reading guidance and selection) groups entries under specific headings such as African Americans, Biography, and Fantasy, with extensive lists of titles under each heading. This work is recommended for all middle school, high school, and public libraries as a reference, reading guidance, and selection tool for students, teachers, and librarians.

CHILDREN'S LITERATURE (GENERAL); YOUNG ADULT LITERATURE (GENERAL)

C*; Y*

78.   **Your Reading: A Booklist for Junior High and Middle School Students**. 10th ed. Ed. by Barbara Samuels and Kylene Beers. National Council of Teachers of English, 1995. 381p. $21.95 pap. 0-8141-5943-5.

This updated list of highly recommended books for middle school/junior high students has been published regularly since 1954. It is compiled by a committee made up of experienced teachers and librarians. The titles selected were all published between 1988 and 1990; because it is not cumulative, earlier editions of *Your Reading* are still useful. Each of the approximately 1,200 entries includes a complete citation and a 25- to 50-word descriptive annotation. Items that have been recommended by other "best books" sources are starred. Books are listed under 24 broad categories and more than 25 subcategories, and then arranged alphabetically by author. Popular series are listed at the end of subject chapters (e.g., Love and Romance). A special section lists the 100 most notable YA books published in the last 25 years. Author, title, and subject indexes are provided. Because this list is highly selective and only includes titles published during a three-year period, it cannot be fairly compared with other retrospective sources. *Your Reading*, as with the other fine reading lists published by the NCTE, is highly recommended for all libraries serving young people.

CHILDREN'S LITERATURE (GENERAL); YOUNG ADULT LITERATURE (GENERAL)

Awards and Prizes

C*; Y

79. Children's Books: Awards and Prizes. Includes Prizes and Awards for Young Adult Books. Children's Book Council, 1993. 404p. $57.50 pap. 0-933633-02-5

This important work has been updated since its inception in 1969. This new edition (the first in six years) contains entries for 191 awards; each entry contains some background information about the award as well as a chronological listing of the winners through 1992. The work is divided into four major sections: U.S. awards selected by adults; U.S. awards selected by young readers; Australian, Canadian, New Zealand, and United Kingdom awards; and selected international and multinational awards. Despite its rather steep price, most libraries that serve children will want to consider purchasing this excellent reference work. *AWARDS AND PRIZES*

C*; Y*

80. The Newbery and Caldecott Awards: A Guide to the Medal and Honor Books. 1997 ed. American Library Association, 1997. 145p. $16. 0-8389-3473-0.

This annual publication lists all Newbery and Caldecott award-winners and runners-up from the inception of the awards (Newbery, 1922; Caldecott, 1938) to 1997. A brief descriptive annotation accompanies each title. Author, illustrator, and title indexes are provided. Obviously, these titles are considered the "cream of the crop" in children's literature and are recommended for all libraries. This handbook provides a great deal of reference information in addition to the complete lists. Every library will want two copies, one for circulating and one for ready-reference at the desk. The book is helpful for reader's advisory and collection development. Also available in quantity are leaflets listing the award-winners for each year. This volume, leaflets, and additional information are available by phoning 1-800-545-2433 or writing to: ALA Order Dept., 50 E. Huron St., Chicago, IL 60611.

AWARDS AND PRIZES; CALDECOTT MEDAL BOOKS; NEWBERY MEDAL BOOKS

C*; Y*

81. The Newbery Companion: Booktalk and Related Materials for Newbery Medal and Honor Books. By John T. Gillespie and Corinne J. Naden. Libraries Unlimited, 1996. 450p. $48. 1-56308-356-6.

Though there are a number of fine works dealing with the Newbery Award books, many also include data on the Caldecott Awards. This well-written volume differs in that it deals exclusively, and in much greater detail, with the Newbery winners and their runners-up. Also, in addition to updating winners and expanding plot summaries, the authors have placed their emphasis on the many ways these special books can be introduced to young people. Following a brief introduction on John Newbery and the medal, the award books are arranged chronologically from 1922 to 1996. Each title includes information under the following headings: Plot Summary, Themes and Subjects, Incidents for Booktalking, Related Titles, About the Book and Author, and Honor Books. Also included are a general bibliography of additional sources and complete author, title, and subject indexes. This work is highly recommended for all libraries that serve children and young adults as a guide to booktalking and other library programming, selection tool, and aid to collection evaluation and development. *NEWBERY MEDAL BOOKS*

Audiovisual Materials

Audio

C; Y; A

82. Audiocassette and Compact Disc Finder. 3rd ed. Ed. by Stephanie Korney. Plexus-NICEM (National Information Center for Educational Media), 1993. 925p. $95. 0-937548-14-6.

This massive yet handy identifying and locational tool contains approximately 40,000 descriptions of audiocassettes and compact discs that focus on the spoken word. Included are educational, documentary, and recreational types. Arranged alphabetically by title, each entry also provides useful information such as running time, format, level, and purchase or rental source. This helpful finding tool is recommended for all libraries developing or maintaining collections of these media, which are growing in popularity. *AUDIOCASSETTES; COMPACT DISCS*

C; Y

83. **Parent's Choice: A Sourcebook of the Very Best Products to Educate, Inform, and Entertain Children of All Ages**. Ed. by Diana Huss Green. Andrews & McMeel, 1993. 208p. $9.95. 0-8362-8036-9.

This work includes books and other sources that recommend the best products for children as determined by the nonprofit Parent's Choice Foundation. The products, for children from infants to young adults, are listed under six categories: toys, books, home videos, audiocassettes, computer programs, and magazines. A descriptive annotation, bibliographic information, price, and age level are indicated for each item listed. A bibliography is appended, and extensive indexes on age, author, producer, company, artist, etc. complete this useful buying guide, which is recommended for all public and school libraries. *AUDIOCASSETTES; COMPUTER SOFTWARE; PERIODICALS; TOYS; VIDEOCASSETTES*

Video and Films

C*; Y*

84. **Best Videos for Children and Young Adults: A Core Collection for Libraries**. By Jennifer Jung Gallant. ABC-Clio, 1990. 185p. $45. 0-87436-561-9.

This recommended list of about 350 nontheatrical videos produced during the past 15 years includes items especially useful for children and young adults from preschool through grade 12. Gallant, who is the AV editor of VOYA, based her selections on content, production quality, and potential use—curricular as well as recreational. All of the selected titles were reviewed favorably. The videos are arranged alphabetically by title, and each entry includes director, producer, distributor, release date, cost, and the like. A brief annotation and suggestions for use and audience level are included. The work is well indexed by subject/title and information on distributors, and video sources are provided. This useful bibliography is a must purchase for all school and public libraries that have or are considering a video collection for children. *VIDEOCASSETTES*

C; Y; A

85. **Bowker's Complete Video Directory, 1995**. Bowker, 1995. 3 vols. $229.95. 0-8352-3586-6.

Video sales, rentals, and public library loans have been increasing dramatically. This revised edition of a very comprehensive directory can be called the "Books in Print" of the video world. More than 107,000 videos are included in this set. Volume 1, "Entertainment," and volumes 2 and 3, "Education/Special Interest," can be purchased separately at $103.45 and $146.95 respectively. The publisher claims that this directory provides "ordering information on more foreign films, Spanish-language films, children's films, silent films, and feature films . . . than anyone else." The set also has many indexes, for title, genre, subject, and more. A similar work is Gale's *Video Sourcebook*, which claims to list more titles but is more expensive. Public libraries developing and maintaining video collections will want one or the other of these sources, but probably not both. School libraries may want to consider purchase at district level. *VIDEOCASSETTES*

C; Y; A

86. **Facets Non-Violent, Non-Sexist Children's Video Guide**. By Virginia A. Boyle. Facets Multimedia; distr. Academy Chicago, 1996. $12.95 pap. 0-89733-420-5.

More than 500 videos suitable for preschoolers through the primary grades are described in this bibliography arranged by title. For each entry, length, age suitability, price, and a descriptive note are supplied. There are subject and age group indexes plus a separate author index for videos based on books. Two other listings available from Facets Video survey adult videos. The first, *Facets That's Entertainment Video Catalog*, covers comedy acts, dance performances, musical theater, play adaptations, and celebrity portraits. The second, *Facets African-American Video Guide*, includes full-length features, historical programs, and documentaries by and about African Americans. *Facets That's*

Entertainment is free but the African American catalog is $10.95. For more information call Facets Video at 1-800-331-6197. *VIDEOCASSETTES*

C; Y; A

87. **Family Video Guide**. By Terry Catchpole and Catherine Catchpole. Williamson Publishing, 1992. 176p. $7.95. 0-913589-64-0.

The Catchpoles have compiled a list of more than 300 films available on video that, in their judgment, are suitable for parents to share with their children. Most of the films were considered nonobjectionable; however, 10 R-rated films are also included for the purposes of family discussion of the "real world." Each film entry contains adequate identifying information for purchase as well as descriptive information. Films are categorized under 15 popular themes, such as race relations. The initial list of 100 titles is deemed suitable for the entire family, regardless of age, and a list of films selected for older children is appended. This inexpensive list is recommended for both public and school libraries. *MOTION PICTURES; VIDEOCASSETTES*

C; Y; A

88. **Film and Video Finder**. 5th ed. National Information Center for Educational Media, 1996. 3 vols. $295.

This huge work now lists and gives information on 92,000 films and videos. Volume 1 allows access to the other two volumes by presenting a subject approach. First there is a subject heading outline and then an extensive subject section, with each film and video listed under subjects by title (with grade level and distributor data). Volume 1 also contains directories to producers and distributors. In volumes 2 and 3, films and videos are listed alphabetically by title. Each listing includes title, edition, physical format, running time, color code, a description of contents, recommended audience or grade level, year of release, and producer or distributor. As a companion paperback volume, NICEM has issued *Index to AV Producers and Distributors* (10th ed. 1996. 350p. $75), which contains a directory of 20,000 producers and distributors of all kinds of nonprint media. Because of their prices and specialized content, these reference works are found only in collections that need extensive material on audiovisual sources. Order from: Plexus Publishing, 143 Old Marlton Pike, Medford, NJ 08055.

MOTION PICTURES; VIDEOCASSETTES

C; Y

89. **Films for Learning, Thinking, and Doing**. By Mary D. Lankford. Libraries Unlimited, 1992. 228p. OP. 0-87287-626-8.

Film titles on such subjects as biography, history, folktales, literature, mythology, science, technology, and guidance are described in this guide that helps teachers and librarians use films effectively and creatively. For each film there are a synopsis, producer's name, format, grade level, classroom activities in a variety of situations, and exercises that can be used to sharpen media skills.

MOTION PICTURES

C; Y

90. **From Page to Screen: Children's and Young Adult Books on Film and Video**. By Joyce Moss and George Wilson. Gale, 1992. 429p. $40. 0-8103-7893-0.

This work covers 750 classic and contemporary works in children's and young adult literature that have been adapted into presentations on about 1,400 films, videos, or laserdiscs. The bibliography is organized alphabetically by the title of the book; some short stories, plays, poems, and folktales are also included. For each title, information is given on the author, publisher, and date, and a brief summary appears. There follows a listing of screen adaptations and, for each of these, data such as title, production information, description of contents, awards, suitability, distributors, price, and format. Appendixes and indexes allow for access to this material by subject, age levels, film titles, distributors, and films for the hearing impaired. An interesting additional feature is that each of the films is rated first by how closely it adheres to the plot and spirit of the original, and second by its overall quality and appeal. Although some of these titles will also be found in *Best Videos for Children and Young Adults* (1990), this listing is unique in its coverage and treatment. It is therefore highly recommended for both children's rooms and school libraries where there is need for this kind of material. *MOTION PICTURES; VIDEOCASSETTES*

C; Y; A
91. The Great Plains National Instructional Television Library (GPN) Catalog. Great Plains National Instructional Television Library, annual. Free.

This annual catalog describes educational products such as videotapes, slides, and videodiscs available to schools (K–12) and colleges. This agency also prepares new and original materials for educational media users. The materials in the catalog are arranged by subject and given lengthy annotations that include running time, price, teachers' guides, and suitability. This listing is updated quarterly with the free GPN Newsletter. Copies of these publications are available from: Great Plains National Instructional Television Library, Box 80669, Lincoln, NE 68501.

VIDEOCASSETTES; SLIDES; VIDEODISCS

C; Y
92. Kids Pick the Best Videos for Kids. By Evan Levine. Citadel Press, 1994. $9.95 pap. 0-8065-1498-1.

Each of the tapes listed in this bibliography is rated twice, first by adult selectors (parents and teachers) and then by young critics (ages 3 to 14) under such criteria as humor, fun factor, social factor, and appropriateness. Particularly interesting are the chapters "Videos Girls Are Especially Crazy About" and "Videos Kids Like but Parents Don't." *VIDEOCASSETTES*

C; Y
93. KidVid: How to Select Kids' Videos for Your Family. By Scott Blakely. HarperCollins, 1995. $10 pap. 0-06-273168-8.

About 1,000 videos are reviewed in this useful bibliography, which is arranged first by age groups and then by category (e.g., music, science/nature, religion). For each entry there is an overall rating using stars, plus comments on educational content, entertainment value, repeatability, and parental cautions. Both fiction and nonfiction films are included. *VIDEOCASSETTES*

C*; Y*
94. Recommended Videos for Schools. Ed. by Tinik I. Roxton and Beth Blenz-Clucas. ABC-Clio, 1992. 184p. $50. 0-87436-688-7.

The focus of this guide is the curriculum rather than entertainment or recreational videos. More than 400 reviews were culled from several recent issues of *Video Rating Guide for Libraries* (now discontinued). They represent the "best recently released educational videos for K–12 audiences." Arranged by subject areas such as math, environment and ecology, performing arts, and social issues, the reviews include a content summary, recommended grade level, use policy, and price. Each entry also receives a rating from 3 to 5 ("good" to "must have"). Full imprint information useful for ordering and cataloging is also provided. This guide differs somewhat from a similar guide by the same publisher: Gallant's *Best Videos for Children and Young Adults*, which lists 350 more public library-oriented videos. *Recommended Videos* is recommended for all school media centers planning or maintaining a video collection. *VIDEOCASSETTES*

C; Y; A
95. VideoHound's Golden Movie Retriever. Visible Ink Press/Gale, annual. 1,500p. $19.95. 0-7876-0781-9.

Averaging about 20,000–25,000 titles a year, this annual list of videos is a spinoff culled from the 125,000+ titles found in the latest edition of *The Video Source Book*. It bills itself as the complete guide to movies on videocassette and laserdisc. The films are listed alphabetically by title. Each entry includes a brief subjective review, running time, color or black-and-white, cast, director, awards, price, distributor, and rating. A large number of special indexes add to the value of this videography: categories in a variety of genres, series, cast, and directors. A distributor guide is also appended. Though this guide contains about three times as many titles, it is similar in purpose and price to Case's *Ultimate Movie Thesaurus*. Both are recommended, and many libraries may want both for reference and collection development. *VIDEOCASSETTES; MOTION PICTURES*

Authors and Illustrators

C; Y
96. **American Writers for Children Since 1960: Poets, Illustrators, and Nonfiction Authors**. Ed. by Glenn E. Estes. Gale, 1987. 430p. (Dictionary of Literary Biography, 61). $128. 0-8103-1739-7.

Continuing the tradition of the excellent DLB series, this standard reference complements two other volumes in the series published by Gale and still in print: *American Writers for Children Before 1900* (1985. $212. 0-8103-1720-6) and *American Writers for Children, 1900-1960* (1983. $112. 0-8103-1146-1). This volume is also similar to others in the series in that it is arranged alphabetically by biographee. It also includes full bibliographical information of all books by and about each author. Its only real limitation is that only 32 authors and illustrators are included. Again, this work is recommended for all libraries that can afford it. *AUTHORS, AMERICAN*

C; Y
97. **Authors of Books for Young People**. 3rd ed. By Martha E. Ward et al. Scarecrow, 1990. 780p. $59.50. 0-8108-2293-8.

This revised and updated edition contains 3,708 entries, incorporates material from the 2nd edition (1971) and its 1979 supplement, and adds almost 300 new entries. Emphasis has been on authors whose biographies have been difficult to locate; therefore, this work tends to supplement rather than duplicate several standard juvenile authors biographical sources such as *Twentieth-Century Children's Writers*. The information generally has been compiled from the files of the Quincy (Illinois) Public Library. The brief entries are arranged in alphabetical order by author's last name. Each entry includes a brief biographical sketch and examples of the author's publications with bibliographic information. While this guide is more useful for reference work than collection building, it is still recommended for most school and public libraries because of the many authors included who are not found in other sources. *AUTHORS*

C; Y
98. **Books by African-American Authors and Illustrators for Children and Young Adults**. By Helen E. Williams. American Library Association, 1991. 270p. $7. 0-8389-0570-6.

Williams, a librarian and professor of children's literature, helps fill a void by providing background information on the contributions of African Americans to children's and young adult literature. She states that her objective in this book is "to provide a representative identification of the books which are written and illustrated by Black writers and artists." The book is divided into four chapters and includes descriptions of 250 books appropriate for children from preschool to grade 3; more than 350 descriptions of books considered appropriate for intermediate grades 5 through 8; more than 700 books that should inform and challenge readers at the senior high level and above; and information about Black illustrators and their works. The more than 1,200 books listed were published from the 1930s to 1990. The big difference between this work and *Black Authors and Illustrators of Children's Books* by Barbara Rollock is the arrangement by age group and the detailed annotations. The price is such that most school and public libraries that own the Rollock work will want both despite the duplication of titles. *AUTHORS, AFRICAN AMERICAN; ILLUSTRATORS, AFRICAN AMERICAN*

C; Y
99. **Books That Invite Talk, Wonder, and Play**. Ed. by Amy A. McClure and Janice V. Kristo. National Council of Teachers of English, 1996. 335p. $19.95. 0-8141-0370-7.

In a series of nearly 40 essays, many well-known authors who write children's literature share their thoughts and discuss how they create the right plot twist, choose the perfect turn of a phrase, or bring their characters to life. Among the writers are Jerry Spinelli, Gary Paulsen, Ashley Bryan, Jane Yolen, Katherine Paterson, and Avi. A variety of genres of children's literature are represented, including historical fiction, folklore, fantasy, nonfiction, poetry, and picture books. Teachers and librarians will find many ideas to use in teaching and library programming in these bibliographical essays. This book is a recommended purchase for all elementary, middle school, and public libraries. *AUTHORS*

C; Y

100. **Children's Literature Review: Excerpts from Reviews, Criticism, and Commentary on Books for Children**. Gale, 1976- . $120/vol.

This extensive and expensive set now numbers more than 40 volumes. Each contains collective criticism on about a dozen authors and illustrators. Along with this extensive critical material are bibliographies of books and other materials by and about the authors under discussion. This is a valuable set, but its price will probably limit its acquisition to large public library collections.

CHILDREN'S LITERATURE (GENERAL); YOUNG ADULT LITERATURE (GENERAL)

C: Y

101. **Contemporary Spanish-Speaking Writers and Illustrators for Children and Young Adults**. By Isabel Schon. Greenwood, 1994. 248p. $49.95. 0-313-29027-X

Information on 249 Spanish-speaking authors and illustrators for young readers is given in this bio-bibliography. Authors from North, South, and Central America are included as well as Spain, the rest of Europe, and Morocco. Entries, which vary from one-half to five pages, include personal data, addresses, career information, awards and honors, a bibliography of the author's works, and critical sources. Quotations from the authors frequently give added depth to the profiles. An appendix of writers and illustrators arranged by country of origin and citizenship and a title index are given. This work will be particularly valuable in schools and libraries trying to develop collections for Spanish-speaking children.

LITERATURE, SPANISH AMERICAN

C; Y

102. **Junior DISCovering Authors: Biographies and Plotlines on 300 Most-Studied and Popular Authors for Young Readers**. Gale/UXL, 1994. CD-ROM. IBM/DOS version, $350. 0-8103-5896-4. Macintosh version, $325. 0-8103-5850-6.

Junior DISCovering Authors provides biographies, portraits, and essays on the lives, careers, and output of each of the 300 highlighted authors. Each entry has about five screens of biographical information, bibliographies of the author's works, media adaptations, and plotlines of major works (with three- or four-sentence summaries). Each plotline is followed by an annotated list of three to five other "books you might like." These are not necessarily by the highlighted author. Therefore, the total of books discussed in the package is in the thousands. Although the emphasis is on contemporary authors like Lloyd Alexander, Judy Blume, and Paul Zindel, there are some entries for adult writers popular with young readers, like Douglas Adams, Stephen King and Mary Higgins Clark, and others for such classic writers as C. S. Lewis and Frances Hodgson Burnett. The appeal level of the authors is roughly from the fifth through ninth grades. Installation is easy, and the disc that accompanies the set clearly explains all the functions. There are many access points: author, title, subject, and character or author personal data (e.g., birth date, birthplace, education, hobbies, awards, nationality, address, politics, religion). For example, one can easily get a list of the writers of science fiction, or those who are African American, or born in Wisconsin. Duplication of authors covered in the parent set *DISCovering Authors* is less than 10 percent. The main database is large (and expensive). It is available in smaller modules at $600 for the first module and $400 for each additional one. Modules available include: *DISCovering Most Studied Authors* (this profiles 350 important, mostly contemporary writers), *DISCovering Multicultural Authors*, *DISCovering Dramatists*, *DISCovering Novelists*, *DISCovering Poets*, and *DISCovering Popular Fiction and Genre Authors*. Two newer releases are *DISCovering Authors: Canadian Edition* and *DISCovering Authors: British Edition*.

AUTHORS

C: Y

103. **Major Authors and Illustrators for Children and Young Adults: A Selection of Sketches from** *Something About the Author*. By Laurie Collier and Joyce Nakamura. Gale, 1993. 6v. $275. 0-8103-7702-0.

The authors of this important reference source have written profiles on 800 of the better-known authors and illustrators of children's books whose works are widely read. The purpose of this work is simply to make data about authors known to patrons of small libraries that cannot afford the much more extensive (and more expensive) *Something About the Author* series. Arranged alphabetically by author, each entry includes a brief biographical sketch, a portrait, a list of writings, and a bibliography of additional information. This should prove to be a useful reference guide and selection aid for school libraries and smaller public libraries as a supplement/complement to the very familiar series *Book of Junior Authors and Illustrators*. *AUTHORS; ILLUSTRATORS*

C* Y*
104. **Seventh Book of Junior Authors and Illustrators**. By Sally Holmes Holtze. H. W. Wilson, 1996. 356p. 0-8242-0874-9.

Kunitz and Haycraft were responsible for the first *Junior Book of Authors* (2nd ed. 1951. $40. 0-8242-0028-4) more than 40 years ago. There have been periodic continuations that are similar in scope and coverage. This, the most current volume, provides detailed biographical sketches, autographs, and portraits of about 250 young adult and children's authors and illustrators, plus lists of their works. The latter is of some value in selection although the primary use of the classic series is to supply basic biographical information. All seven volumes are in print. *AUTHORS*

C; Y
105. **Something About the Author**. Gale. $92/vol.

There are now about 90 volumes in this set that covers more than 10,000 authors and illustrators. Entries are of two kinds. The first gives only a brief introduction to the subject and his or her work; the second gives in-depth profiles that extend over several pages and are illustrated with photographs, dust jacket art, and, when appropriate, examples of the subject's illustrations. In addition to career and personal data, these entries also include excerpts from letters and diaries, detailed chronologies, and author comments. For each of these entries there are two bibliographies, the first of primary sources and the second of secondary biographies and critical information. These can be of value in collection development. Each volume contains biographical material on 100–140 children's authors and artists. There are two other series that also contain bibliographic material although each is primarily a source for biographical information. *Yesterday's Authors of Books for Children* (2 vols. $93/vol.) is a set that highlights authors and illustrators from early times to 1960, and Something About the Author Autobiography series ($92/vol.), which now has more than a dozen volumes, contains autobiographical essays by about 20 authors and illustrators of books for young people. These excellent series are unfortunately often too expensive for individual school or public libraries to acquire, but perhaps they can be purchased for school district collections, large public libraries, and, certainly, universities that support children's literature courses. Also see entries for two companion series *Authors and Artists for Young Adults* and *Major Authors and Illustrators for Children and Young Adults*. *AUTHORS*

C
106. **Twentieth-Century Children's Writers**. Ed. by Laura Standley Berger. 4th ed. St. James Press, 1995. 1,256p. $132. 1-558-62177-6.

Y
107. **Twentieth-Century Young Adult Writers**. Ed. by Laura Standley Berger. St. James Press, 1994. 830p. $132. 1-558-62202-0.

The two volumes cited above are similar in scope, purpose, and format. The updated 4th edition of *Children's Writers* concentrates on authors for children age 10 and under. Almost 800 entries are included in its main section, 100 fewer than in the earlier edition. Most of those dropped have been added to the companion volume, *Twentieth-Century Young Adult Writers*. The main portion of both works covers English-language writers whose works were published generally after 1900. Following a brief biographical sketch is a list of all of the author's publications (even adult titles). A signed critical essay completes each entry. Appended are lists of nineteenth-century writers and brief entries for foreign-language writers. A title index completes the work. There are many similar works available. These two volumes of the St. James Twentieth-Century Writers series may serve as either a supplement/complement to titles such as *Major Authors and Illustrators for Children and Young Adults*, *Seventh Book of Junior Authors and Illustrators*, and *Something About the Author*. These important reference aids are all useful for collection development in school, academic, and public libraries, though smaller libraries may not need or be able to afford all. *AUTHORS*

C; Y

108. **Writers for Children: Critical Studies of Major Authors Since the Seventeenth Century**. By Jane M. Bingham. Scribner's, 1988. 720p. $100. 0-684-18165-7.

This critical guide examines 84 writers from the seventeenth to the early twentieth century whose books have become classics for young people. The entries are arranged alphabetically by author; each entry, which averages about six or eight pages, includes biographical information and a critical essay. These are followed by a bibliography of primary and secondary works. A detailed index to the authors and all books and stories mentioned is provided. This well-written book is recommended for academic, public, and school libraries as a reference book and as a guide to collection development. *AUTHORS*

Biographical Sources

C; Y

109. **Biographical Index to Children's and Young Adult Authors and Illustrators**. By David V. Loertscher. Libraries Unlimited, 1993. 400p. OP. 0-931510-47-3.

Over 13,000 international authors, illustrators, poets, filmmakers, and cartoonists from both collective and single biographies are included in this up-to-date index. Audiovisual resources are also included. More than 1,500 biographical works are indexed, including the standard adult and juvenile reference sources: *Contemporary Authors*, *Something About the Author*, and the well-known Wilson author series. Each entry includes name, birth/death year, and country or state of birth, as well as a list of additional sources of information. Find a copy of this comprehensive guide and use as a handy reference tool and aid to collection development. *AUTHORS; ILLUSTRATORS*

C; Y

110. **Hooray for Heroes! Books and Activities Kids Want to Share with Their Parents and Teachers**. By Dennis Denenberg and Lorraine Roscoe. Scarecrow, 1994. 255p. $27.50. 0-8108-2846-4.

This bibliography of biographies is arranged by age groups: preschool (ages 3–5), primary (ages 6–8), intermediate (ages 9–11), and young people (ages 12–14). Within each group there are two sections: "Ordinary People in Extraordinary Situations" and "Biographies." In each of these sections, biographies are arranged by the name of the subject. For each entry, bibliographic information is given; sometimes a short annotation and an indication of the book being received favorably are provided. Those books that were recommended by the National Council for the Social Studies in their annual notable books list are highlighted. A separate section describes activities like crafts, food, music, and drama that can be used in conjunction with reading biographies. A few collective biographies are analyzed separately, and there are separate indexes for series, subjects, and biographers. *BIOGRAPHY*

Computer Technology

Software

C; Y; A

111. **CD-ROM for Librarians and Educators: A Resource Guide to Over 800 Instructional Resources**. 2nd ed. By Barbara Head Sorrow and Betty S. Lumpkin. McFarland, 1996. 416p. $45 pap. 0-7864-0176-1.

This is a bibliography of 800 instructional CD-ROMs (up from 300 in the first edition) that range in intended users from kindergarten through college, with some for an adult audience. The packages are arranged by subject. For each entry the material supplied includes title, producer, format, subject, price, grade level, hardware and software needed, distributor, and a description of the contents. The annotations are not critical, but inclusion in the bibliography suggests a recommendation. Introductory material contains a general explanation of CD-ROMs, a glossary, a suggested reading list, policies for purchasing, and a review of search techniques. A list of CD-ROM distributors is also provided. This excellent guide will be particularly helpful in acquisition work although in some cases prospective purchasers of a particular product might wish to consult more extensive reviews for fuller evaluations. Also see the entry below for *CD-ROM for Schools* and the one for Patrick R. Dewey's *303 CD-ROMs to Use in Your Library*.

CD-ROMS; COMPUTER SOFTWARE

C*; Y*

112. **CD-ROM for Schools: A Directory and Practical Handbook for Media Specialists**. By Pam Berger and Susan Kinnell. Eight Bit Books, 1994. $29.95 pap. 0-910465-13-7.

Hailed by reviews as "a five-star winner" and "a gold mine of information," this guide supplies a clear, readable introduction to CD-ROMs and how to make intelligent decisions concerning hardware, software, networking, and selection. The first chapters also cover such topics as establishing policies and procedures, the impact of CD-ROMs on staffing and instruction, and how to establish evaluation management (helpful journals and online services are cited). After indicating their criteria for selection, the authors list a core collection of 100 top titles, with the 10 best starred. For each there is an annotation giving details on hardware requirements, vendor information, an analysis of content, and such practical aspects as ease of use and price. An additional 200 CD-ROMs are also listed with ample, though less extensive, background material. In a separate chapter, all 300 titles are indexed by curriculum and grade levels. There follows a 30-page glossary of terms. Though specifically geared to schools, this excellent guide will also be useful in public libraries. The publisher's name and address are: Eight Bit Books, 462 Danbury Rd., Wilton, CT 06897. If ordering direct, include $3 for shipping and handling.

CD-ROMS; COMPUTER SOFTWARE

C; Y

113. **The Computer Museum Guide to the Best Software for Kids**. HarperPerennial, 1995. $16. 0-06-273376-1

This is an excellent guide for choosing good software titles on such subjects as reading, recreation, discovery, and exploration. Each entry is arranged by subject and well annotated. Supplementary information includes age guides, ratings for each piece of software, lists of the best, and indexes.

COMPUTER SOFTWARE

C; Y

114. **The Frugal Youth Cybrarian: Bargain Computing for Kids**. By Calvin Ross. American Library Association, 1996. 175p. $25. 0-8389-0694-X.

Designed to help school librarians build useful software libraries with little or no money, this practical guide shows how to identify, find, and download low-cost educational shareware and freeware applications and to acquire inexpensive CD-ROMS, hardware, and databases. These lists are applicable for DOS, Windows, and Macintosh platforms. There are guides to valuable BBS and Internet sites and online services plus step-by-step instructions on how to download and use what you find. For the novice there is also a succinct guide to the Internet with explanations of such areas as the World Wide Web, BBS, ftp, and online services. This guide is both a budget stretcher and a handy manual on using available computer resources in the classroom.

COMPUTER SOFTWARE; FREE MATERIALS

C; Y; A

115. **Gale Directory of Databases**. Gale, 1996. 2 vols. $340. 0-8103-5749-0.

Though this set is too expensive for a school or small public library, professionals should be aware of it when information about databases is required. This set describes more than 10,400 databases available worldwide in a variety of formats. For each entry, information is given on producer names and contacts, content, subject covered, language, update frequency, geographical coverage, availability, and cost. Volume 1 covers more than 5,800 online databases; volume 2, "portable" formats (i.e., CD-ROM, diskette, magnetic tape, batch access, and handheld products). There are separate lists of database producers, online services, and vendors, each with helpful directory information. Each volume is available separately; volume 1 (0-8103-9068-X) is $230, and volume 2 (0-8103-9129-5) is $150. There is also a CD-ROM version of the entire set (0-8103-8241-5) priced at $600.

DATABASES; CD-ROMS; ONLINE DATABASES

C; Y; A

116. **Games and Entertainment on CD-ROM: The Ultimate Guide to Home CD-ROM Entertainment**. By Regina Rega and Matthew Finlay. Mecklermedia, 1994. 250p. $29.95 pap. 0-88736-967-7.

A spinoff from Mecklermedia's *CD-ROMs in Print*, this directory lists and describes more than 1,300 games and home entertainment titles. The word "entertainment" is defined broadly to include such topics as cookbooks, children's books, gardening, and sports. This is a handy, easily used guide to subjects on CD-ROMs popular with all ages of library patrons. *CD-ROMS; GAMES*

C*; Y*

117. **Only the Best, 1993: The Annual Guide to the Highest-Rated Educational Software, Preschool–Grade 12**. By Shirley Boes Neill and George W. Neill. Association for Supervision and Curriculum Development, 1993. $22.

Earlier editions of this guide were published by Bowker. The present volume is part of an annual listing of microcomputer software programs that have received the highest rating from many evaluation services in the United States and Canada. The entries are first listed alphabetically, and this list serves as a title index. Annotated entries have a brief description noting system compatibility, usage tips, and grade level. They are then listed under broad headings such as arts, early childhood education, foreign language, language arts, mathematics, science, and typing. Each entry also includes cost and ordering information. There is a cumulative guide on disk (Mac or IBM): *Only the Best, 1985-93* for $99. Details are available from Curriculum/Technology Resource Center, Association for Supervision and Curriculum Development, 1250 N. Pitt St., Alexandria, VA 22314.

COMPUTER SOFTWARE; MICROCOMPUTERS

C; Y

118. **Scholastic Software Catalog, K–12**. Scholastic, annual. Free.

This annual listing describes software programs that are recommended by Scholastic and available for purchase through them. Arranged by subject, entries give a description of the software, grade level, price, producer, and more. There are title and subject indexes. Send to: Scholastic Software Catalog, 2931 E. McCarthy St., Jefferson City, MO 65102. *COMPUTER SOFTWARE*

C; Y

119. **That's Edutainment: A Parent's Guide to Educational Software**. By Eric Brown. Osborne/McGraw-Hill, 1996. 400p. $29.95. 0-07-882083-9.

In the first part of this interesting and much-needed selection aid, Brown discusses edutainment (the meshing of learning and multimedia), important educational software companies, the role of software in the schools, and multimedia system components. Following this overview are lengthy reviews of Brown's selection of the 100 best titles on floppy disk and CD-ROM. Each entry includes ratings and evaluations. A CD-ROM with demos of highly recommended items is included with the volume. Though designed for home use, this guide will be very useful for most schools and many public libraries as a reference source and selection aid. Many libraries may want to consider a circulating copy. *COMPUTER SOFTWARE*

Internet

C; Y; A

120. **The Complete Internet Companion for Libraries**. By Allen C. Benson. Neal-Schuman, 1995. 432p. $49.95. 1-55570-178-7.

In five large sections, this valuable guide defines the Internet, explaining hardware and software requirements, important applications like e-mail and the World Wide Web, library use, and its effects on patrons and their needs. For resources development there is a selective list of Internet assets and services, including file types and the software that creates them. Also included are library discussion lists and documents in the EFF Library Policy Archive. A free 75-page supplement on the World Wide Web is included with the purchase of the parent volume. *INTERNET*

C; Y

121. **Dial Up! Gale's Bulletin Board Locator**. Gale, 1996. 1,081p. $49. 0-7876-0364-3.

Information on 10,000 U.S. bulletin boards available by dial-up access is contained in this directory. Contact information, target audiences, fees, sign-on limits, a contents description, and modem speeds and settings are included for each entry. Bulletin boards are arranged by state, then by area code, and then alphabetically. Many topics are included, such as entertainment, sports, government, and travel. A special section lists the bulletin boards by various online services, including America Online, CompuServe, DELPHI, Genie, and Prodigy. There is also a master alphabetically arranged index by title and a topical index that supplies access by subject.   *COMPUTER BULLETIN BOARD*

C*; Y*; A*

122. **Educator's Internet Companion: Classroom Connect's Complete Guide to Educational Resources on the Internet**. By Gregory Giagnocavo et al. Wentworth Worldwide Media, 1995. 227p. $39.95 pap. 0-932577-10-5.

This excellent guide is both an introduction to the educational resources available to elementary and high schools via the Internet and a manual on how to use them in classroom learning experiences. Chapter 1 supplies 30 lesson plans at various levels (e.g., one is on chemistry in the senior high grades; another is on life in space for K–3) and shows how to integrate the Internet logically and naturally into these teaching units. Ways to modify the units for different grade levels are given. Chapter 2 explores eight sites via gopher, telnet, ftp, and World Wide Web, and chapter 3 lists many education-related sites arranged by gopher, telnet, etc. The top 50 sites are described in chapter 4, and chapter 5 details searching techniques. There are many useful appendixes. An instructional video and a disk are included in the package. Highly recommended for both libraries and teachers' professional collections. The publisher is Wentworth Worldwide Media, 1866 Colonial Village Ln., Lancaster, PA 17605-0488.   *INTERNET*

C; Y

123. **Gopher It! An Internet Resource Guide for K–12 Educators**. By Gail Cooper and Gary Cooper. Libraries Unlimited, 1996. 122p. $20. 1-56308-486-4.

Gopher sites on the Internet are administered by educational institutions, foundations, and government agencies. They tend to be more reliable and professional than other sites. They are also usually textual in nature and can be downloaded without the reformatting and reconfiguration that web sites often entail. This directory is arranged by 250 curriculum topics that help the user find lesson plans, teaching materials, research reports, and funding opportunities. Entries include descriptions of the resources on the site. There are also many cross-references to facilitate the use of this timely directory.   *INTERNET*

C; Y

124. **The Internet and Instruction: Activities and Ideas**. 2nd ed. By Ann E. Barron and Karen S. Ivers. Libraries Unlimited, 1998. In press. pap. 1-56308-613-1.

The authors have provided an easy-to-use guide to telecommunications in general and the Internet in particular. The core of the book consists of ideas and activities for the classroom (grades 4 through 12) that are detailed in chapters arranged by curriculum areas such as social studies and math. Through these projects, students are encouraged to explore the Internet independently and pursue individual interests in a variety of subject areas.   *INTERNET*

C; Y

125. **Internet for Library Media Specialists**. By Carol Mann Simpson. Linworth, 1995. 144p. OP. 0-938865-39-0.

After a general history on the nature of the Internet, sample screens are pictured to explain distinct features and characteristics. There are separate chapters on developing policies for Internet use with children and young adults, how to introduce the Internet to students and faculty (with reproducible transparencies), and tips on how to use it in various subject areas. Though this is not a directory of useful sites, it gives important background information.   *INTERNET*

C; Y

126. **The Internet for Newbies: An Easy Access Guide**. By Constance D. Williams. Libraries Unlimited, 1996. 129p. $20. 1-56308-483-X.

This helpful guide is not a directory of resources but a manual for beginning users that explains what is involved in the Internet and gives guidance on how to find its sites and use the materials they contain. It covers such Internet systems as the World Wide Web, ftp, gophers, and telnet. Because the emphasis is on using these resources in classrooms, this book will be useful in schools at all levels, from elementary through high school. *INTERNET*

C*; Y*

127. **The Internet Resource Directory for K–12 Teachers and Librarians**. 97/98 ed. By Elizabeth B. Miller. Libraries Unlimited, 1998. 250p. $25 pap. 1-56308-617-4.

This is a new edition of the well-received first edition that appeared in 1994. The author says that her book is "a starting point for teachers and school library media specialists to use in designing individual directories of Internet resources." A brief introductory chapter covers features such as e-mail, telnet, ftp, gopher, and the World Wide Web. Then the book provides a directory to more than 600 discussion groups, electronic books and newspapers, lesson plans, and other teaching resources arranged under broad curriculum areas with many subdivisions. Entries include access methods, addresses, how each is accessed, login information, and an annotation giving details about the contents. Each resource was carefully chosen using criteria centered around usefulness, accuracy, suitability, and update policy. All are free. Designed specifically for educators, this book is a useful addition to all school media centers; some public libraries will have a need for this material as well. *INTERNET*

Free and Inexpensive Materials

C*; Y*

128. **Educators Guide to Free Materials**. Educators Progress Service, annual.

There are now 11 volumes in the *Educators Guide to Free Materials*. They fall into four guide categories: audiovisual, printed materials, computer materials, and mixed media dealing with specific subjects.

Audiovisual:
128.1   **Educators Guide to Free Videotapes** (1996–97 ed. $27.95).
        This volume lists 2,621 videotapes in various formats that are available to schools on a free rental basis.
128.2   **Educators Guide to Free Films, Filmstrips, and Slides** (1996–97 ed. $36.95).
        There are a total of 1,713 free films, filmstrips, slides, audiotapes, and audiodiscs listed. Most must be returned after use, but some can be kept permanently.

Printed Materials Guides:
128.3   **Elementary Teachers Guide** (1996–97 ed. $26.95).
        A directory of 1,942 free posters, flyers, maps, brochures, booklets, etc.
128.4   **Educators Index of Free Materials** (1996–97 ed. $47.95).
        Geared towards the high school level and above, this work lists 2,277 materials that are free for the asking.
128.5   **Educators Guide to Free Teaching Aids** (1996–97 ed. $45.50).
        This is a listing of more than 2,000 of the best free printed materials and five sample teaching units in a loose-leaf binder format.

Computer Materials:
128.6   **Guide to Free Computer Materials** (1996–97 ed. $38.95).
        This directory includes disks, flyers, videos, books, and other materials related to computing, along with a glossary of 1,000 terms and hundreds of pages of shareware.

Mixed Media Guides:

128.7   **Educators Guide to Free Science Materials** (1996–97 ed. $27.95).

128.8   **Educators Guide to Free Guidance Materials** (1996–97 ed. $28.95).

128.9   **Educators Guide to Free Home Economics and Consumer Education Materials** (1996–97 ed. $25.95).

128.10   **Educators Guide to Free Social Studies Materials** (1996–97 ed. $29.95).

128.11   **Educators Guide to Free Health, Physical Education, and Recreation Materials** (1996–97 ed. $27.95).

Each of these subject guides contains listings of videotapes, films, audiotapes, and hundreds of printed materials available free.

All of the titles in this series have the same arrangement. A table of contents provides a curricular classification for the materials. The body of each work contains information on every title arranged under various subject areas plus an indication of age suitability. This is followed by several indexes: title, subject, and source and availability. Here are given names and addresses of each of the organizations from which materials can be obtained and details concerning any limitations on use. Most of these audiovisual materials are available for free rental for limited periods of time and must be returned on a fixed schedule. Each of these sections is printed on a different colored paper to facilitate use. These guides, like others in the series, have been in use for many years in America's schools and libraries and are available on a 15-day free approval basis. The materials listed have been screened to insure that they are bias-free and without excessive commercialism. These books have been found to be extremely useful in collection development in both schools and public libraries. Inquiries and orders should be sent to: Educators Progress Service, Dept. D, 214 Center St., Randolph, WI 53956.

FREE MATERIALS; FILMS; FILMSTRIPS; SLIDES; AUDIOTAPES;
VIDEOCASSETTES; VERTICAL FILE MATERIALS; SCIENCE; GUIDANCE;
HOME ECONOMICS; CONSUMER EDUCATION; SOCIAL STUDIES; HEALTH;
PHYSICAL EDUCATION; RECREATION; COMPUTER SOFTWARE

C; Y

129.   **Free (and Almost Free) Things for Teachers**. By Susan Osborn. Perigee Books/Berkley Publishing, 1993. $8.95 pap. 0-399-51795-2.

Although many of the 200 resources listed in this bibliography are print items, there are several nonprint, like a handheld miniplanetarium. Maximum cost is $5. In addition to descriptions of contents, complete ordering information is given in this useful little guide.

FREE MATERIALS; VERTICAL FILE MATERIALS

Y; A

130.   **Free and Inexpensive Career Materials: A Resource Directory**. By Cheryl S. Hecht. Garrett Park Press, 1995. unpaged. $19.95 pap. 1-880774-09-7.

This work lists 821 organizations and agencies that supply career information in the form of pamphlets and leaflets for $5 or under. They include trade and professional organizations, federal and state agencies, academic departments, foundations, companies, and publishers. Each entry includes an address, telephone number, titles of materials, any cost, and, in many cases, a brief description of the item. Preceding this list is an index of 250 occupations and subjects with references to the organizations that supply useful materials on that topic. Unfortunately, this index could be more thorough. Nevertheless, this inexpensive guide will be helpful in building vertical file collections of career materials.

OCCUPATIONS; VOCATIONAL GUIDANCE;
VERTICAL FILE MATERIALS; FREE MATERIALS

C; Y

131.   **Smithsonian Resources Guide for Teachers**. Smithsonian Institution, 1994. Free ($2 for 10 or more copies).

More than 400 mostly free or inexpensive educational items from about 40 museums and organizations affiliated with the Smithsonian are listed in this guide. Agencies represented include the National Science Resources Center, the National Gallery of Art, the Kennedy Center for the Performing Arts, and

Reading Is Fundamental. Divided into four subject areas (the arts, language arts, science, and social studies), entries include posters, pamphlets, audiotapes, and videotapes. There are author, subject, and media indexes. To order, contact: Office of Elementary and Secondary Education, Arts and Industries Bldg., Room 1163, MRC 402, Smithsonian Institution, Washington, DC 20560.

FREE MATERIALS; VERTICAL FILE MATERIALS

Language and Literature

General and Miscellaneous

C; Y

132. **Approaches to Literature Through Subject**. By Paula Kay Montgomery. Oryx, 1993. 243p. (Oryx Reading Motivation Series). $29.50 pap. 0-89774-774-7.

Outlined in this book are many methods that can be used to motivate middle grade and junior high students to read by hooking them on books dealing with high-interest subjects. Both fiction and nonfiction titles are used as examples, and some of the topics covered are people, things, and historical and current events. In the companion volume by Mary Elizabeth Wildberger, *Approaches to Literature Through Authors* (Oryx, 1993. $29.50. 0-89774-776-3), various authors (and a few illustrators) like Beverly Cleary, Betsy Byars, Walter Dean Myers, Cynthia Voigt, and even William Shakespeare are used to interest prospective readers. Both books contains many examples of models to follow, plus extensive lists of student materials and resources, and aids for the teacher, all of which can be used for collection development. These books will be particularly useful in middle and junior high schools and, perhaps, in some children's rooms in public libraries. *LITERATURE—STUDY AND TEACHING*

C*; Y*

133. **Books in Spanish for Children and Young Adults: An Annotated Guide, Series VI**. By Isabel Schon. Scarecrow, 1993. 305p. $38.50. 0-8108-2622-4.

This much-awaited update includes children and young adult books published in Spanish, as well as bilingual and translated books. Most of the titles in this comprehensive bibliography were published from 1989 to 1991. The scope and format are similar to the previous editions. It is intended for teachers, librarians, and parents as an aid in selecting books in Spanish from preschool through high school levels. The titles are arranged by country and then by topic such as fiction, music, and art. Each entry contains full bibliographic information, a brief description, and a critical annotation dealing with theme, style, and reader appeal. Earlier volumes, designated as Series II, III, IV, and V, are also still available. Schon, a professor of library science at Arizona State University, is also the author of *A Basic Collection of Children's Books in Spanish*, which includes about 500 titles arranged by subject. The titles complement each other and are recommended for all school and public libraries that support bilingual programs or serve a large Spanish-speaking population. *CHILDREN'S LITERATURE, SPANISH; SPANISH LITERATURE; YOUNG ADULT LITERATURE, SPANISH.*

C; Y

134. **A Critical Handbook of Young Adult and Children's Literature**. 5th ed. By Rebecca J. Lukens. Addison-Wesley, 1994. 352p. $26. 0-06-501108-2.

This is an excellent guide to criteria for evaluating children's and young adult literature under such chapter headings as character, setting, plot, theme, and style. Each chapter ends with a list of recommended books, each of which can serve as a checklist and guide for purchasing quality titles. There are also extensive bibliographies in appendixes that list prize-winning books.

CHILDREN'S LITERATURE (GENERAL); YOUNG ADULT LITERATURE (GENERAL)

C; Y

135. **Fiction Index for Readers 10–16: Subject Access to Over 8,200 Books (1960–1990)**. By Vicki Anderson. McFarland, 1992. 480p. $43.50. 0-89950-703-4.

This is an index by subject to books of fiction published from 1960 through 1990 for children ages 10 through 16. More than 225 subjects are listed, and there are detailed subject and title indexes.

Although this work is not evaluative or selective, it is a way of locating novels through the subject approach. For very large children's literature collections.

CHILDREN'S LITERATURE (GENERAL); YOUNG ADULT LITERATURE (GENERAL)

C; Y

136. Fiction Sequels for Readers 10 to 16: An Annotated Bibliography of Books in Succession. By Vicki Anderson. McFarland, 1990. 150p. $21.95 pap. 0-89950-519-8.

This listing of fiction sequels involves about 350 authors and 1,500 titles of books read in the upper elementary and junior high grades. Some of the titles are out-of-print but are available in many libraries. There is an alphabetical arrangement by author, with each of the books in the author's series listed in order and given a short annotation. There is no indication of grade or interest level, but a title index supplies author names and the position of the title in the series. This work contains about twice as many authors as *Sequences*. It will have value both in children's reading guidance and in collection development. *SEQUELS*

C; Y

137. Gender Positive! A Teachers' and Librarians' Guide to Nonstereotyped Children's Literature. By Patricia L. Roberts et al. McFarland, 1993. 206p. $24.95 pap. 0-89950-816-2.

More than 200 books in which gender roles are positive and nonstereotyped are listed in this guide. It covers titles suitable for use in kindergarten through eighth grade. For each entry there are descriptive annotations plus one or more classroom-related activities. *SEXISM*

C; Y

138. Great Books for Girls: More than 600 Books to Inspire Today's Girls and Tomorrow's Women. By Kathleen Odean. Ballantine, 1997. 416p. $12.50 pap. 0-345-40484-X.

Aimed at raising a girl's self-image, this entertaining and useful bibliography annotates more than 600 books where girls are the central characters and show strength and resourcefulness. Beginning with picture books and extending into popular adult titles, this annotated list will help librarians who are looking for girls' books of quality and appeal. *WOMEN IN LITERATURE; FEMINISM*

C*; Y

139. Index to Poetry for Children and Young People, 1988–1992. By G. Meredith Blackburn III. H. W. Wilson, 1994. 400p. $58. 0-8242-0861-7.

This series of poetry indexes began in 1942; the original edition was edited by John E. and Sara W. Breton (1942. $43. 0-8242-0021-7). This was followed by the first supplement (1954. $30. 0-8242-0022-5) and second supplement (1965. $30. 0-8242-0023-3). Additional volumes cover the years 1964–1969 (1972. $30. 0-8242-0435-2); 1970–1975 (1978. $38. 0-8242-0621-5); 1976–1981 (1983. $38. 0-8242-0681-9); and 1982–1987 (1989. $48. 0-8242-0773-4). The present volume indexes more than 100 poetry collections published between 1988 and 1992 that contain poetry suitable for young people from elementary through high school. About 7,500 poems are listed by title, first line, author, and subject, with the fullest information given in the title entry. There is a listing of the 123 books analyzed with complete bibliographic materials and an annotation of the contents. Because the books analyzed were chosen by librarians and children's literature specialists, this list is valuable for selection purposes. This is an excellent reference book for libraries serving children and young adults. *POETRY*

C; Y

140. Inviting Children's Responses to Literature: Guides to 57 Notable Books. By Amy A. McClure and Janice V. Kristo. National Council of Teachers of English, 1994. 145p. $12.95 pap. 0-8141-2379-1.

For each of the notable 57 books highlighted there is a suggested grade level (preschool through junior high), a plot summary, many teaching suggestions and activities, and a list of related books. The activities encourage students to use discussion, writing, reading, and listening to respond to the stories. The books display a wide range of interests and genres and include such favorites as Paula Fox's *One-Eyed Cat*, Alexandra Day's *Frank and Ernest*, and Virginia Hamilton's *The People Could Fly*.

CHILDREN'S LITERATURE (GENERAL); LIBRARY PROGRAMS

C; Y
141. **Let's Hear It for the Girls: 375 Great Books for Readers 2–14**. By Erica Bauermeister and Holly Smith. Penguin, 1997. 191p. $10.95. 0-14-025732-2.

Each of the 375 annotated titles in this bibliography furnishes an entertaining reading experience and features a heroine that can serve as a suitable role model. Running the gamut from picture books to young adult novels, this is an entertaining list to browse through and will be useful for both collection development and reading guidance.   *WOMEN IN LITERATURE; FEMINISM*

C; Y
142. **Literature of Delight: A Critical Guide to Humorous Books for Children**. By Kimberly Olson Fakih. Bowker, 1993. 269p. $40. 0-8352-3027-9.

Fakih identifies almost 1,000 humorous books that are useful as a bridge to literacy and learning in working with youngsters ages 3 to 14. Two-thirds of the fiction and nonfiction titles were published within the past 10 years, and most are readily available. The works are arranged within chapters, which include "Nonsense and Absurdity," "Satire," "Parody," "Spoofs and Send-Ups," "Poetry and Rhyme," "Just Plain Silly," and more. The useful volume is indexed by title, author, subject, character, and grade level. It is recommended for reference, reading guidance, programming, and collection building for most school and public libraries.   *HUMOROUS STORIES*

C*; Y*
143. **Plays for Children and Young Adults: An Evaluative Index and Guide. Supplement 1: 1989–1994**. 2nd ed. By Rashelle S. Karp and June H. Schlessinger. Garland, 1996. 369p. $65. 0-8153-1493-0.

This index/guide identifies and evaluates more than 2,100 plays, written from 1989 to 1994, that may be produced by or for young people, ages 5 to 18. The word "plays" is broadly interpreted; coverage includes plays, choral readings, scenes, musicals, reader's theater, and skits. Many other indexes were screened in choosing plays for this index, including, for example, Wilson's *Play Index* and *Index to Children's Plays in Collections, 1975–1984*. Plays are arranged alphabetically by title. Each entry provides a grade-level range for the audience and actors, a description of the set, playing time, royalty information, name of the playwright, and the original title if adapted. Full bibliographic information is provided for plays that appear as a single volume or part of an anthology or periodical. Five indexes facilitate use of this valuable reference/collection building aid. Its predecessor includes more than 3,000 plays published from 1975 to 1989 and is still available (598p. $83. 0-8240-6112-8). Both editions are highly recommended for most school, public, and academic libraries.   *DRAMA*

C; Y
144. **Recommended Reading List**. Comp. by the Los Angeles Science Fantasy Society, 1993. Free.

In order to promote reading and fight illiteracy, the Children's Literature Committee of the Los Angeles Science Fantasy Society has compiled a recommended list for young people age nine to teenaged with an interest in imaginative literature (science fiction and fantasy). For more information on the work of this society, write to Galen A. Tripp, Children's Literature Committee, at the address below. For a free copy of this recommended list send a SASE to: Recommended Reading List, c/o LASFS, 11513 Burbank Blvd., North Hollywood, CA 91601-2309.   *FANTASY; SCIENCE FICTION*

C; A; Y
145. **Research and Professional Resources in Children's Literature: Piecing a Patchwork Quilt**. Ed. by Kathy G. Short. International Reading Association, 1995. 288p. $20.95. 0-87207-126-X.

Teachers, researchers, and librarians now have a valuable resource that brings together in one handy guide important current research and reference information on children's literature. The authors of this compilation are all experienced teachers, librarians, or university professors. This inexpensive guide should prove helpful to those attempting to identify research on a topic or strategies for using literature or children's books on specific subjects. Therefore, it is recommended for most public libraries and the professional collection of elementary schools.

REFERENCE BOOKS; CHILDREN'S LITERATURE (GENERAL)

C; Y

146. **Survival Themes in Fiction for Children and Young People**. 2nd ed. By Binnie Tate Wilkin. Scarecrow, 1993. 200p. $27.50. 0-8108-2676-3.

In this edition, about 300 books published between 1982 and 1992 dealing with survival are examined through extensive annotations that cover the plots as well as social and psychological issues. The works are divided into three sections: the individual (aloneness, feelings, images of self and others, and sexuality); pairings and groupings (friendship, peer pressure, and families); and world views (the environment, religion, politics, war and peace, and the celebration of life and death). Each section has a list of related films and program ideas. *SURVIVAL*

C; Y

147. **A Teacher's Guide to Folklife Resources for K–12 Classrooms**. American Folklife Center, Library of Congress, 1994. 36p. free.

Resources that deal with the folklife of many communities involve oral history, traditions, and crafts, among other things. The American Folklife Center at the Library of Congress has compiled a handy guide identifying and indicating the availability of this rich source of cultural information. This brief bibliography contains print and audiovisual sources as well as a listing of national, regional, and state agencies that offer folklife programs and resources. This aid is designed for use with students from kindergarten through grade 12 and is recommended for all school and public libraries. Single copies are available for free; multiple copies are available for the nominal cost of shipping and handling. Write to: The Library of Congress Educational Initiative, American Folklife Center, Washington, DC 20540-8100. *FOLKLIFE; INSTRUCTIONAL MATERIALS*

Specific Genres

Fantasy and Science Fiction

C*; Y*; A

148. **Fantasy Literature for Children and Young Adults: An Annotated Bibliography**. 4th ed. By Ruth Nadelmen Lynn. Bowker, 1995. 1,150p. $52. 0-8352-3456-8.

This is an annotated list of 4,800 English and American fantasy novels and collections of short stories published between 1900 and 1994 for young people in grades 3 through 12. Part 1 lists them in 10 sections by type of fantasy such as ghost, time travel, and animal, and then by author. Both in- and out-of-print books are included. A total of 29 reviewing sources have been checked, and recommendation symbols are used to denote books of superior and outstanding quality. Also included is a one-sentence annotation for each title. Part 2, the research guide, lists secondary sources for the use of adults. This is divided into four sections: "Reference and Bibliography," "History and Criticism," "Teaching Resources," and "Author Studies." There are author and illustrator, title, and subject indexes. This is a valuable tool for every elementary and high school plus children's rooms in public libraries. *FANTASY*

C; Y

149. **Science Fiction, Fantasy, and Horror Writers**. By Mariel MacNee. Gale/UXL, 1995. 2 vols. $38. 0-8103-9865-6.

The lives and works of 80 of the most popular writers of science fiction, fantasy, and horror for children and young adults are covered in this set. The range of subjects is wide. Writers for children include L. Frank Baum, Norton Juster, and E. B. White; for young adults there are such authors as Lois Duncan, Natalie Babbitt, and Christopher Pike; classic writers include Mary Shelley and Robert Louis Stevenson; and examples of writers for adults are Poul Anderson, Stephen King, Kurt Vonnegut, Anne Rice, and J. R. R. Tolkien. Each entry includes vital information, a portrait, an easily read lengthy biography, critical comments on the author's works, quotes from critics and the author, a list of the author's salient works ("Best Bets" boxes highlight the most important), photographs of book jackets and movie stills, and a bibliography of sources. There are also appendixes, including lists of Hugo and

Nebula awards, and author, title, and subjects indexes. This attractive reference set also has value in collection development particularly because of its selective bibliographies.

SCIENCE FICTION; FANTASY; HORROR—FICTION; AUTHORS

Historical Fiction

C; Y; A

150. **Historical Figures in Fiction**. By Donald K. Harman and Gregg Sapp. Oryx, 1994. 368p. $45. 0-89774-718-6.

Historical figures from Abigail Adams to Emiliano Zapata are arranged alphabetically in this comprehensive guide to characters in historical fiction. About 1,500 people are listed and 4,200 novels are cited. The publication dates range from 1940 to 1993, but about half were published before 1970. Symbols are used to indicate novels for children and young adults. Bibliographic information and a list of review citations are supplied for each title. There are indexes by author title and by the occupations of the subjects. *HISTORICAL FICTION*

C*; Y*

151. **Recreating the Past: A Guide to American and World Historical Fiction for Children and Young Adults**. By Lynda G. Adamson. Greenwood, 1994. 494p. $55. 0-313-29008-3.

While the focus of this bibliography may be on American historical fiction, all historical periods from prehistory to the contemporary period are adequately represented in this comprehensive list of 970 recommended titles for young people grades 1–10. About 200 award-winning fiction titles are included. A number of adult titles suitable for young adults are also cited. Actually, this work contains more than 15 separate annotated bibliographies arranged by historical time periods; they are then further arranged in alphabetical order by author. Each entry includes full bibliographic data and a descriptive annotation that includes reading and grade levels, historical event, plot, theme, and current availability. An important bonus of this work are the seven appendixes that include lists of titles by readability and interest levels; protagonists of or plots from minority groups; sequels with same characters in a series; important historical dates; famous groups or people appearing in works; and country and date of setting. This well-developed bibliography is an excellent guide for collection development in the area of historical fiction. It is recommended for all libraries serving children and young adults. *HISTORICAL FICTION*

Multiculturalism

General and Miscellaneous

C*; Y

152. **Culturally Diverse Library Collections for Children**. By Herman L. Totten et al. Neal-Schuman, 1994. 304p. $35 pap. 1-55570-140-X.

A total of 1,300 books are recommended for the development of multiethnic collections in elementary and middle schools. The bibliography is divided into four large sections: African American, Hispanic American, Asian American, and Native American. Under these headings there are further divisions by genre: general nonfiction, biographies, folklore, fiction for younger and middle readers, reference works, and scholarly works for adults. For each entry, full bibliographic information is given plus a brief annotation and suggested ages or grades. There are also indexes by author, illustrator, and title. This is a well-organized, reliable guide to building multiethnic collections.

MULTICULTURALISM; AFRICAN AMERICANS;
HISPANIC AMERICANS; ASIAN AMERICANS; NATIVE AMERICANS

C; Y*

153. **Culturally Diverse Library Collections for Youth**. By Herman L. Totten et al. Neal-Schuman, 1996. 220p. $35 pap. 1-55570-141-8.

A companion to the above title, this bibliography of recommended books and videos covers 780 titles. The work is arranged into four major sections about African Americans, Native Americans,

Hispanic Americans, and Asian Americans. The latter is further subdivided into Chinese Americans, Japanese Americans, etc. There is a fifth section on multiethnic materials. Each section has separate listings for biographies; fiction; folklore, literature, and poetry; reference and scholarly works; general nonfiction; and videos. Each title is annotated with full bibliographic data and suggested ages and grades. The annotations vary widely in length. A few out-of-print and not recommended items are included. Indexes are by author, title, and subject.   *MULTICULTURALISM; AFRICAN AMERICANS; ASIAN AMERICANS; NATIVE AMERICANS; HISPANIC AMERICANS*

C; Y

154. **Dealing with Diversity Through Multicultural Fiction**. By Lauri Johnson and Sally Smith. American Library Association, 1993. 106p. $20. 0-8389-0605-2.

Although not especially a collection-building tool, this report on an exciting program to dispel racial stereotypes through reading fiction and engaging in planned follow-up activities contains a valuable bibliography of the titles that were used successfully. The title of the study was Project Equal, and its purpose was to expose existing negative attitudes towards cultural differences through both carefully selected contemporary realistic fiction (the criteria are included) and well-structured participatory activities like role playing, book discussions, and writing journals. The target group was middle schoolers in a New York private school. This account of the project from planning through execution can serve as an inspiring model for other librarians and teachers who want to counter racial, gender, and cultural discrimination. The bibliography of books used in the program will be an essential backup resource.   *MULTICULTURALISM*

C; Y

155. **Developing Multicultural Awareness Through Children's Literature: A Guide for Teachers and Librarians, Grades K–8**. By Patricia L. Roberts and Nancy Lee Cecil. McFarland, 1993. 216p. $24.95 pap. 0-89950-879-0.

The authors have compiled an interesting bibliography of about 240 titles of multicultural fiction, folk literature, and biography suitable for elementary through junior high school students. The titles are intended to portray positive cultural differences and "modify cultural stereotypes." The titles are listed under five sections: African Americans, Asian Americans, European Americans, Latino Americans, and Native Americans. Each section is further divided by grade levels: K–3 and 4–8. Each listing contains complete bibliographic information and a descriptive annotation. Many of the entries cite a target activity and possibly a list of related books-to-read activities. This relatively inexpensive work should prove to be a useful addition to most multicultural materials collections in schools and public libraries.   *MULTICULTURALISM*

C*; Y

156. **Exploring Diversity: Literature Themes and Activities for Grades 4–8**. By Jean E. Brown and Elaine C. Stephens. Teacher Ideas Press, 1996. 225p. $23 pap. 1-56308-322-1.

Religious, racial, and generational diversity are explored in this bibliography of multicultural books. It is divided into five main areas: "Heritage: Understanding Our Past"; "Identity: Seeking a Sense of Self"; "Identity: A Sense of Belonging"; "Getting Along with Others: Family"; and "Getting Along with Others: Friends." The well-chosen fiction, nonfiction, and biography titles are well annotated. Themes, discussion questions, and activities are included as well as a professional reference section. Useful for both collection development and development of multicultural curriculum units in upper elementary and junior high, this volume is a fine complement to Hazel Rochman's *Against Borders* (ALA, 1993, $25. 0-8389-0601-X).   *MULTICULTURALISM*

C; Y; A

157. **Guide to Multicultural Resources, 1997–1998**. Highsmith, 1997. 584p. $49. 0-917846-83-4.

This useful directory and bibliography lists more than 3,000 organizations, resources, and government agencies involved in a variety of multicultural activities that includes such groups as African Americans, Asian or Pacific Americans, Hispanic Americans, and Native Americans. A useful guide for all types of libraries.   *MULTICULTURALISM*

C; Y

158. **Immigrants in the United States in Fiction: A Guide to 705 Books for Librarians and Teachers, K–9**. By Vicki Anderson. McFarland, 1994. 143p. $29.50. 0-89950-906-1.

The society, history, and customs of people who were born outside the United States and later emigrated to America are covered in this bibliography of books for elementary and junior high schools. Arranged by various nationalities, entries supply bibliographic information, grade level, and a brief annotation. Most selections were published between 1965 and 1993.

MULTICULTURALISM; IMMIGRATION

C; Y

159. **Kaleidoscope: A Multicultural Booklist for Grades K–8**. By Rudine Sime Bishop. National Council of Teachers of English, 1994. 168p. $14.95 pap. 0-8141-2543-3.

Concentrating on African Americans, Asian Americans, Hispanic Americans/Latinos, and Native Americans, this bibliography of 400 titles celebrates America's cultural diversity. The chapters are arranged by themes and subjects (e.g., poetry, the arts, ceremonies and celebrations, history, people to know, and places to go) rather than by ethnic groups. The entries are for fiction and nonfiction titles published between 1990 and 1992 and include several picture books for the primary grades. There are comprehensive paragraph-length annotations plus indexes by book awards, authors, illustrators, titles, and subjects. Continuations of this useful title have been promised. *MULTICULTURALISM*

C; Y

160. **Many Faces Many Voices: Multicultural Literary Experiences for Youth**. Ed. by Anthony Manna and Carolyn Brodie. Highsmith, 1992. 200p. $29. 0-917846-12-5.

Actually, this interesting work is a collection of papers and workshop presentations from the annual Virginia Hamilton Conference held at Kent State University. Contributors included a number of children's and young adult authors. In addition to the bibliographies accompanying each presentation, annotated bibliographies of multicultural and multiethnic books for young adults and children are appended, as well as sources for additional multicultural publications. This list, with its very specific focus, is recommended for all libraries building collections of multicultural materials for young people.

MULTICULTURALISM

C; Y

161. **The Multicolored Mirror: Cultural Substance in Literature for Children and Young Adults**. Ed. by Merri V. Lindgren. Highsmith, 1992. 195p. $29. 0-917846-05-2.

Many questions were raised during a 1991 conference of the Cooperative Children's Book Center. The papers, presented by many noted authors, are published in this series of essays dealing with many aspects of our cultural heritage as portrayed in children's and young adult literature. Much of what is included in this brief account will be of value to teachers and librarians as they get more and more involved in the role of multicultural literature in our changing society. Undoubtedly, the most valuable part of this book are the lengthy and detailed bibliographies of multicultural literature. They are useful as both reference and collection development aids, and perhaps they justify the acquisition of this interesting work. *MULTICULTURALISM*

C; Y

162. **Multicultural Children's and Young Adult Literature: A Selected Listing of Books Published Between 1980–1990 by and About People of Color**. 3rd ed. Comp. by Ginny Moore Kruse and Kathleen T. Horning. Diane Publishing, 1993. 78p. $35. 1-56806-323-7.

This bibliography was compiled and distributed by the Cooperative Children's Book Center at the University of Wisconsin, Madison. The carefully selected and annotated books are recommended as being "high quality children's and young adult books innovative in style, important in theme, and/or unusual in insight." The books are arranged in alphabetical order by author under such subjects as "Seasons and Celebrations," "Issues in Today's World," and "Picture Books." This excellent bibliography is recommended for all public and elementary school libraries. *MULTICULTURALISM*

C*; Y*

163. **Our Family, Our Friends, Our World: An Annotated Guide to Significant Multicultural Books for Children and Teenagers**. By Lynn Miller-Lachmann. Bowker, 1992. 709p. $46. 0-8352-3025-2.

This very comprehensive guide claims to be global in scope; it deals with cultures, politics, geography, and pressing issues facing people from around the neighborhood to around the world. It includes more than 1,000 books published in English from the United States and Canada since 1970. Each chapter includes an introductory summary, a map, and an annotated list of books for grades preschool through 12. A similar work that is not much more than an oversized pamphlet is Kruse and Horning's *Multicultural Children's and Young Adult Literature*. The publisher of *Our Family* claims to have the first work of its kind; it certainly is the most extensive and timely book currently available on a very hot topic. It is highly recommended for all school and public libraries building collections in this area.
MULTICULTURALISM

C; Y

164. **Serving Linguistically and Culturally Diverse Students: Strategies for the School Library Media Specialist**. By Melvina Azar Dame. Neal-Schuman, 1993. 186p. $25. 1-55570-116-7.

Linguistically and culturally diverse populations often cause special concerns for libraries and schools serving these children. This guide examines their special needs in materials and services. It gives many suggestions on how to create activities and programs for them and pointers on integrating them into the regular curriculum. Many bibliographies and lists of suitable resources are included.
MULTICULTURALISM

C*; Y*

165. **This Land Is Our Land: A Guide to Multicultural Literature for Children and Young Adults**. By Alethea K. Helbig and Agnes Regan Perkins. Greenwood, 1994. $49.95. 0-313-28742-2.

Over 800 titles, 560 in great detail, are reviewed in this up-to-date bibliography of multicultural, multiethnic literature. All of the entries were published between 1985 and 1993 (60 percent since 1990). The reading/age levels of the selections range from picture book age to high school students. In this comprehensive guide, the authors have attempted to keep current and to provide worldwide coverage to the literature about and of African American, Asian American, Hispanic American, and Native American traditions and experiences. The work is divided into the four major ethnic categories, then further subdivided by chapters on fiction, oral tradition, and poetry. Each title has been evaluated on literary values such as plot, style, and characterization. A similar book that is much less comprehensive in its coverage is Kruse and Horning's *Multicultural Literature for Children and Young Adults*. Both titles are recommended for all school and public libraries as aids to collection development and reference work.
MULTICULTURALISM

C; Y; A

166. **Venture into Cultures: A Resource Book of Multicultural Materials and Programs**. Ed. by Carla D. Hayden. American Library Association, 1993. 166p. $25 pap. 0-8389-0579-X.

This multimedia-multicultural guide is organized around major cultural groups found in the United States, such as African American, Arabic, Hispanic, Jewish, and Native American. Each chapter contains a brief overview of the cultural background and traits and availability of resources. Each section also has an annotated bibliography; many include audiovisual materials, ideas for programs, food preparation, games, crafts, and lists of resources and vendors. Although this is intended primarily for elementary and middle schools, it would also be useful for higher levels. A bibliography of sources useful to adults is also included. An index by culture completes this work, which is recommended for every school and public library.
MULTICULTURALISM

African Americans

C; Y

167. **The Black Experience in Children's Literature—1994**. New York Public Library, 1995. 64p. $5 pap. 0-87104-726-8.

More than 450 briefly annotated titles dealing with the African American experience are listed in this inexpensive guide. The titles, ranging in age from preschool to junior high school level, are divided into four geographical areas: the United States, South and Central America and the Caribbean, Africa, and England. A list of Coretta Scott King Award winners is also included. The titles are accessible through an author/title index. Copies are available for $5 plus a $1 shipping and handling charge (bulk orders are also available) from: *The Black Experience*, Office of Branch Libraries, New York Public Library, 455 5th Ave., New York, NY 10016.   *AFRICAN AMERICANS*

C; Y

168. **Telling Tales: The Pedagogy & Promise of African American Literature for Youth**. By Dianne A. Johnson. Greenwood, 1990. 184p. (Contributions in Afro-American and African Studies, 134). $45. 0-313-27206-9.

This critically annotated work deals with the contributions of writers from 1920 to 1990, including works by W. E. B. DuBois, children's fiction by Langston Hughes and Arna Bontemps, and the writings and illustrations of John Steptoe and others. Recommended for most libraries, especially those supporting an African American or African studies program or those serving a large population of African Americans.   *AFRICAN AMERICAN LITERATURE*

Hispanic Americans

C*; Y*

169. **Best of the Latino Heritage: A Guide to the Best Juvenile Books About Latino People and Cultures**. By Isabel Schon. Scarecrow, 1996. 304p. $37.50. 0-8108-3221-6.

Schon, a leading authority on Hispanic books for children, has compiled a guide based on her previous volumes: Series I to IV of *A Hispanic Heritage* and Series V after the name changed to *A Latino Heritage*. Criteria were established to determine the best books, including the presentation of the material, the quality of the art and writing, and the appeal to children at various ages. Key points were appeal and accuracy. The selected books are arranged by country and include full bibliographic data, a descriptive annotation, critical comments, and a recommended grade level. This best book list is recommended for all libraries serving young people, especially those with a large Latino population.   *HISPANIC AMERICANS*

C: Y

170. **Introduccion a la Literatura Infantil y Juvenil**. By Isabel Schon and Sarah Corona Berkin. International Reading Association, 1996. 182p. $19.95. 0-87207-144-8.

Available only in a Spanish-language edition, this work explains why children's literature is significant and lists many different and recommended Spanish-language books available to youngsters. Each of the 12 chapters explores a different type of book and includes a comprehensive bibliography of books listing appropriate reading levels from beginning readers through young adult. The hundreds of titles include publications (from both North and South America) of original titles and translations into Spanish from other languages.   *SPANISH LITERATURE*

C*; Y*

171. **A Latino Heritage, Series V: A Guide to Juvenile Books About Latino People and Cultures**. By Isabel Schon. Scarecrow, 1995. 210p. $32.50. 0-8108-3057-4.

The latest contribution to this excellent series (which was formerly titled *A Hispanic Heritage*) lists more than 200 juvenile books published from 1990 to 1994, suitable for readers in grades 1 through 12, that deal with Latino people and cultures. The books are arranged in chapters with geographical divisions such as Argentina, Spain, and the United States. Each entry contains bibliographic information, an evaluative and descriptive annotation, and grade and audience indicators. Asterisks mark those books especially recommended. There is an author, title, and subject index. This is a fine collection development tool in school and public libraries that stress Hispanic studies. Three of the four earlier volumes in the series are still available (under the title *A Hispanic Heritage*): *Series II* (1985. $20.00. 0-8108-1727-6), *Series III* (1988. $20.00. 0-8108-2133-8), and *Series IV* (1991. $22.50. 0-8108-2462-0). Also, the best from all five series are compiled by Schon in a volume described elsewhere in this guide under the title *The Best of the Latino Heritage*. HISPANIC AMERICANS

Native Americans

C; Y

172. **American Indian Reference Books for Children and Young Adults**. 2nd ed. By Barbara J. Kuipers. Libraries Unlimited, 1995. 230p. $25. 1-56308-258-6.

Kuipers, an experienced educator and library media specialist, has worked with Native Americans for many years. Her aim here was to compile a collection of titles that present an accurate portrayal of American Indians. This compilation of more than 200 recommended and relevant nonfiction materials is intended for children and young adults grades 3–12. Each entry provides full bibliographic data and indicates subject area and reading level. The annotations, which are lengthy, discuss the strong and weak points of each book and suggest possible curriculum use. A specially devised evaluation guide and checklist to ensure objectivity and avoid stereotypes is also provided. This much-needed bibliography is recommended for most school and public libraries, especially those working with a Native American population. NATIVE AMERICANS; REFERENCE BOOKS

C; Y

173. **How to Teach About American Indians: A Guide for the School Library Specialist**. By Karen D. Harvey et al. Greenwood, 1995. 240p. $35. 0-313-29227-2.

This is a general guide on how to teach and learn about Native Americans, their culture, history, and present conditions. This helpful volume also supplies accurate information on the subject, recommends appropriate library resources, and gives guidelines on how to select instructional materials and use them effectively. There are also some model lesson plans appended. NATIVE AMERICANS

C; Y; A

174. **Native American Checklist**. Comp. by Barbara Beaver. Bookpeople, 1992. 20p. Free.

This interesting checklist may be only 20 pages in length, but it lists more than 900 titles dealing with almost every aspect of the life and contributions of Native Americans. Among the many topics included are art, history, literature, religion, travel, and women. Separate lists of children's books and audiovisual materials are provided. This list is free to schools and libraries and can be requested by sending an SASE to: Bookpeople, 7900 Edgewater Dr., Oakland, CA 94621. NATIVE AMERICANS

C; Y

175. **Native Americans in Fiction: A Guide to 765 Books for Librarians and Teachers, K–9**. By Vicki Anderson. McFarland, 1994. 180p. $31.50. 0-89950-907-X.

This bibliography serves as a very comprehensive checklist; however, brief annotations are provided. The more than 700 books are arranged alphabetically by tribes. Entries contain publisher, author, date, and grade designations. Author, title, and subject indexes are also included. This bibliography would be useful for identifying works for interlibrary loan purposes as well as a possible acquisition guide for elementary and junior high school and public libraries. NATIVE AMERICANS

C; Y

176. **Through Indian Eyes**. Ed. by Beverly Slapin and Doris Seale. New Society Publishers/New Society Educational Foundation, 1992. 336p. $49.95; $24.95 pap. 0-86571-212-3; 0-86571-213-1 pap.

There are more than 300 separate and diverse native cultures in the United States, and the job of identifying and acquiring materials related to these cultures is often overwhelming. This handbook/bibliography is intended to make it possible for librarians, teachers, and parents to become familiar with and select quality children's books dealing with the Native American experience. This work is an expansion of the authors' earlier edition, which is still in print and still useful: *Books Without Bias: Through Indian Eyes*. 2nd ed. (1988. $25. 0-9625175-0-X). Of the present edition, more than one-third of the text consists of book reviews of titles from standard sources as well as less-familiar presses. A resources section lists information on acquiring print and nonprint materials, curriculum materials, and periodicals, all ranging from preschool through high school level. Finally, a well-selected bibliography by and about Native Americans completes this volume, which is recommended for every school and public library. *NATIVE AMERICANS*

Reading Guidance

General and Miscellaneous

C*; Y*
177. **The Best: High/Low Books for Reluctant Readers**. By Marianne Laino Pilla. Libraries Unlimited, 1990. 100p. OP. 0-87287-532-6.

The 374 high/low titles included in this list were chosen on the basis of quality, reading level, and, most important, on how they would appeal to young people in grades 3 to 12. Reluctant readers are defined by the author, an experienced children's librarian, as those reading two levels or more below grade level. Fiction and nonfiction titles are included; detailed criteria for inclusion are clearly stated in the well-written introduction. Titles are arranged alphabetically by author and numbered. Each entry includes full bibliographical data, a brief annotation, and grade and reading levels. Title, subject, and grade/reading level indexes complete this useful tool. Find a copy of this brief, inexpensive guide for all libraries serving children and young adults. *HIGH INTEREST–LOW VOCABULARY BOOKS*

C*; Y*
178. **Best Books for Developing Moral and Family Values**. Ed. by Gregory Wolfe and Suzanne Wolfe. Bowker, 1997. 600p. $65. 0-8352-3833-4.

Based on the premise that books can affect one's attitudes and behavior, the editors have compiled a list of more than 700 fully annotated titles relating to family life intended for readers between the ages of 7 and 14. The annotations are aimed at professionals and parents concerned with what children are reading. The important words in the title are "family" and "values" because the titles were carefully selected to depict a healthy family life to impressionable youth. Family, as defined by the editors, includes single-parent households, step-siblings, step-parents, grandparents, and adoptive parents. This interesting work is recommended for any library serving young people. *VALUES*

C*; Y*
179. **The Best of Bookfinder: Selected Titles from Volumes 1–3**. By Sharon Spredemann Dreyer. American Guidance Service, 1992. 451p. $49.95 pap. 0-88671-439-7.

Booklist states that *The Best of Bookfinder* "lays the foundation for bibliotherapy work with children. Highly Recommended." More than 675 fully annotated titles from volumes 1–3 of *Bookfinder* (the time-tested standard aid for bibliotherapy, now in its 4th volume) are included in this relatively inexpensive and invaluable reference tool. The titles are arranged under the general areas of psychological, developmental, and behavioral topics. Complete author, title, and subject indexes are provided. This work is particularly recommended as a selection tool for the smaller library that might not be able to afford most of the titles cited in the first three volumes of *Bookfinder*. *BIBLIOTHERAPY*

C; Y
180. **BookBrain and BookWhiz**. SIRS, The Knowledge Service, 1995. 1 CD-ROM, 1 floppy disk. $175. Annual update $75.

Two popular reading incentive programs have been combined on one CD-ROM to produce a database of 3,200 annotated titles for children and young adults in grades K–9. The program can be used independently by students or with guidance from a librarian or teacher. The contents are arranged in three major grade groups: 1–3, 4–6 and 7–9, which are searchable by author, title, or subject. Pictures, text, sound, and animation are used to motivate students. The program is in English with a Spanish-language option. The program can be customized by either adding or deleting titles, and children can add their own comments to the books they have read. Despite its steep cost, this interactive reading motivational program that offers many opportunities for reading guidance and collection development is recommended for most school and public libraries.   *READING GUIDANCE; COMPUTER SOFTWARE*

C*; Y*

181.   **The Bookfinder 4: When Kids Need Books: Annotations of Books Published 1983 Through 1986**. By Sharon Spredemann Dreyer. American Guidance Service, 1989. 642p. $89.95; $44.95 pap. 0-913476-50-1; 0-913476-51-X pap.

Published since 1977 and now in its 4th edition, *The Bookfinder* is becoming a basic guide for reading guidance and bibliotherapy. Its main intent is to match books to the special needs and problems of young people ages 2–15. *Bookfinder 4* indexes and analyzes 731 titles published through 1986. Titles are arranged alphabetically by author; full bibliographic data, including in-print status, are given. This data are followed by subject headings, a lengthy descriptive annotation, and a critical comment. The subject index includes about 450 psychological, behavioral, social, and developmental topics of real concern to young people and notes the age level of each book. A special bonus of this edition is a revised statement on bibliotherapy and an updated list of selection aids and professional books. Author and title indexes complete this useful guide. This special aid is highly recommended for all libraries serving young people. See also *The Best of Bookfinder*.   *BIBLIOTHERAPY*

C; Y; A

182.   **Guiding the Reader to the Next Book**. By Kenneth Shearer. Neal-Schuman, 1996. 221p. $39.95. 0-55570-209-0.

Though not a bibliography, this handy guide provides good background information and useful tips on organizing and delivering good reader's advisory services. There are sections on giving expert reading guidance to children and young adults, how to display books, and how to classify fiction for maximum use. An appendix lists and describes reader's advisory sources on the Internet.   *READING GUIDANCE*

C*; Y*

183.   **100 World-Class Thin Books, or What to Read When Your Book Report Is Due Tomorrow**. By Joni Richards Bodart. Libraries Unlimited, 1993. 204p. $27.50. 0-87287-986-0.

Every school and many public librarians have been confronted with the problem of recommending a "good, thin book" for a student who is desperate because of an impending deadline. Bodart, of booktalk fame, has provided librarians with a solution. All of the titles in this bibliography are 200 pages or less, and all are highly recommended and suitable for middle school and high school students. All entries contain bibliographic data as well as information on grade level, theme, genre, related subject area and whether or not a paperback is available. Much of this data is also provided in the well-developed indexes. Subject areas chosen are timely and meant to catch the attention of students, particularly those who may be reluctant readers. This long-awaited bibliography is a must purchase as a quick reference tool and selection aid for all libraries working with young people.   *YOUNG ADULT LITERATURE (GENERAL); READING GUIDANCE*

C; Y; A

184.   **What Do I Read Next? A Reader's Guide to Current Genre Fiction**. 7th ed. Gale, 1996. 525p. $105. 0-8103-6450-6.

Begun in 1991, this annual publication is designed to help librarians and patrons locate new titles in the popular fantasy, western, romance, horror, mystery, and science fiction genres. Each area has an introduction written by an editor who is well informed in that area. Titles are arranged by author within genre sections. Nearly 2,000 recent titles are included in the 7th edition. Each entry describes a separate book, including publisher and date; series name and number, if appropriate; main characters; time and geographical setting; story type and a brief plot synopsis; review citations; other works by the author; and similar books by different authors. Most of the titles will have been reviewed within 11 months of the publication date of each volume. A very special feature of this innovative work is the inclusion of seven indexes: title, series name, names of main characters, time setting, geographic setting, type of story, and author. This book includes all levels but focuses on adult-level books. It is well thought through and highly recommended for all public libraries that do extensive reader's advisory work and can afford the cost. A CD-ROM cumulative version is also available for $495. (See next entry.) Gale also publishes two other titles that are similar in purpose and format but intended for young people. They are much less expensive and recommended for school libraries and children's and young adult departments of public libraries: *What Do Children Read Next?* and *What Do Young Adults Read Next?*

READING GUIDANCE

C; Y; A
185. **What Do I Read Next? CD-ROM**. Gale, 1996. Windows stand-alone version. Annual subscription with quarterly updates. $495. 0-7876-0535-2.

With more than 52,000 recommended fiction and nonfiction titles and more than 15,000 added each year, this CD-ROM database is designed to reduce the time involved to find the right book for the right reader of any level. Based on the popular print version (see above entry) this cumulative list includes books in the seven popular genres: mystery, romance, science fiction, fantasy, horror, western, and historical. All entries contain author and publication date; most identify characters, settings, and time periods and classify the title by genre. About 75 percent include plot summaries. Quarterly updates keep the reader informed of new releases. This database will serve well and is recommended as a reference, reader's advisory, and selection aid for all public libraries that can afford the cost.

READING GUIDANCE

C; Y
186. **What Else Should I Read? Guiding Kids to Good Books, Vol. 2**. By Matt Berman. Libraries Unlimited, 1996. 215p. $24. 1-56308-419-8.

When kids ask the common question, "Do you have any other books like the one I just read?," Berman, a third and fourth grade teacher, provides possible answers in this handy bibliography. Thirty more book webs with linkage to nearly 800 recommended books for young readers are added to his earlier volume 1 (*What Else Should I Read?* Libraries Unlimited, 1995. $24.50. 1-56308-241-1), which also contained 30 topic webs with links to 50 more titles and is still readily available. Books are accessed through a variety of directions, such as subject, author, or genre. The books are intended for readers in grades 3 though 8. This bibliography is recommended for elementary and middle school libraries and young people's departments of public libraries. *READING GUIDANCE*

Booktalking

C*; Y*
187. **Booktalking Series**. Ed. by Joni Richards Bodart. H. W. Wilson.

Bodart, perhaps the most renowned authority on booktalking and children's and young adult literature, has edited a large number of time-tested works over the years that have aided librarians, teachers, reading specialists, and others working with children and young adults. All have been widely acclaimed and are highly recommended. In addition to the many volumes in the *Booktalking Series* published by Wilson, two volumes by Bodart published by Libraries Unlimited are also available: *The New Booktalker*, Volume 1, 1992, and Volume 2, 1993. Current and retrospective titles in the Wilson series still in print include:

187.1   **Booktalking the Award Winners: Young Adult Retrospective Volume** (1996. 210p. $32. 0-8242-0877-3). 460 titles.

187.2   **Booktalking the Award Winners: 1993–1994** (1995. 192p. $32. 0-8242-0876-5). 213 titles.

187.3   **Booktalking the Award Winners: 1992–1994** (1994. 224p. $32. 0-8242-0866-8). 250 titles.

187.4   **Booktalk! 5** (1993. 294p. $32. 0-8242-0836-6). 320 titles.

187.5   **Booktalk! 4: Selections from the Booktalker for All Ages and Audiences** (1992. 320p. $32. 0-8242-0835-8). 350 titles.

187.6   **Booktalk! 3: More Booktalks for All Ages and Audiences** (1988. 386p. $32. 0-8242-0764-5). 500 titles.

187.7   **Booktalk! 2: Booktalking for All Ages and Audiences** (1985. 408p. $32. 0-8242-0716-5). 260 titles, plus in-depth instruction on preparing and presenting talks of your own.

187.8   **Booktalking with Joni Bodart** (Videocassette. 1986. 28 minutes. Color VHS with viewer's guide. 0-8242-0741-6).

BOOKTALKS

C*; Y*

188.   **Middleplots 4: A Book Talk Guide for Use with Readers Ages 8–12**. By John T. Gillespie and Corinne J. Naden. Bowker, 1994. 434p. $42. 0-8352-3346-0.

Like the earlier volumes in this series, titled *Introducing Books*, *Introducing More Books*, and *Introducing Bookplots 3*, this book is intended as a manual on introducing good books to children in the middle grades. It highlights important themes and suggests techniques for using 80 classic and contemporary titles, plus hundreds of additional resources listed. The selections are arranged in eight categories such as adventure and mystery, fantasy and science fiction, school and friendship, humor, and other lands and peoples. Each entry includes a plot summary, thematic material, booktalk material, and information about the author. Thorough author, title, and subject indexes as well as cumulative indexes to the earlier volumes are included. This volume and its companion Bowker titles *Primaryplots*, *Juniorplots*, and *Seniorplots* are excellent sources for booktalking and as selection aids in collection development for all school and public libraries.   *BOOKTALKS*

C*; Y

189.   **The New Booktalker**. By Joni Richards Bodart. 2 vols. Libraries Unlimited. Vol. 1, 1992. 110p. OP. 1-56308-087-7. Vol. 2, 1993. 109p. OP. 1-56308-087-7.

In addition to a number of articles offering practical guidelines and suggestions on booktalking, several hundred ready-to-use booktalks are included in these two volumes by, perhaps, the best-known authority on booktalks. Ratings on popularity, quality, and grade level of the selected titles are also included. The booktalks are intended for grades 1–12. Seven indexes (author, title, subject, genre, grade-level, paperback format, and contributors) should make accessing the right booktalk for the right group an easy task. Though out-of-print, additional collections of booktalks by Bodart are published by H. W. Wilson and can be found under the title *Booktalking Series*.   *BOOKTALKS*

C*; Y*

190.   **Tales of Love and Terror: Booktalking the Classics, Old and New**. By Hazel Rochman. American Library Association, 1987. 128p. $22 pap. 0-8389-0463-7.

Rochman demonstrates how to promote the pleasure of reading through booktalking. In a convincing introduction, she emphasizes the importance of booktalking. She contends: "The best booktalks are about those books I love and want to share . . . always the emphasis is on pleasure." Rochman uses the thematic approach to booktalking; many titles are recommended throughout the text. As well, a series of lists are provided in the appendix arranged by themes and genres. Rochman's scope and style are quite different from Joni Bodart's *Booktalk! 3*, but the two titles complement each other, and both are recommended. Dorothy Broderick, in VOYA, 10/87, stated: "*Tales of Love and Terror* belongs in every library." An accompanying videocassette (which can be used independently) is also available.

BOOKTALKS

Reference Books

C*; Y*; A*

191. **Encyclopedias, Atlases, and Dictionaries**. Ed. by Marion Sader and Amy Lewis. Bowker, 1995. 575p. $85. 0-8352-3669-2.

This volume combines and updates two earlier publications: *Reference Books for Young Readers* (1988) and *General Reference Books for Adults* (1988). It reviews 200 reference works arranged in four major sections: encyclopedias, atlases, dictionaries, and electronic versions of these works on CD-ROM, floppy disks, and online. Each section is introduced by an essay that outlines the criteria used for evaluation and gives pointers to consider before making a purchase for home or library. Following this introduction are the critical reviews divided into two parts: adult and juvenile. Reviews vary in length from one-and-a-half to four pages and are written by experienced librarians. The reviews are detailed, comprehensive, and complete. Useful charts allow quick comparisons of titles by scope, level, illustrations, cost, etc. Facsimile pages from encyclopedias and dictionaries are also included. Glossaries explain terms such as "guide words" and "Boolean search." The extensive coverage on electronic reference works includes a section titled "What to Look for in Electronic Reference Works." Coverage ends with the 1993 or 1994 edition of each title. This book will be useful in libraries both as a collection development tool and as a consumer buying guide.

ENCYCLOPEDIAS; DICTIONARIES; ATLASES; CD-ROMS; REFERENCE BOOKS

C*; Y*

192. **Guide to Reference Books for School Media Centers**. 4th ed. By Margaret Irby Nichols. Libraries Unlimited, 1992. 450p. $40. 0-87287-833-3.

This work identifies more than 2,000 reference works that are in-print and "designed specifically for the juvenile and young adult market." The titles are arranged in 54 subject categories. For each entry there is full bibliographic information, including price, a grade level indication, an annotation, and review citations. In addition to standard print sources, this guide also covers review journals, nonprint and computer selection aids, library organizations, and media skills material. There are subject and title indexes. This is an excellent selection guide, particularly for junior and senior high school libraries.

REFERENCE BOOKS

C; Y; A

193. **Kister's Best Dictionaries for Adults and Young People: A Comparative Guide**. By Kenneth F. Kister. Oryx, 1992. 438p. $39.95. 0-89774-191-9.

After an interesting background introduction that covers 61 pages and such subjects as the history, evaluation, purposes, types, and contents of dictionaries, there follows an intensive, thorough review of 132 adult titles and 168 others suitable for children and young adults. Specialized dictionaries such as thesauri are not included. In the evaluations, many examples are excerpted from the dictionaries, and there are quotes from reviews. Tables and charts are often used for comparative purposes, and the final evaluations are frank and to-the-point. There are several appendixes including listings of reviews journals, publications on language, and a bibliography of books and articles on dictionaries. This book will be extremely valuable in all types of libraries when giving advice to patrons on purchasing a dictionary. It will also help in building the library's own collection of dictionaries.   *DICTIONARIES*

C; Y; A

194. **Kister's Best Encyclopedias: A Guide to General and Specialized Encyclopedias**. 2nd ed. By Kenneth F. Kister. Oryx, 1994. 520p. $42.50. 0-89774-744-5.

As well as 77 general encyclopedias, this excellent reference book evaluates more than 800 special subject encyclopedias and 44 foreign-language encyclopedias in nine languages. After introductory sections on criteria used in evaluation and on the world of encyclopedias, there is a large segment on general encyclopedias, subdivided by size of set and intended audience. Within this area there are also separate sections on electronic encyclopedias and important titles now out-of-print. Each entry contains an evaluative review that can vary from a single page to more than 10, depending on the importance of the works. There are also evaluation of sample articles. Useful comparative charts and an overall rating

(A to F) for each work complete the sections. The subject encyclopedias segment is divided into 30 subject areas (e.g., music, computer and electronic sciences) and contains briefer reviews. A bibliography of works about encyclopedias, a directory of publishers and distributors, and an index complete this volume. It is useful both in choosing encyclopedias for the library and in helping parents make suitable purchases for their homes. *ENCYCLOPEDIAS*

C*; Y*; A*

195. **Purchasing an Encyclopedia: 12 Points to Consider**. 5th ed. By the Editorial Board of *Reference Books Bulletin*. American Library Association, 1996. 48p. $7.95. 0-8389-7823-1.

Reviews of eight print multivolume and six CD-ROM encyclopedias are included in this new edition, which pays particular attention to the changes from previous editions. The book is written by an editorial board of *Reference Books Bulletin*. Each encyclopedia is evaluated according to 12 stated criteria: age level, authority, arrangement, subject coverage, objectivity, recentness, quality, style, bibliographies, illustrations, physical format, and special features. This handy guide is recommended for all libraries as a reference tool for use by parents, teachers, and librarians and as a helpful selection aid. *ENCYCLOPEDIAS*

C; Y; A*

196. **Recommended Reference Books for Small and Medium-Sized Libraries and Media Centers, 1998**. Ed. by Bohdan S. Wynar. Libraries Unlimited, 1998. In press. 1-56308-625-5.

This excellent guide is now in its 16th annual edition. This particular volume reviews almost 530 titles chosen by the editor as the most valuable reference books of the previous year. The number represents about a third of the titles that were originally reviewed in *American Reference Books Annual* (ARBA). RRB makes it convenient for librarians to locate new references in a given field because of its subject arrangement. All of the lengthy and generally well-written reviews are signed by the reviewers, who are usually librarians, college professors, or subject specialists. They are also coded with a C, P, or S, designating a recommendation for college, public, or school libraries. This relatively inexpensive guide is highly recommended for all libraries. Previous editions are also available for reference and collection development. *REFERENCE BOOKS*

C*; Y*

197. **Reference Sources for Children's and Young Adult Literature**. By Deborah Rollins and Dona Helmer. Booklist Publications/American Library Association, 1996. 56p. $7.95. 0-8389-7838-X.

More than 150 books dealing with children and young adult literature are included in this handy reference source. This work is an updated and expanded version of two bibliographies that originally appeared in the "Reference Books Bulletin" section of *Booklist*. Included are bibliographies, biographical sources on writers and illustrators, lists of media adaptations, awards, review sources, and selection aids. This short and inexpensive resource is recommended for all librarians serving children and young adults. *REFERENCE BOOKS*

C; Y; A*

198. **Reference Sources for Small and Medium-Sized Libraries**. 5th ed. Ed. by Jovian P. Lang. American Library Association, 1992. 317p. $40 pap. 0-8389-3406-4.

This new edition of what is becoming a standard work was produced under Lang's editorial guidance and an ad hoc committee of ALA's Reference and Adult Services Division. With almost 2,000 entries, this newly revised edition contains an "approximate increase of 75 percent in number of new entries over the previous edition." This classified and annotated bibliography not only updates the standard sources but also includes "reference materials for children and young adults . . . sources in other formats, such as microforms and databases." The cutoff date is 1990; however, some newer editions have a 1991 imprint. Though the title is similar, Lang's work differs from an equally useful work by Wynar: *Recommended Reference Books for Small and Medium-Sized Libraries and Media Centers, 1996*. Wynar's work is an annual edition with newer titles drawn from the best of ARBA, whereas the Lang work is retrospective with irregular updates. Therefore, both titles are highly recommended for school media centers and public libraries. *REFERENCE BOOKS*

C*; Y*; A*
199. **Wilson Indexes**. H. W. Wilson.

The Wilson indexes have been a basic ingredient in reference services worldwide for about 100 years. Their important role as directional/locational tools for reference and research in a variety of subject areas and levels is unquestioned. Equally important, but not recognized or used fully, is their value as selection tools. All of the Wilson indexes have an appended list of "Sources Indexed," usually providing full bibliographic information. Many libraries use these lists to evaluate or build up their collections, in particular subject areas or in certain types of materials (short stories, plays, periodicals, etc.). Also, many libraries attempt to acquire as many of the sources as possible in order to alleviate patron frustration in seeking information. The major indexes currently available and recommended for libraries serving young adults are listed below. They are also cited, with detailed annotations, elsewhere in this guide, under specific subject areas (consult the author/title index for entry number). It is suggested that the publisher be contacted (1-800-367-6770) for latest prices and availability in other formats (e.g., online, CD-ROM, MARC-tape, computer software).   *SERVICE BASIS*

The following indexes are priced according to the number of periodicals indexed that are held by the library or on the library's expenditure for books:

  199.1 **Book Review Digest**. 1905- . ISSN 0006-7326.
        More than 7,000 reviews from about 90 selected periodicals annually.

  199.2 **Education Index**. 1929- . ISSN 0013-1385.
        400 periodicals, yearbooks, and monographic series; especially recommended for professional collections.

  199.3 **General Science Index**. 1978- . ISSN 0162-1963.
        150 periodicals covering all areas of science from astronomy to zoology.
                                                                        FLAT-RATED INDEXES

The following indexes are priced on an annual subscription at the rate indicated in the Wilson catalog:

  199.4 **Biography Index**. 1946- . ISSN 0006-3053.
        Indexes about 2,700 periodicals and over 2,000 books annually.

  199.5 **Essay and General Literature Index**. 1900- . ISSN 0014-083X.
        Indexes collections and anthologies.

  199.6 **Play Index**. 1949- . ISSN 0554-1054.
        Indexes more than 30,000 plays since 1949.

  199.7 **Readers' Guide to Periodical Literature**. 1900- . ISSN 0034-0464.
        Indexes about 240 popular periodicals.

  199.8 **Short Story Index**. 1900- . ISSN 0360-9774.

  199.9 **Vertical File Index**. ISSN 0042-4439.
        Issued 11 times a year; described under Periodicals.
                                                                                INDEXES

Science and Mathematics

General and Miscellaneous

C; Y
200. **Integrating Aerospace Science into the Curriculum: K–1**. By Robert D. Ray. Teacher Ideas Press, 1992. 191p. $21.50 pap. 0-87287-924-0.

This is a book of ideas, activities, and projects that teachers can use to teach aerospace science to students in all public school grades. Of particular value to librarians are the many bibliographies and resource listings that follow groups of activities. The materials are fairly current and are recommended for inclusion in school and library collections; therefore, the work is of some value in collection development.   *SCIENCE; AEROSPACE SCIENCE*

C; Y

201. **Integrating Science Through Children's Literature: Over Land and Sea**. By Carol M. Butzow and John W. Butzow. Libraries Unlimited, 1995. 193p. $23 pap. 0-87287-946-1.

Aimed at a middle school audience (grades 4 through 7), this book uses popular children's novels such as *Sarah, Plain and Tall*; *Julie of the Wolves*; and *The Island* to teach scientific concepts involving air, weather, the tundra, deserts, fossils, oceans, and lakes. Each chapter centers on a single book, and there are at least eight pages in each of the chapters devoted to science projects related to the subject matter and themes explored in the book. Many activities require only paper and pencil; others, like growing plants and using a compass, require more materials and preparation.   *SCIENCE*

C*; Y

202. **Read to Succeed in Science and Math: A Bibliography for Families**. By AAAS Science Library Institute. American Association for the Advancement of Science, 1996. 10p. Free.

Designed for use by parents, this up-to-date bibliography includes more than 125 recommended science books for children (all but three or four were published during the 1990s). The list of books is preceded by a four-page introduction that discusses the importance of science and offers many practical tips to parents to encourage children to read and foster an interest in science and math. The book titles, which are not annotated but were reviewed by science experts, are arranged in alphabetical order by title under three main categories: Biography, Science Story Books, and Hands-On Science Books. Though listed as books for children, many titles are also suitable for young adults. The authors state that "This list is just a starting point. More recommended books can be found in *Science Books and Films' Best Books for Children*" (which was also published by the AAAS). This short but excellent list is recommended for all libraries serving children and young adults, and is available free by writing to: Directorate for Education and Human Resources Programs, American Association for the Advancement of Science, 1200 New York Ave., NW, Washington, DC 20005.   *SCIENCE; MATHEMATICS*

C; Y*; A

203. **A Reference Guide for Botany and Horticulture**. By Ronald G. Simon. Instructional Media Institute, 1996. 508p. $39.95 pap. 0-9653962-0-7.

More than 300 sources are represented in this outstanding list of instructional materials in botany and horticulture. Primarily a bibliography for adults and high school students, the book does have a short section appended of materials for elementary schools. The materials are listed according to such formats as books, CD-ROMs, software, manuals, kits, models, posters, slides, videodiscs, and videotapes. For each title there are adequate bibliographic material and an annotation. A source directory and indexes are also included. This is a useful purchasing guide for school and public libraries.

BOTANY; HORTICULTURE

C*; Y*

204. **Science Books and Films' Best Books for Children, 1992–1995**. By Tracy Gath and Maria Sopsa. American Association for the Advancement of Science, 1996. 286p. $24. 0-87168-586-8.

All of the listed works were originally reviewed during 1992–1995 in *Science Books and Films*, a review journal of the highly regarded American Association for the Advancement of Science. Only those books that received a "highly recommended" or "recommended" rating are included in this compilation; therefore, this list represents the finest science books for children published recently. The citations are arranged first by broad subject area, such as technology and engineering, and then by more specific headings, such as aeronautics. Complete bibliographic data is provided as well as recommended interest and grade levels. The lengthy, detailed reviews make this bibliography particularly interesting to science teachers. An author and title index completes this bibliography, which should be very valuable for collection development in elementary, middle, and junior high schools as well as public libraries. An earlier compilation, *Science Books and Films' Best Books for Children, 1988–91* (AAAS, 1992. $40), is also available. Inquiries can be addressed to: American Association for the Advancement of Science, 1200 New York Ave., NW, Washington, DC 20005.   *SCIENCE*

C*; Y*

205. **Science Books for Young People**. By Carolyn Phelan. Booklist/American Library Association, 1996. 88p. $9.95 pap. 0-8389-7837-1.

Drawn from *Booklist* reviews, this annotated list of 500 of the best and most recent books for children from kindergarten through eighth grade will help in collection building and evaluation. The selections are excellent and cover the pure sciences from astronomy to zoology.   *SCIENCE*

C; Y

206. **Science Experiments and Projects Index**. By Lisa Holonitch. Highsmith, 1994. 324p. $40. 0-917846-31-1.

The staff of the children's division of the Columbus, Ohio, Public Library was involved in compiling this list of 8,400 science experiments and projects found in 400 books published between 1980 and 1993 and suitable for students in grades K–12. Arranged by subject, each entry is identified and its location given, including page numbers. A bibliography of the books analyzed appears at the back. Unfortunately, grade levels are not indicated, which hinders this work's use for collection development.   *SCIENCE—EXPERIMENTS*

C; Y

207. **Science Experiments Index for Young People**. 2nd ed. By Mary Ann Pilger. Libraries Unlimited, 1996. 400p. $60. 1-56308-341-8.

This is an index to the projects and experiments found in about 1,500 titles. In addition to coverage of the pure physical sciences, some books related indirectly to the sciences (e.g., mathematics projects, those involving food and nutrition) are included. The main section is arranged by subject headings. Each experiment is briefly described, a book number is given, and the specific pages in the book are provided. Grade levels are not given for the experiments. The second section lists, by number, the books analyzed and gives full bibliographic information. This section can be of value in developing library collections. This edition contains entries on nearly 500 new children's science books but retains some coverage from the previous edition, *Science Experiments Index for Young People* (Libraries Unlimited, 1988. 240p. OP. 0-87287-671-3), and its companion volume, *Science Experiments Index for Young People, Update 91* (Libraries Unlimited, 1991. OP. 0-87287-858-9), both of which are still in print. The index is recommended for both elementary and middle school libraries. Also use *Science Fair Project Index* (1992), though it is not as up-to-date.   *SCIENCE-EXPERIMENTS*

C; Y

208. **Science Fair Project Index, 1985–1989: For Grades K–8**. By Cynthia Bishop et al. Scarecrow, 1992. 555p. $55. 0-8108-2555-4.

This index is intended for use by teachers, librarians, and students in the elementary grades to locate material on science fair projects found in 195 books published between 1985 and 1988. Almost all areas of science and many areas of technology are covered. Two earlier compilations, *Science Fair Project Index, 1981–1984* (Scarecrow, 1986. $55.00. 0-8108-1892-2) and *Science Fair Project Index, 1973–1980* (Scarecrow, 1983. $59.50. 0-8108-1605-9), are still available. All are of use in school collections to locate material on science fair projects, but their value for collection development is now limited by their age. See also *Science Experiments Index for Young People* (1996).   *SCIENCE—EXPERIMENTS*

Environment

C; Y

209. **Developing Environmental Awareness Through Children's Literature: A Guide for Teachers and Librarians, K–8**. By Nancy Lee Cecil. McFarland, 1996. $28.50 pap. 0-7864-0221-0.

There are more than 200 books included in this bibliography that portray characters who respect their environment and act on their beliefs. The books are organized under five basic genres: contemporary fiction, folklore, historical fiction, biography, and fantasy. Full bibliographic data are given for each entry plus a descriptive annotation and an indication of the appropriate grade level. There are author, title, and subject indexes.   *ECOLOGY; ENVIRONMENT*

C*; Y*

210.   **E for Environment: An Annotated Bibliography of Children's Books with Environmental Themes**. Bowker, 1992. 306p. $42. 0-8352-3028-7.

This bibliography contains 517 of the best fiction and nonfiction titles published on environmental topics for children from preschool through age 14. The major areas covered are fostering positive attitudes about the environment, ecology, environmental issues, people and nature, and learning activities. Each entry is helpfully annotated with material on contents and age suitability. Emphasis is on recently published materials. An appendix lists the best titles for older students and adults. Access to this material is simplified by author, title, and subject indexes. This will be an extremely useful collection development tool in elementary and middle schools.   *ECOLOGY; ENVIRONMENT*

C; Y

211.   **The World of Water: Linking Fiction to Nonfiction**. By Phyllis J. Perry. Libraries Unlimited, 1995. 149p. $21.50. 1-56308-321-3.

Perry has developed a handy curriculum enrichment book designed to assist teachers in their planning of units of study for grades 5–9 involving the world of water—oceans, rivers, lakes, etc. The work is based on the premise that fiction can serve as a link to nonfiction titles in all areas of curriculum. Entries for each fiction book contain setting, major characters, other books by the author, plot summary, and multidisciplinary activities. Nonfiction includes a short summary and possible topics for further student study. The entries are organized under five major themes: ships, diving, and treasure; animals and plants that live in and around the sea; survival in the world of water; environmental concerns; and additional resources. This interesting and inexpensive work is recommended for every elementary school media center and professional library as a teaching enrichment tool and aid for selection.   *WATER*

Sex Education

C; Y; A

212.   **For Sex Education, See Librarian: A Guide to Issues & Resources**. By Martha Cornog and Timothy Perper. Greenwood, 1996. 408p. $45. 0-3133-29022-9.

Nearly 600 recommended books involving sex education are listed and annotated in this comprehensive bibliography. The titles are suitable for a wide age range, from children through adults. Coverage also includes guidelines for materials selection, access, programming, processing, and how to cope with censorship and vandalism.   *SEX EDUCATION*

C; Y*

213.   **Out of the Closet and into the Classroom: Homosexuality in Books for Young People**. 2nd ed. By Marjorie Lobban and Laurel A. Clyde. Bowker, 1996. 150p. $35 pap. 1-875589-86-4.

More than 120 titles are listed in this fully annotated bibliography dealing with an important and timely topic. A discussion of sexual activity and awareness is an incidental part of the book and is not explicit or overemphasized. Entries are arranged alphabetically by author. Most of the books are intended for preteens and young adults; however, six picture books for two- to five-year-olds are also included. Also, while most of the titles are fiction and deal with male homosexuality (gay sex), almost 25 percent are concerned with lesbian sex. A special feature of the book are seven appendixes that include stories with homosexual main characters; books that just mention homosexuality or use homosexual terms; and books by homosexual authors. This book is recommended for collection development and for reading guidance and reference use by teachers/librarians/parents. It is recommended for all school and public libraries.   *HOMOSEXUALITY*

C; Y; A

214.   **Studies in Human Sexuality: A Selected Guide**. 2nd ed. By Suzanne G. Frayser and Thomas J. Whitby. Libraries Unlimited, 1995. $85. 1-56308-131-8.

More than 1,000 entries are included in this guide to the best in English-language books on human sexuality. There are about 500 new entries in this edition. Topics covered include medicine, psychology, anthropology, sociology, religion, law, history, literature, and the arts plus such issues as sex abuse, rape, sexual harassment, AIDS, homosexuality, and prostitution. Entries get extensive annotations. A coding system suggests reading levels (i.e., professional, popular, children's, and young adults). There are thorough indexes in this excellent guide to nonfiction publications. This resource would be useful in large professional collections. *SEX EDUCATION*

Social Studies

C; Y

215.   **Africa in Literature for Children and Young Adults: An Annotated Bibliography of English-Language Books**. By Meena Khorana. Greenwood, 1994. 368p. $59.95. 0-313-25488-5.

Nearly 700 English-language books set in Africa and published from 1873 to 1994 are described in this annotated bibliography. An additional 120 titles are noted in the annotations. The work reflects how Africans and others have defined, interpreted, and promoted Africa, its cultures and peoples, its religions and beliefs. The titles, which are arranged by genres (traditional literature, fiction, poetry, drama, biography and autobiography, and informational books) within six geographic regions of Africa, are evaluated as to sensitivity to multicultural concerns. Many of the works are from African publishers. The well-written annotations include recommended grade levels and range from 100 to 400 words in length. A list of Afrocentric book distributors is provided as well as author, illustrator, title, and subject indexes. This bibliography will be useful to school and public libraries for evaluating older materials as well as for collection development. *AFRICA*

C*; Y*

216.   **American History for Children and Young Adults: An Annotated Bibliographic Index**. By Vandelia VanMeter. Libraries Unlimited, 1990. 350p. $32.50. 0 87287-731-0.

Almost 3,000 fiction, nonfiction, and biographical titles arranged chronologically by time period and subject are listed in this important collection tool for American history. Each entry includes full bibliographic data, a brief annotation, and a suggested grade level. Also very useful to school and public librarians are the author, title, subject, and grade level indexes. *UNITED STATES—HISTORY*

C; Y; A

217.   **Black History Month Resource Book**. Ed. by Mary Ellen Snodgrass. Gale, 1993. 430p. $34.95. 0-8103-9151-1.

Snodgrass has compiled a rich source book of almost 350 activities that help elementary and secondary schools (and libraries serving young people) publicize and commemorate Black History month in February each year. The activities are arranged in broad subject areas such as art and architecture, cooking, religion, sewing and fashion, speech and drama, myth, and storytelling. Each specific entry includes age or grade level, procedures, materials, estimated cost, and a list of sources. Of special interest is the extensive list of books, articles, films, computer software, resource centers, and the like. The appendixes include a series of indexes such as entry name, age/grade level, and budget estimates. There is no subject index, but the general arrangement helps in accessing specific items. This work is recommended for all libraries—school, public, religious institutions, museums, etc.—serving young people and interested in promoting Black History Month.

AFRICAN AMERICANS; BLACK HISTORY MONTH

C; Y; A

218.   **Celebrating Women's History: A Women's History Month Resource Book**. By Mary Ellen Snodgrass. Gale, 1996. 517p. $44.95. 0-7876-0605-7.

More than 300 activities and projects, from games to arts and crafts activities, display ideas, and tributes to various individuals, highlight this resource book on creative ways to celebrate Woman's History Month in March. These activities are arranged in 29 subject chapters like art, geography, literature, and science. In addition to age/grade level, budget, and procedures, each entry has a list of sources, mostly books and videos. For collection development, there is also an appendix listing museums, newsletters, publishers, and sources of various media. *WOMEN'S HISTORY MONTH; WOMEN*

C; Y
219. **Explorers and Exploration: The Best Resources for Grades 5 Through 9**. By Ann Welton. Oryx, 1993. 192p. $29.95 pap. 0-89774-799-2.

Each of the 10 chapters in this book covers a specific episode or period in exploration from the last 1,000 years. Brief introductory material for each section introduces personalities, causes, locales, and important events. Following this material, there are detailed annotated bibliographies of fiction and nonfiction titles with suggestions on how to use each title with students. This valuable tool can help librarians locate books to enhance the curriculum in the area of social studies. *EXPLORERS*

C*; Y
220. **Exploring the United States Through Literature**. Oryx, 1994–1995. 7 vols. $24.95/vol.

Each of the volumes in this set (see listing below) covers a specific region of the United States and is divided alphabetically into state sections. There are subdivisions by format, including nonfiction, biography, fiction, periodicals, computer programs, videos, audiocassettes, maps, atlases, and filmstrips. Topics covered include geography, history, regional literature and culture, famous people, and folklore. Each entry contains full bibliographic information, an evaluative description of contents, and suggestions for use. The titles (usually about 700 per volume) are for use with children from grades K–8. Appendixes include lists of professional resources and directories of publishers, producers, and vendors. There are also author, title, and subject indexes. The titles are:

220.1 **Great Lakes States**. By Kathy Howard Latrobe. Oryx, 1994. 168p. $24.95 pap. 0-89774-731-3.
States covered: Illinois, Indiana, Michigan, Minnesota, Ohio, and Wisconsin.

220.2 **Mountain States**. By Sharyl G. Smith. Oryx, 1994. 176p. $24.95 pap. 0-89774-783-6.
States covered: Colorado, Idaho, Montana, Nevada, Utah, and Wyoming.

220.3 **Northeast States**. By P. Diane Frey. Oryx, 1995. 280p. $24.95 pap. 0-89774-779-8.
States covered: Connecticut, Delaware, District of Columbia, Maine, Maryland, Massachusetts, New Hampshire, New Jersey, New York, Pennsylvania, Rhode Island, and Vermont.

220.4 **Pacific States**. By Carol A. Doll. Oryx, 1994. 168p. $24.95 pap. 0-89774-771-2.
States covered: Alaska, California, Hawaii, Oregon, and Washington.

220.5 **Plains States**. By Carolyn S. Brodie. Oryx, 1994. 136p. $24.95 pap. 0-89774-762-3.
States covered: Iowa, Kansas, Missouri, Nebraska, North Dakota, and South Dakota.

220.6 **Southeast States**. By Linda Veltze. Oryx, 1994. 224p. $24.95 pap. 0-89774-770-4.
States included: Alabama, Arkansas, Florida, Georgia, Kentucky, Louisiana, Mississippi, North Carolina, South Carolina, Tennessee, Virginia, and West Virginia.

220.7 **Southwest States**. By Pat Tipton Sharp. Oryx, 1994. 120p. $24.95 pap. 0-89774-765-8.
States included: Arizona, New Mexico, Oklahoma, and Texas.
GEOGRAPHY; UNITED STATES

C*; Y*
221. **Learning About the Holocaust: Literature and Other Resources for Young People**. By Elaine C. Stephens et al. Library Professional Publications/Shoe String Press, 1995. 188p. $29.50; $18.50 pap. 0-208-02398-4; 0-208-02408-5 pap.

Following a brief historical overview of the Holocaust, the authors, all university professors, have compiled a comprehensive and annotated bibliography of nearly 300 titles appropriate for kindergarten through high school. The work is arranged by chapters on various types of materials including nonfiction, photoessays, maps, personal narratives, poetry, biography, drama, and fiction. Within each genre the items are arranged by level. Each entry includes bibliographic citation, quotes from the text, descriptive summary, and suggestions for teachers and librarians who work with young people. A final section includes lists of organizations and institutions, curriculum guides, journals, and nonprint resources. This useful bibliographic guide is recommended as a selection aid, collection development tool, and teaching aid for teachers and librarians at all levels. *HOLOCAUST; JEWS*

C; Y

222.   **Nuclear Age Literature for Youth: The Quest for a Life-Affirming Ethic.** By Millicent Lenz. American Library Association, 1990. 315p. $32.50 pap. 0-8389-0535-8.

The purpose of this interesting work is to identify and analyze books for children and young adults that deal with the fears and anxieties over nuclear war and its aftermath. Identification is also made of the development in literature of a new kind of hero, a biophile—a "lover of the total life system." Critical analyses and plot summaries are provided for many titles, which will help teachers develop units on peace and help librarians acquire related materials. This unique text is recommended for school and public libraries for reference and collection development.   *NUCLEAR WARFARE; PEACE*

C; Y

223.   **Peoples of the American West: Historical Perspectives Through Children's Literature.** By Mary Hurlbut Cordier and Maria A. Perez-Stable. Scarecrow, 1989. 230p. $22.50. 0-8108-2240-7.

The focus of this annotated bibliography of almost 100 children's books is on the westward movement and the winning of the West during the latter part of the nineteenth century. There is some preliminary information on the importance of making history live through children's literature, but the heart of the book is the bibliographic entries, which are divided into broad topics such as homesteading, overland journeys, immigrants and immigration, Native Americans, and the American Southwest. Titles are further subdivided by grade level. This brief book is recommended for all elementary and middle school libraries and public libraries serving young people.   *WEST (U.S.); WESTWARD EXPANSION*

C; Y

224.   **War and Peace Literature for Children and Young Adults: A Resource Guide to Significant Issues.** By Virginia A. Walter. Oryx, 1993. 171p. $27.50. 0-89774-725-9.

This resource guide is more than a bibliography. Walter devotes a great deal of the book to discussing developmental needs of young people and relating them to problems with evolving an understanding of such events as the Holocaust, concentration camps, and the bombing of Hiroshima. Other issues discussed, all within the framework of a bibliography, include the futility and nobility of war, survival, heroism, and propaganda. The sections on peace and conflict resolution are especially well developed. Bibliographic citations are adequate. Other strong features of this work include an annotated list of resources for adults and four complete indexes. Kennemer's book *Using Literature to Teach Middle Grades About War*, another worthwhile resource on the same subject, was published in 1993; however, it has a narrower focus, both in level and in coverage. Nevertheless, both books are recommended as reference guides and as aids for collection development in school and public libraries.   *PEACE; WAR*

C; Y

225.   **The Ways of War: The Era of World War II in Children's and Young Adult Fiction.** By M. Paul Holsinger. Scarecrow, 1995. $57.50. 0-8108-2925-X.

Holsinger has compiled a comprehensive bibliography of more than 1,000 titles with World War II as the main theme or backdrop setting and that are appropriate for young people. These are books that portray the horrors of war but at the same time allow for a rich reading experience. Each entry in this narrowly focused bibliography includes publication information, a detailed annotation, and an evaluation symbol based on a four-star rating. Title, geographic, and thematic indexes complete this interesting work. Recommended for most libraries serving young people.   *WORLD WAR II—FICTION*

C; Y

226.   **World History for Children and Young Adults: An Annotated Bibliographic Index.** By Vandelia VanMeter. Libraries Unlimited, 1992. 425p. OP. 0-87287-732-9.

This unique bibliography identifies and describes more than 2,000 fiction and nonfiction books appropriate for children in grades K–12 dealing with world events. Each title has been reviewed favorably. The entries are arranged by time periods, then subdivided by subject. Full bibliographic data, a brief annotation, and recommended grade level are also provided for each entry. Find a copy of this reference guide for all libraries that serve or work with young people.

WORLD HISTORY; HISTORICAL FICTION

Special Audiences

C; Y

227. **The Juvenile Collection**. Recording for the Blind and Dyslexic, 1996. $29.95.

Y; A

228. **The Adult Collection**. Recording for the Blind and Dyslexic, 1996. $49.95.

These catalogs list about 75,000 audiotapes and computer disks that are available from the recording center for the blind and dyslexic. They include textbooks, professional books, computer manuals, and volumes of general literature. About 3,000 new titles are added per year. These lists allow access by author, title, and subject. They can be bought together for $69.95, or singly at the prices listed above. Orders can be placed with: Recording for the Blind and Dyslexic, 20 Roszel Rd., Princeton, NJ 08540. *BLIND; DYSLEXIC*

C; Y

229. **Portraying Persons with Disabilities: An Annotated Bibliography of Fiction for Children and Teenagers**. 3rd ed. By Debra E. J. Robertson. Bowker, 1992. 482p. $39.95. 0-8352-3023-6.

This selective annotated bibliography lists more than 650 fiction titles that help promote understanding and acceptance of the disabled. The selected titles are intended for young people between the ages of 5 and 18. This work updates the earlier editions by Baskin and Harris: *Notes from a Different Drummer* (1977. $21.95. 0-8352-0978-4) and *More Notes from a Different Drummer* (1984. $35.00. 0-8352-1871-6). This volume serves as a companion volume to *Portraying Persons with Disabilities: An Annotated Bibliography of Nonfiction for Children and Teenagers* (see next entry). This work is recommended for all school and public libraries as a tool for bibliotherapy, reading guidance, and collection development. *DISABILITIES*

C; Y

230. **Portraying Persons with Disabilities: An Annotated Bibliography of Nonfiction for Children and Teenagers**. By Joan Brest Friedberg et al. Bowker, 1992. 385p. $39.95. 0-8352-3022-8.

This work describes and evaluates 350 nonfiction titles about individuals with disabilities. It is written for youngsters ages two and up and serves as a companion volume to *Portraying Persons with Disabilities: An Annotated Bibliography of Fiction for Children and Teenagers*. This selection also updates the much earlier *Accept Me as I Am*. Both titles are highly recommended as guides to bibliotherapy, reading guidance, and collection building for all school and public libraries. *DISABILITIES*

C; Y; A

231. **A Reader's Guide for Parents of Children with Mental, Physical, or Emotional Disabilities**. 3rd ed. By Cory Moore. Woodbine House, 1990. 248p. $14.95 pap. 0-933149-27-1.

This guide to up-to-date information about disabilities has several focuses. First, it is designed to help parents find current information about living with a disabled child as well as information about specific conditions. Second, it is intended to supply a list of books written for children and young adults for librarians and other professionals to use in bibliotherapy work. For each disability discussed in the second section of the book, there are a list of basic readings and sources for additional information. The volume concludes with publishers' addresses and indexes of organizations and agencies (a good source for vertical file information), authors and editors, titles, and subjects. Most of the sources cited are dated in the 1980s. All include full bibliographic information and a concise annotation. There are several similar sources on the topic, but none as broad-based. For example, Friedberg's *Accept Me as I Am* is an excellent bibliography but deals only with nonfiction titles and is five years older. Moore's book is inexpensive; it deserves to be in every school and public library as a reference tool and as a selection aid. *DISABILITIES; MENTAL HANDICAPS; PHYSICAL HANDICAPS*

C; Y

232. **Understanding Abilities, Disabilities, and Capabilities: A Guide to Children's Literature**. By Margaret F. Carlin et al. Libraries Unlimited, 1991. 114p. OP. 0-87287-717-5.

This innovative bibliography includes books, films, and other nonprint media covering more than 40 handicapping conditions. All of the items are appropriate for children ages 2–18. The entries include bibliographic information and an indication of readability and suggested age level. The annotations, which are both descriptive and critical, are quite lengthy and are useful for booktalks. Copies of this book, on an important subject, should be found for all school and public libraries.

DISABILITIES; MENTAL HANDICAPS; PHYSICAL HANDICAPS

Sports, Hobbies, and Recreation

C

233. **Crafts Index for Young People**. By Mary Anne Pilger. Libraries Unlimited, 1992. 288p. OP. 1-56308-002-8.

Pilger has consulted more than 1,000 books in order to compile this index of craft projects; they are listed in the back of the work in numerical order. The individual craft entries are listed by subject in alphabetical order; each entry contains the number and page of the master list. Find a copy to serve as a starting point for building up a collection of craft books for elementary school and children's departments of public libraries. *HANDICRAFTS*

C; Y; A

234. **The Crafts Supply Sourcebook: A Comprehensive Shop-by-Mail Guide**. 3rd ed. By Margaret A. Boyd. Betterway Publications, 1994. 286p. $16.95 pap. 1-55870-355-1.

This is an omnibus item that contains material on 2,600 suppliers of craft products plus coverage for information sources. Part 1 lists suppliers under such subject areas as stained glass craft, jewelry making, sculpture, wine and beer making, model railroading, and photography. Part 2 does the same for every variety of needlecraft. The third part, called "Resources," contains general information about crafts and gives a useful list of books, other publications, and associations. This volume will have many uses in public libraries and in art programs in schools. *HANDICRAFTS*

C; Y

235. **Fun for Kids II: An Index to Children's Craft Books**. By Marion F. Gallivan. Scarecrow, 1992. 482p. $42.50. 0-8108-2546-5.

Fun for Kids (Scarecrow, 1981. $25. 0-8108-1439-0), the original volume in this series, was published in 1981. This continuation of the parent volume indexes more than 300 craft books published between 1981 and 1990 for youngsters in preschool through the eighth grade. The first part of this book is a listing of the books indexed; the second is a subject index with reference to the author of the book, appropriate page numbers, grade level suitability and the material needed. Last, there is an index to the kinds of material used (e.g., burlap). This work will be a great help to everyone responsible for providing craft activities for children and for librarians. It can also be used as an acquisition tool.

HANDICRAFTS

C; Y; A

236. **Sport on Film and Video: North American Society for Sport History Guide**. By Judith A. Davidson and Daryl Adler. Scarecrow, 1993. 204p. $32.50. 0-8108-2739-5.

This filmography briefly describes the content of each of the recommended films and videos. The films cover an amazing range of sports and interests, and each film has been proven effective in a classroom situation. Age suitability from elementary through adult is indicated.

MOTION PICTURES; VIDEOCASSETTES; SPORTS

III

Sources for Children (Preschool–Grade 6)

General and Miscellaneous

C*
237.   **Adventuring with Books: A Booklist for Pre-K–Grade 6**. 10th ed. Ed. by Julie M. Jensen and the Committee on the Elementary School Booklist of the National Council of Teachers of English. National Council of Teachers of English, 1993. 603p. $19.95 pap. 0-8141-0079-1.

This newest edition of an excellent bibliography describes and categorizes 1,800 of "the best" children's books published between 1988 and 1992, an increase of about 50 since the earlier 1989 edition. Fiction, nonfiction, and picture book titles are chosen on the basis of literary and artistic quality and overall accuracy. This edition includes more titles for the very young. Each entry includes basic bibliographic information, recommended age and grade levels, and a brief annotation. Books are arranged into 20 broad categories. Added bonuses include a chapter on book awards and book lists; a directory of publishers; and author, illustrator, title, and subject indexes. This outstanding standard bibliography belongs in every elementary school and public library.

CHILDREN'S LITERATURE (GENERAL); PICTURE BOOKS

C*
238.   **Best Books for Children: Preschool Through Grade 6**. 5th ed. By John T. Gillespie and Corinne J. Naden. Bowker, 1994. 1,411p. $65. 0-8352-3455-X.

This greatly expanded and updated 5th edition of highly selected books for children includes more than 15,500 fully annotated individual titles; almost 4,500 additional titles are mentioned in the annotations. Entries are arranged under eight very broad subject or curriculum areas, then sublisted under more specific topics. Each entry includes author, title, grade level, illustrator, publisher, date, price, ISBN, and a brief annotation. Almost one-third of the book consists of extremely useful indexes: author, illustrator, title, and subject/grade/reading level. This valuable basic tool is highly recommended for collection development and reading guidance for all libraries serving children or those that work with children from preschool through middle school.   *CHILDREN'S LITERATURE (GENERAL)*

C*
239.   **The Best in Children's Books: The University of Chicago Guide to Children's Literature, 1985–1990**. 4th ed. By Zena Sutherland. University of Chicago, 1991. 616p. $37.50. 0-226-78064-3.

Sutherland, former editor of the highly regarded *Bulletin of the Center for Children's Books*, has continued the high standards of reviewing in this most recent edition of *The Best in Children's Books*. Three earlier editions cover the time periods 1966–1972, 1973–1978, and 1979–1984 and are still useful and in print. This edition includes almost 1,200 titles all chosen on the basis of literary merit, and all originally reviewed in the *Bulletin*. Titles are arranged alphabetically by author. Each entry includes plot, type of illustration, reading level, and complete ordering information. Titles of special distinction are so identified. The six indexes are an added strength of this guide: title, developmental values, curricular use, reading level, subject, and type of literature. This well-known bibliography is highly recommended as a reading guidance, reference, and collection development aid for teachers, librarians, parents, and others working with children. *CHILDREN'S LITERATURE (GENERAL)*

C*

240.   **Bibliography of Books for Children**. Ed. by Helen Shelton. Association for Childhood Education International (ACEI), 112p. annual. $15.

This standard bibliographic reference tool has been published since 1937. In this edition, entries are arranged into various sections by type, i.e., picture books, fiction, nonfiction, reference sources, and periodicals. Fiction is alphabetical by author; nonfiction is listed by Dewey Decimal Classification. Each entry provides full bibliographic information as well as a reading level and a brief annotation. This inexpensive work is highly recommended for all libraries that serve children and those working with children. *CHILDREN'S LITERATURE (GENERAL)*

C*

241.   **Books for Children**. By Margaret N. Coughlan. Children's Literature Center of the Library of Congress, U.S. Government Printing Office, annual. $1.

With all the authority of the venerable Library of Congress, Coughlan and a committee of children's book specialists from school and public libraries have compiled this annual list of the finest in children's books. Actually each year about 100 are chosen out of 3,000–4,000 considered. The books are arranged by approximate age group, then in alphabetical order by title. A supplementary list of "Also Worthy of Note," books to which it is difficult to assign an age label, is an added bonus. Any school or public library should consider purchasing this list in quantity and distributing it to parents, teachers, and other adults. Certainly, the titles are highly selective and the price is right. The lists for the past few years are available for $1 each from: Superintendent of Documents, U.S. Government Printing Office, Department 39-LC, Washington, DC 20402. *CHILDREN'S LITERATURE (GENERAL)*

C

242.   **Books to Share: Notable Children's Books of [year]**. Office of Children's Services, Westchester (NY) Library System, annual.

This list of children's books is selected by a group of children's librarians. Approximately 100 titles are chosen per year. Titles are arranged under seven popular categories and have brief notes. The Westchester Library System may also have available similar selected lists for nominal costs, such as *Reading for the Fun of It: A Guide to Books for Children with Learning Disabilities* ($3.50), and *Sharing the World's Magic: A Guide to Folk Literature for Children with Learning Disabilities* ($3.00). Above titles and a list of others currently in-print are available from: Judith Rovenger, Westchester Library System, 8 Westchester Plaza, Elmsford, NY 10523. *CHILDREN'S LITERATURE (GENERAL)*

C*

243.   **Children and Books**. 9th ed. By Zena Sutherland. Addison Wesley Longmans, 1997. 800p. $56.59. 0-673-99733-2.

This has become a standard text on children's literature, and rightly so because it gives a thorough and tasteful introduction to all aspects of this subject. It is now organized into four broad areas: "Knowing Children and Books," "Exploring the Types of Literature," "Bringing Children and Books Together," and "Areas and Issues." All parts contain helpful bibliographies, but because the second part deals with specific authors and their works, the bibliographies here can serve as buying guides to the best in children's literature. There are also valuable bibliographies on selection aids and on recommended readings that explore special topics. Appendixes include a directory of publishers and children's book awards. There are author, title, illustrator, and subject indexes. Highly recommended for all children's literature collections. *CHILDREN'S LITERATURE (GENERAL)*

C

244. **Children's Books [year]: 100 Books for Reading and Sharing**. By the New York Public Library's Children Book Committee. New York Public Library, annual. 16p. $3 pap.

This annotated listing of 100 outstanding new books is arranged by three levels of readers plus sections of picture books, poetry, and folk and fairy tales. The latest edition is available for $3 plus $1 postage from the Office of Branch Libraries, NYPL, 455 Fifth Ave., New York, NY 10016. Also available is a retrospective look at important children's books, annotated and arranged by decade: *Children's Books, 1911–1986: Favorite Children's Books from the Branch Collections of the New York Public Library*. This is available from the same address for $5.   *CHILDREN'S LITERATURE (GENERAL)*

C*

245. **Children's Books of the Year**. By the Child Study Children's Book Committee. Bank Street College, annual. $6.

The Child Study Children's Book Committee is composed of educators, librarians, authors, illustrators, and other specialists. Each year since 1916, it has prepared a list of the year's recommended children's books suitable for readers from preschool through age 14. The works (usually about 600 per issue) are high in quality and grouped by age suitability or by special subjects (e.g., poetry). There are tips for parents and author, illustrator, and title indexes. This book list can be obtained for a check for $6 made out to Child Study Children's Book Committee and sent to: Committee at Bank Street College of Education, 610 W. 112 St., New York, NY 10025. Back issues are available, as are other specialized book lists.   *CHILDREN'S LITERATURE (GENERAL)*

C

246. **Children's Books to Own**. By the Children's and Youth Services Department. Detroit Public Library, annual. 16p. $1 pap.

This booklet, aimed chiefly at parents, annotates and gives age and interest levels for a select group of children's books suitable for the home library. Paperback editions are included. The booklet is available for a check for $1 made out to Detroit Library Commission and sent to: Public Relations Department, Detroit Public Library, 5201 Woodward, Detroit, MI 48202.

CHILDREN'S LITERATURE (GENERAL)

C*

247. **Children's Catalog**. 17th ed. H. W. Wilson, 1996. 1,400p. $105. 0-8242-0893-5.

This is a mainstay for supplying authoritative material for collection development in elementary schools and children's rooms in public libraries. Compiled by specialists in children's library work from around the United States, the current volume lists and annotates more than 6,000 titles for grades pre-K through six. The first section lists nonfiction works arranged by Dewey Decimal numbers. Section two is for fiction books arranged by author's last name. There are separate sections for story collections and easy books. Each entry contains full bibliographic and cataloging information plus excerpts, usually two, from reviews. The first is descriptive and the second critical. The second half of the book is given over to a huge author, title, subject, and analytical index. There are more than 7,000 analytical references to short stories or specific parts of nonfiction books. Purchase of the main volume also entitles the owner to four annual paperback supplements listing more than 500 titles each and covering 1997, 1998, 1999, and 2000. This title is useful for evaluating collections as well as serving as a selection and purchasing tool. Highly recommended.   *CHILDREN'S LITERATURE (GENERAL)*

C

248. **Children's Choices for [year]**. By the International Reading Association and the Children's Book Council Joint Committee. International Reading Association, annual. free.

The first *Children's Choices* appeared in the November 1975 issue of *The Reading Teacher*. The list continues to appear annually in this periodical, but reprints are available from the International Reading Association. It is a preferential selection of newly published books selected by about 10,000 young people scattered around the United States in five teams. The 100+ titles are arranged by broad age groups and are annotated with descriptive comments and quotes from young reviewers. There are no indexes. New annual listings are usually available in October. There are now two companion reprints.

Young Adults' Choices (selected by the same team method) appears first in the September issue of *Journal of Reading* and contains approximately 30 well-annotated titles. *Teachers' Choices* is found in the November issue of *The Reading Teacher* and lists, with annotations, about 25 titles that teachers find useful in curriculum use. These attractive pamphlets are available free from the International Reading Association, 800 Barksdale Rd., Newark, DE 19714-8139 for a self-addressed stamped 9"x12" envelope. Postage for the *Children's* list is for four ounces first class and two ounces for the other two. Bulk copies are available at the following rates: 10 copies, $6; 100 copies, $45; 500 copies, $170.

CHILDREN'S LITERATURE (GENERAL); YOUNG ADULT LITERATURE (GENERAL)

C*; Y
249.   **Children's Classics: A Book List for Parents**. Horn Book, 1990. 20p. $3.

This pamphlet recommends classics in the field of literature for both children and young adults. It is available for $3 with $.50 postage to Horn Book, 14 Beacon St., Boston, MA 02108.

CHILDREN'S LITERATURE (GENERAL); YOUNG ADULT LITERATURE (GENERAL)

C*
250.   **Children's Literature in the Elementary School**. 6th ed. By Charlotte S. Huck and Susan Hepler. Brown and Benchmark, 1996. 800p. $45. 0-697-27960-X.

This highly respected text on children's literature gives an excellent survey of the kinds of children's literature and ways of making it central to a school's curriculum. Each chapter contains valuable bibliographies of books and materials about children's literature or lists of quality titles for children. These lists can serve as a bibliography for a basic collection in school and public libraries.

CHILDREN'S LITERATURE (GENERAL)

C
251.   **Dictionary of American Children's Fiction, 1859–1959: Books of Recognized Merit**. By Alethea K. Helbig and Agnes Regan Perkins. Greenwood, 1985. 640p. $79.50. 0-313-22590-7.

This alphabetically arranged reference work contains entries under author, title, and major characters for 420 award-winning children's books of more than 5,000 words (picture books are excluded) published between 1859 and 1959. The entries for titles are the longest and give plot summaries and critical evaluations. Author entries give brief biographical information, and character entries describe the characters and their roles in the novel. An extensive, excellent index section includes characters not mentioned in the main body, settings by place and time, subjects, and themes. This valuable reference tool can be helpful in developing historical collections of children's literature. There are continuation volumes by the same two authors that are similar in organization and presentation: *Dictionary of American Children's Fiction, 1960–1984: Recent Books of Recognized Merit* (1986. $79.50. 0-313-25233-5); *Dictionary of American Children's Fiction, 1985–1989: Recent Books of Recognized Merit* (1993. $59.95. 0-313-27719-2); and *Dictionary of American Children's Fiction, 1990–1995: Books of Recognized Merit* (1997. $79.00. 0-313-28763-5). Also see the authors' *Dictionary of British Children's Fiction: Books of Recognized Merit* and *Dictionary of Children's Fiction from Australia, Canada, India, New Zealand, & Selected African Countries*.   *CHILDREN'S LITERATURE (GENERAL)*

C
252.   **Dictionary of British Children's Fiction: Books of Recognized Merit**. By Alethea K. Helbig and Agnes Regan Perkins. Greenwood, 1989. 2 vols. $150. 0-313-22591-5.

Some 1,626 entries in this work analyze 387 prize-winning British books published from 1687 to 1985. Only works of 5,000 words or more were included, thus omitting picture books. There are entries for authors, titles, and major characters. Title entries have the greatest amount of information, including both British and American editions, a plot summary, and critical comment. Author entries give biographical material and a bibliography of principal works. Character entries are for identification purposes. There is a lengthy index (more than 200 pages) that includes subject and thematic references and a listing of books by time and setting. This reference work will be valuable where historical information on children's literature is needed. It can also serve as a tool for collection development. This is a companion piece to the authors' *Dictionary of American Children's Fiction*.

CHILDREN'S LITERATURE (GENERAL)

C

253.   **Dictionary of Children's Fiction from Australia, Canada, India, New Zealand, and Selected African Countries: Books of Recognized Merit**. By Alethea K. Helbig and Agnes Regan Perkins. Greenwood, 1992. 459p. $89.50. 0-313-26126-1.

This companion volume to the authors' *Dictionary of American Children's Fiction* and *Dictionary of British Children's Fiction* profiles 263 important books by 164 authors with entries that cover authors, titles and plot summaries, important characters, settings, and themes. About half of the books have appeared in American editions. Appendixes list the books by country and by prizes won. A fine volume for students of children's literature interested in its international aspects.

CHILDREN'S LITERATURE (GENERAL)

C

254.   **Educator's Companion to Children's Literature. Vol. 1: Mysteries, Animal Tales, Books of Humor, Adventure Stories, and Historical Fiction**. By Sharron L. McElmeel. Libraries Unlimited, 1995. 153p. $23.50 pap. 1-56308-329-9.

Five genres popular with young readers are explored in this manual on how to promote learning through reading. In each section a principal book and several related titles are recommended along with a number of activities useful for both classroom teachers and librarians. A companion volume, *Educator's Companion to Children's Literature. Vol. 2: Folklore, Contemporary Realistic Fiction, Fantasy, Biographies, and Tales from Here and There* (Libraries Unlimited, 1996. 160p. $24 pap. 1-56308-330-2), examines five other genres in a similar format. Though not specific selection aids, the recommendations in these works are reliable and can be used to evaluate collections.

CHILDREN'S LITERATURE (GENERAL)

C*

255.   **The Elementary School Library Collection: A Guide to Books and Other Media**. 20th ed. By Linda L. Homa. Brodart, 1996. 1,200p. $139.50. 0-87272-105-1.

This highly respected, reliable selection aid for school library collection development now contains more than 12,000 print and nonprint titles and covers preschool through grade six, including more than 2,000 titles new to this edition. For each of these recommended titles are given bibliographic information, cataloging and ordering information, a descriptive annotation, interest and reading levels, and acquisition priority (phase 1, 2, or 3). Titles available in large print and titles available from the National Library for the Blind and Physically Handicapped are also indicated. Selections are made with the help of a committee of specialists. The basic arrangement is first by Dewey Decimal number for nonfiction titles, followed by fiction and easy books. Professional materials are included, and lists of media for preschool children, books for beginning readers, and recommended titles in publisher and author series are appended. Extensive author, title, and subject indexes are provided. New editions appear every two years. This excellent, highly recommended source for basic collection development is unique in the scope of material included and in its indication of priority purchasing. ESLC is available in traditional book format and on a CD-ROM in single or networkable versions searchable from 16 access points (e.g., author, title, series, reading level). For more information contact Brodart, 500 Arch St., Williamsport, PA 17705.   *CHILDREN'S LITERATURE (GENERAL); AUDIOVISUAL MATERIALS;*
CD-ROMS; COMPUTER SOFTWARE

C

256.   **Eyeopeners II: Children's Books to Answer Children's Questions About the World Around Them**. By Beverly Kobrin. Scholastic, 1995. 305p. $6.95 pap. 0-590-48402-8.

This guide, a revised and updated edition of *Eyeopeners* (1988), describes about 800 nonfiction titles for grades K through 8 with many tips on interesting ways they can be used to bring children and books together. The bibliography is preceded by a section on the importance of reading and suggestions on how to encourage quality reading. The books are organized by subjects such as dinosaurs, cars, and music as well as by problem topics like death, sex, alcoholism, and divorce. All materials are annotated and were in print as of 1995. There is an index by authors and illustrators, titles, and detailed subjects. This bibliography is intended both for parents and teachers as well as librarians and therefore contains material with which experienced librarians might already be familiar. However the author's enthusiasm helps make this book a delight to read and it still has many uses including collection development. The earlier edition, though now out-of-print, may still be valuable (Penguin, 1988. $10.95 pap. 0-14-046830-7). *CHILDREN'S LITERATURE (GENERAL)*

C
257.   **Great New Nonfiction Reads**. By Sharron L. McElmeel. Libraries Unlimited, 1995. 224p. $21 pap. 1-56308-228-4.

The author, a school librarian, has compiled a bibliography of 140 nonfiction main titles chosen for their authenticity, appeal, accuracy, and recentness that can by used as read-alouds or for independent reading with children in grades 1 through 6. After an introduction on choosing and using informational books, there are two main sections. The first lists about 120 books under alphabetically arranged subjects from "Adopting" to "Wounds and Injuries." One book is included under each topic with several others mentioned in the entry in a section called "Connections." Entries also include bibliographic information, age and grade levels, series information, and a detailed summary. Similar information is supplied in the second section on biographies. Each section has its own author and title index, with complete indexes by author, title, and subject at the back. About 600 titles are included. As well as a selection aid, this bibliography will be useful for teachers and librarians in giving reading guidance.

CHILDREN'S LITERATURE (GENERAL); NONFICTION

C*
258.   **More Exciting, Funny, Scary, Short, Different, and Sad Books Kids Like About Animals, Science, Sports, Families, Songs, and Other Things**. Ed. by Frances Laverne Carroll and Mary Meacham. American Library Association, 1992. 192p. $18 pap. 0-8389-0585-4.

This volume updates and complements an earlier title that is still useful but no longer in-print: *Exciting, Funny, Scary* . . . (1985). There is very little duplication with the older title, and, as before, the list of titles favored by children was submitted to the editors by practicing librarians. These titles, which are intended primarily for youngsters in grades 2–5 (with a number stretching into junior high level), are arranged under 75 popular topics, each containing about 4–12 titles. Books in each category are arranged in alphabetical order by title; each contains a brief annotation. Author-title and subject indexes are provided. This inexpensive volume is useful for booktalks, reading guidance work, and, of course, collection development; it is recommended for all libraries that serve or work with children.

CHILDREN'S LITERATURE (GENERAL)

C*
259.   **More Kids' Favorite Books: A Compilation of Children's Choices, 1992–1994**. Children's Book Council/International Reading Association, 1995. 132p. $8. 0-87207-130-8.

More than 300 annotated titles are included in this brief bibliography, which is based on the International Reading Association's annual Children's Choices lists that appear in the *Reading Teacher*. A companion bibliography dealing with teenagers—*More Teens' Favorite Books*—is also available through the IRA. The selections and evaluations for this children's edition were solicited from 10,000 kids ages 4 to 13, from every section of the United States. The titles are arranged by five suggested reading levels. Annotations were written by the youngsters themselves. Title, author, and illustrator indexes complete this list of favorite books, which is recommended as an aid to promoting reading and as a selection tool for public and school libraries. To order send a check payable to International Reading Association to: Order Department, International Reading Association, 800 Barksdale Rd, Box 8139, Newark, DE 19714-8139. *CHILDREN'S LITERATURE (GENERAL)*

C
260.   **The New York Times Parent's Guide to the Best Books for Children**. By Eden Ross Lipson. Times Books/Random House, 1991. 464p. $15 pap. 0-8129-1688-3.

According to the author, this revised and updated book "is for people who know and love particular children and want them to grow up loving particular books." Lipson, the Children's Book Review editor of *The New York Times*, has compiled a handy guide to almost 2,000 titles for every age group from preschool to middle school. They are indexed under 55 topics such as picture books, religion, funny books, and dinosaur books for babies. This book is popular and inexpensive, and it will help parents and their local libraries select good books for children. For that purpose, this list is recommended for all libraries that serve children.   *CHILDREN'S LITERATURE (GENERAL); READING GUIDANCE*

C*

261.   **Popular Reading for Children III: A Collection of Booklist Columns**. Ed. by Sally Estes. American Library Association, 1992. 64p. OP. 0-8389-7599-2.

This short volume is a gold mine of retrospective bibliographies of popular books for children that have appeared in *Booklist* between 1986 and 1991. They are the "books kids want on the subjects kids care about," including dragons and dinosaurs, eerie reading, historical fiction, humor, and things that go bump in the night—it's all here. This guide could be used in conjunction with its companion volume *Popular Reading for Young Adults*. This handy and inexpensive list is recommended for all libraries that work with children.   *CHILDREN'S LITERATURE (GENERAL)*

C

262.   **Reading Is Fundamental**.

RIF is a nationwide organization dedicated to the promotion of reading, especially for the very young in areas of our country that are considered disadvantaged. They have published a number of worthwhile pamphlets, reading lists, and guides. Four recent publications include:

262.1   **Encouraging Young Writers**

262.2   **Building a Family Library**

262.3   **Family Storytelling**

262.4   **Summertime Reading**

These lists are available for $.50 each or $15 for 100. For these lists and other information write to: RIF, 600 Maryland Ave., SW, Ste. 500, Washington, DC 20024.

CHILDREN'S LITERATURE (GENERAL); STORYTELLING

C

263.   **Tried and True: 500 Nonfiction Books Children Want to Read**. By George Wilson and Joyce Moss. Bowker, 1992. 300p. $34.95. 0-8352-3026-0.

The 500 child-tested titles chosen for this list were selected by a panel of librarians, educators, and children. The books are intended for work with children ages 4 to 8. The volume is organized by grade level into groups of books that children will read for enjoyment, and books children will read for research. The books are then further divided into specific subject categories. Each entry includes full bibliographic information, reading level, and a brief annotation. All entries are indexed by author, title, subject, and reading level. The compilers of this work are also the authors of *Books for Children to Read Alone*, another list of tried-and-true books. Both titles are recommended for all elementary school and public libraries.   *CHILDREN'S LITERATURE (GENERAL)*

Audiovisual Materials

C

264.   **All Ears: How to Use and Choose Recorded Music for Children**. By Jill Jarnow. Viking/Penguin, 1991. 210p. $9.95 pap. 0-67082-313-9.

This is an annotated guide to recordings for children intended for parents, teachers, and children's librarians. In addition to the list of recommended titles, the guide contains brief profiles of popular stars, such as Rosenshontz and Sharon, and recognizes the contributions of such early leaders as Ella Jenkins and Pete Seeger. Entries are indexed by subject and age. Recommended for elementary school and public libraries serving children.   *MUSIC; PHONORECORDINGS*

C

265.   American Library Association's Best of the Best for Children: Software - Books - Magazines - Video. Ed. by Denise Perry Donavin. Random House, 1992. OP. 0-679-40450-3; 0-679-74250-6 pap.

Booklist reviewer Donavin has compiled and edited this very comprehensive guide of more than 1,500 items considered "the best" for children from preschoolers through early teens. In addition to the materials noted in the subtitle, the volume also includes toys, games, cassettes, and travel activities. Donavin has drawn on the expertise of the reviewers as well as the youth divisions of the American Library Association for her selections. The annotated entries are arranged thematically and then by format. This work is highly recommended for use as a reference tool and selection aid by teachers, parents, and librarians who work with children of all ages.

CHILDREN'S LITERATURE (GENERAL); PERIODICALS; TOYS; GAMES; INSTRUCTIONAL MATERIALS

C

266.   Buyer's Guide to Children's Software. High/Scope Press, 1995. 196p. $19.95 pap. 0-929816-96-X.

More than 600 reviews are included in this volume on software for children ages three to seven. Also included is information about the software market and descriptions of the High/Scope Award for Excellence winners. For each entry there are descriptions, evaluations, and producers' addresses. Screen samples are given for the majority of the programs discussed. Special features in this guide include a computer terminology glossary, a description of the evaluation process, and a directory of national software manufacturers. This work will be very useful in elementary and preschool libraries. For information on price and ordering write: High/Scope Educational Research Foundation, 600 N. River St., Ypsilanti, MI 48198-2898.   *COMPUTER SOFTWARE*

C

267.   Children's Jukebox: A Subject Guide to Musical Recordings and Programming Ideas for Songsters Ages One to Twelve. By Rob Reid. American Library Association, 1995. 270p. $25. pap. 0-8389-0650-8.

Approximately 2,400 children's songs are organized and listed under 35 subject headings from Anatomy to Weather. The author, a children's librarian, has "kid tested" many of these songs in his own library. Approximately 400 to 500 songs get extensive annotations, summaries, programming tips, and suggested age and interest levels. For collection development, there is a list of the recordings that are analyzed with an indication of the 20 that made it into the "Robbie Award Hall of Fame." Performers, dates and recording numbers, and companies are indicated in the discography. Appendixes include a list of children's musical videos and related sources and a bibliography of books that can be used with the songs. There is also an index by song title. In short, this is a very useful resource for classrooms, homes, and libraries to build music collections for youngsters.   *SONGS; MUSIC; DISCOGRAPHY*

C

268.   Children's Media Market Place. 4th ed. By Barbara L. Stein. Neal-Schuman, 1995. 397p. $49.95 pap. 1-55570-007-1.

About every five years a new edition of this directory of sources related to children's media appears. Although much of the material included will facilitate the accession process in children's collection, this is not primarily a bibliographic reference book (except for three sections on periodicals for children, parents, and professionals and a bibliography of selection tools). The first part, "Directory of Children's Media Sources," covers such areas as publishers, audiovisual and software producers, wholesalers, bookstores, book clubs, literary agents, museums, and personnel in state libraries and library organizations. The second part has a names and numbers index. Information for each entry in part 1 includes names, addresses, and related material. There are 21 resource sections, each of which contains a fantastic collection of material related to items suitable for preschool through twelfth grade.

INSTRUCTIONAL MATERIALS

C*

269. **Great Videos for Kids: A Parent's Guide to Choosing the Best**. By Catherine Cella. Citadel, 1992. 144p. $7.95 pap. 0-8065-1377-2.

This catalog of the best videos for children covers a variety of topics like animation, book-based videos, family topics, folk and fairy tales, holidays, and instructional films. Each is annotated, and in a preface the criteria used to judge these videos is outlined. The appendixes have interesting lists of "the best," like the best videos with positive Black roles and the best with positive female roles. This work will be useful in public libraries and elementary schools for use with parents, teachers, and collection building. *VIDEOCASSETTES*

C

270. **Growing Up with Music: A Guide to the Best Recorded Music for Children**. By Laurie Sale. Avon, 1992. 256p. $10 pap. 0-380-76211-0.

This guide to recommended musical cassettes and CDs is organized into chapters that deal with such subject as lullabies, baby and toddler music, recordings for preschoolers, recordings for ages 4 through 10, holiday music, classical music, and recordings in French and Spanish. Recordings in each chapter are listed alphabetically by artist, and each citation is annotated. This work will be helpful in building collections in children's rooms and elementary schools.

MUSIC; COMPACT DISCS; AUDIOCASSETTES; DISCOGRAPHY

C

271. **Index of Songs on Children's Recordings**. By Barbara Snow. Staccato Press, 1993. 210p. $30. 0-9636149-0-8.

A total of 674 tapes, records, and CDs are analyzed in this index to more than 7,300 songs. The work is divided into six sections: an alphabetical list of recordings indexed; the discography (which gives title, performer, label, date, and song titles on the disc); a song title index; a performer index; a producer/distributor index; and recording awards. Although this guide does not rate the recordings listed, it is invaluable for identifying recordings, songs, and their performers. The address of the publisher is: Staccato Press, 278 Hambletonian Dr., Eugene, OR 97401. *SONGS; DISCOGRAPHY*

C*

272. **Kits, Games, and Manipulatives for the Elementary School Classroom: A Sourcebook**. By Andrea C. Hoffman and Ann M. Glannon. Garland, 1993. 5,132p. $99. 0-8240-5342-7.

This unique sourcebook was produced by two librarians who recognized the importance of tactile and hands-on materials as classroom resources. About 1,400 available kits, games, and manipulatives are arranged within five subject categories: reading and language arts, mathematics, social studies, science and health, and arts. Helpful information such as grade level, price, format, and source is provided under each entry. Extensive and useful descriptor, author, and title indexes are also provided. A directory of sources completes the work. This "catalog" should be available in every elementary school media center as well as academic libraries with elementary school education programs.

GAMES; INSTRUCTIONAL MATERIALS

Authors and Illustrators

C*

273. **Black Authors and Illustrators of Children's Books: A Biographical Dictionary**. 2nd ed. By Barbara Rollock. Garland, 1992. 252p. $35. 0-8240-7078-X.

Rollock, a former Coordinator of Children's Services at the New York Public Library, has updated this much-needed reference tool by adding 35 new entries to this edition and revised most of the original 115 biographies to create what is really a bio-bibliography. The authors and illustrators that are included in the "Bibliographical Sources and References" are added bonuses and helpful for both reader's advisory work and collection development. Of particular interest are the four appendixes: awards and honor books, publishers' series, publishers and bookstores, and distributors. A detailed index completes the work. This standard reference work is recommended for all school and public libraries serving children. *AUTHORS, AFRICAN AMERICAN; ILLUSTRATORS, AFRICAN AMERICAN*

C
274. **Children's Authors and Illustrators: An Index to Biographical Dictionaries**. 5th ed. By Joyce Nakamura. Gale, 1995. 811p. $156. 0-8103-2899-2.

This is not so much a collection-building tool as a guide to locating biographical material on 30,000 children's authors and illustrators. However, the listing of the 650 reference books analyzed to find the 200,000 biographical entries included might be of value in making children's librarians aware of the variety of biographical sources available in the field of children's literature.

AUTHORS; ILLUSTRATORS

Awards and Prizes

C
275. **Children's Book Awards International: A Directory of Awards and Winners, from Inception to 1990**. By Laura Smith. McFarland, 1992. 671p. $82. 0-89950-686-0.

This guide is arranged by country, from Argentina to Yugoslavia, and lists more than 400 awards that are or have been given in the field of children's literature. Each award is described with such information as sponsor, date of inception, award provisions, and conditions. There follows a listing of winners that supplies only bibliographic information. The four indexes allow access by authors, awards, illustrators, and titles. A comparable title is *Children's Literature Awards and Winners: A Directory of Prizes, Authors, and Illustrators*, which lists 211 awards. *Newbery and Caldecott Medalists and Honor Book Winners* supplies better information on these two American awards. However, this international directory will be useful in libraries that need broad coverage of children's literature or where multicultural material is in demand.

AWARDS AND PRIZES

C
276. **Children's Literature Awards and Winners: A Directory of Prizes, Authors, and Illustrators**. 3rd ed. Gale, 1994. 678p. $94. 0-8103-6900-1.

This describes 300 awards for excellence in children's literature given in the United States and internationally. Part 1 is a directory that describes the awards and lists, with full bibliographic material, the winners and runners-up as of the early 1990s. Part 2 alphabetically lists authors and illustrators and the awards they have won. Part 3 is a bibliography of materials (e.g., books, articles) about these awards, and part 4 consists of indexes by author, illustrator, subject, title, and award. This work deserves a place in large public libraries and curriculum centers where it can serve many purposes, including evaluating collections for possible new acquisitions.

AWARDS AND PRIZES

C*
277. **Coretta Scott King Award and Honor Books: From Vision to Reality**. By Henrietta M. Smith. American Library Association, 1994. 130p. $25. 0-8389-3441-2.

To celebrate 25 years of the annual Coretta Scott King awards, this bibliography was created to help librarians and teachers use books already in their libraries and to build collections of important books that deal with the African American experience. This award honors distinguished works by African American authors and illustrators of children's books. In addition to historical background, the prizewinning and honor books are discussed in reverse chronological order from 1994 to 1969 (the illustration award was begun in 1974). For each entry, there are bibliographical details, contents notes, themes, quotes, and reasons for winning. Nineteen beautiful color plates are scattered within the text. Two interviews (one with author Patricia McKissack and the other with artist Pat Cummings) are included, and there are biographies and portraits of the winners. A valuable addition to library resources.

CORETTA SCOTT KING AWARD; AWARDS AND PRIZES

C
278. **Literary Laurels, Kids' Edition: A Guide to Award-Winning Children's Books**. Hillyard, 1996. 136p. $11.95. 0-9647361-1-X.

Every children's book title receiving an award from that award's inception to 1995 or 1996 is highlighted in this highly focused volume. Thirty-three children's book awards in the United States and

Great Britain are included. The awards are indexed by age level and specialty. This handy and unique compilation includes well-known awards, such as Caldecott, Newbery, Horn Book, Coretta Scott King, and Carl Sandburg, plus many more. Each of the more than 1,200 books are indexed by author, illustrator, and title. This title serves as a companion volume to Laura Carlson's *Literary Laurels: A Reader's Guide to Award Winning Fiction* (Hillyard, 1996. 80p. $9.95. 0-9647361-0-1), which includes all age groups but mainly adult. The *Kids' Edition* deserves to be in every library serving children, especially those that can't afford the more comprehensive and more expensive titles such as *Children's Books: Awards and Prizes* or *Children's Literature Awards and Winners*.   *AWARDS AND PRIZES*

Language and Literature

C

279.   Developing Learning Skills Through Children's Literature: An Idea Book for K–5 Classrooms and Libraries. Volume 1. By Mildred Knight Laughlin and Letty S. Watt. Oryx, 1986. 288p. $30 pap. 0-89744-258-3.

This handbook describes how to implement literature-based teaching using thematic or cross-curricular units based on quality contemporary and classic literature. The authors describe a wide range of books and activities designed to help motivate children to enjoy literature. There is also a sequel, *Developing Learning Skills Through Children's Literature, Volume 2* (Oryx, 1994. 320p. $30 pap. 0-89774-746-1), which contains nine detailed literature-based lesson plans for each grade level from K through 5, each dealing with a different topic or theme, a particular author, or books of a specific genre. Included are reading lists, author biographies, and group activities.

LITERATURE—STUDY AND TEACHING

C

280.   Index to Fairy Tales, 1987–1992: Including 310 Collections of Fairy Tales, Folktales, Myths, and Legends with Significant Pre-1987 Titles Not Previously Indexed: Sixth Supplement. By Joseph W. Sprug. Scarecrow, 1994. 602p. $59.50. 0-8108-2750.

The *Third Supplement, 1949–1972* (1973. $52.50. 0-8108-2011-0), the *Fourth Supplement, 1973–1977* (1979. $29.50. 0-8108-185-5), and the *Fifth Supplement, 1978–1986* (1989. $49.50. 0-8108-2194-X) of this respected index to collections of folk and fairy tales are still in print. The sixth supplement covers 310 collections published chiefly between 1980 through 1991. The main body of the work is a listing of titles and subjects in a single alphabet, with title entries containing the main information. This listing is preceded by a list of the collections analyzed. The work has an illustrious history that dates back more than 60 years. It continues to be an important literature reference work for both school and public libraries.   *FOLKTALES; FOLKLORE; MYTHOLOGY*

C

281.   Literature-Based Moral Education: Children's Books and Activities. By Linda Leonard Lamme et al. Oryx, 1992. 145p. $24.50 pap. 0-89774-723-2.

This timely and much-needed bibliography of children's books and instructional activities on moral education was compiled by university professors in elementary education. The books selected deal with self-esteem, responsibility, sharing, truthfulness, solving conflicts, perseverance, patience, and many other related topics. They are arranged in broad thematic chapters. Entries include an annotation that suggests possible classroom, library, or home use. Recommended grade levels are also suggested. The book is recommended for all children's and elementary school libraries for use by teachers, librarians, and parents.   *MORAL EDUCATION; VALUES*

C

282.   Literature-Based Reading: Children's Books and Activities to Enrich the K–5 Curriculum. By Mildred Knight Laughlin and Claudia Lisman Swisher. Oryx, 1990. 168p. $29.95. 0-89774-562-0.

This handbook offers practical suggestions and examples of using literature rather than textbooks for elementary school classroom reading instruction. For each model unit many activities, such as role playing and art projects, are suggested. Though this title is not intended as a selection aid, the books suggested for use will make excellent additions to school libraries. There are two other similar guides by Laughlin for the same age group: *Literature-Based Art and Music* (1992. $29.92. 0-89774-661-9) and *Literature-Based Social Studies* (1991. $27.50. 0-89774-605-8).

LITERATURE—STUDY AND TEACHING

C; A
283. **Using Children's Books in Reading/Language Arts Programs: A How-to-Do-It Manual for Library Applications**. By Diane D. Canavan and Lavonne Hayes. Neal-Schuman, 1992. 192p. $29.95. 1-55570-101-9.

This how-to-do-it manual also serves as a bibliography to enrich a whole language classroom. The major sections deal with such topics as books with repetitive language, rhythm and rhyme, and rebus stories; books for developing vocabulary through word play, concepts, and literature; and books dealing with parts of speech, plot, setting, and point of view. The final chapter features titles dealing with reading, libraries, books, and writing. This short volume is recommended for all elementary school and many public libraries as a reference tool, programming guide, and guide to collection building.

LITERATURE—STUDY AND TEACHING

C; Y
284. **Using Picture Storybooks to Teach Literary Devices: Recommended Books for Children and Young Adults. Vol. 2**. By Susan Hall. Oryx, 1994. 256p. $24.95. 0-89774-582-5.

Volume 1 of the same title was published in 1990 and is still useful and available. This new volume, with its 300 new selections, can be used as a stand-alone. Hall presents a convincing case for the use of quality picture storybooks to teach literary devices such as alliteration, allusion, ambiguity, metaphor, and satire. Following a number of brief introductory chapters, lists of picture storybooks are alphabetically arranged under each literary device, which is also carefully defined. Each entry contains full bibliographic information, an annotation, and an example of the highlighted technique. An index of authors and titles is also provided. Recommended for school library media centers at all levels for use by teachers and as a library guide for reference and collection building.

PICTURE BOOKS; LITERATURE—STUDY AND TEACHING

Multiculturalism

C
285. **Basic Collection of Children's Books in Spanish**. By Isabel Schon. Scarecrow, 1986. 230p. $25. 0-8108-1904-X.

Schon, a professor of library science and perhaps the leading authority on Spanish books for children, has compiled an excellent bibliography of more than 500 titles in Spanish intended for Spanish-speaking children from preschool through grade 6. This basic list complements Schon's excellent series *Books in Spanish for Children and Young Adults*, and it should prove immensely helpful as a buying guide for the busy school or public librarian (especially those not fluent in the Spanish language or unfamiliar with the body of literature that exists but is not reviewed in standard sources). Titles are arranged topically into nonfiction, fiction, easy books, reference books, and professional books. A brief descriptive note and a recommended grade level are provided. There are also author, title, and subject indexes as well as an appendix of dealers of books in Spanish. This bibliography is a must purchase for all school and public libraries if they have a large Spanish-speaking population or are serving those studying Spanish as a second language.

CHILDREN'S LITERATURE, SPANISH; SPANISH LITERATURE

C
286. **Connecting Cultures: A Guide to Multicultural Literature for Children**. By Rebecca L. Thomas. Bowker, 1996. 689p. $40. 0-8352-3760-5.

This is a comprehensive subject index to more than 1,600 titles published between the 1970s and late 1990s and suitable for use with preschoolers through the sixth grade. Included are fiction titles, folktales, poetry, and songbooks that reflect a diversity of cultures, current interests, and timely topics.

Each entry has complete bibliographical information, including publication date and ISBN, a cultural designation, use levels, subjects, and a summary. Very good as an evaluative checklist for collections and as a resource builder.   *MULTICULTURALISM*

C; A

287. **Cultures Outside the United States in Fiction: A Guide to 2,875 Books for Librarians and Teachers**. By Vicki Anderson. McFarland, 1994. 414p. $42.50. 0-89950-905-3.

The 2,875 books included in this extensive bibliography were found in several excellent collections used by the author. They are arranged alphabetically by 150 countries or geographical regions. Each entry includes author, publication date, grade level, a brief annotation, and subject headings. Most books were published since 1965 although some classics are included. The descriptions are nonevaluative, and there is no indication of interest level or in-print status of the books. In spite of these limitations, this work will have value as a checklist of materials in the field.   *MULTICULTURALISM*

C

288. **A Guide to Children's Books About Asian Americans**. By Barbara Blake. Scholar, 1995. 215p. $49.95. 1-85928-014-5.

Part 1 of this book is a narrative history and cultural survey of Asian peoples and an account of their immigration to the United States. Many countries are covered, including China, Japan, the Philippines, Vietnam, India, Pakistan, and Bangladesh. Part 2, the bibliography, is arranged first by geographical areas, then by fiction and nonfiction, with separate lists for the primary and upper elementary grades. Titles have received at least one recommendation and were published between 1970 and 1993. Bibliographic information, a list of subjects, and a brief annotation accompany each entry. Unfortunately, inadequate indexing prevents maximum use of this otherwise valuable reference work. See also *Our Family, Our Friends, Our World* and *This Land Is Our Land*.   *ASIAN AMERICANS*

C

289. **Libros en Espanol Para los Pequenos (Children's Books in Spanish)**. New York Public Library, 1993. 47p. $5. 0-685-70977-9.

This special list of bilingual books is an updating of the 1990 edition with the same title and developed as a project of the DeWitt-Reader's Digest project "Connecting Libraries and Schools Project" (CLASP). The focus of the collection is on books written in Spanish from Spain and Latin America. Each entry gives country of origin, full bibliographic information, and a brief annotation. Age levels are also indicated. Those books translated are listed with English titles; bilingual books list both English and Spanish titles. Though designed for the New York Public Library Branch Libraries to meet the needs of the large and diverse Spanish-speaking population of New York City, this special list can be useful and is recommended for all children's libraries with large Spanish-speaking populations.
                                    BILINGUAL BOOKS; SPANISH LITERATURE

C

290. **Light a Candle! The Jewish Experience in Children's Books**. New York Public Library, 1993. 8p. $4. 0-87104-721-7.

This annotated bibliography of 108 titles celebrates Jewish life, past and present. It was compiled by a committee of children's librarians at the New York Public Library. The work is divided into six sections: Celebrations and Observances; Tales of Tradition; Journeys—To a New Life; In Many Lands...; The Holocaust; and New Lives, New Hopes. Copies cost $4 plus $1 shipping charges for 1–5 copies and $1.25 for 6–10 copies. Write to: Office of Branch Libraries, New York Public Library, 455 5th Ave., New York, NY 10016.   *CHILDREN'S LITERATURE, JEWISH; JEWS*

C*; Y

291. **Multicultural Children's Literature: An Annotated Bibliography, Grades K–8**. By Beth Beutler Lind. McFarland, 1996. 250p. $34.50. 0-7864-0038-2.

More than 1,100 fiction and nonfiction titles written for young people in grades K–8, arranged by four major ethnic groups, and published since 1980 are listed in this annotated bibliography. The selections are arranged first by ethnic groups (African Americans, Asian Americans, Hispanic Americans, and Native Americans) and then by grade levels (K–3 or 4–8). They are further subgrouped under each grade level as follows: informational nonfiction, biographies/autobiographies, historical/realistic fiction, and folklore/myths/legends. Each entry includes a brief annotation and complete bibliographic information. This book is recommended for all libraries serving children along with two similar bibliographies that do not duplicate each other and are included in this guide: Thomas's *Connecting Cultures*, with more than 1,600 titles, and Helbig and Perkins's *This Land Is Our Land*, with fewer titles but lengthy critical and descriptive annotations.   *MULTICULTURALISM*

C*

292. **Multicultural Picture Books: Art for Understanding Others**. By Sylvia Marantz and Kenneth Marantz. Linworth, 1994. 150p. $29.95. 0-938865-22-6.

This work by the Marantzes is unique in that it is the only one that focuses almost entirely on identifying and analyzing illustrations in picture books for their portrayal of many cultures in American society. Included are representatives of Asian, Middle Eastern, African (including African-American, Caribbean, and Latin American), Native American, and some European ethnic cultures (mostly Russian Jewish). The book starts with a discussion on why children should be exposed to picture books depicting various cultures, as well as the evaluation of multicultural picture books. Then for each culture the authors list folktales and stories of the past, contemporary life, and books about personal experiences of various immigrant groups. Each entry contains a brief summary and a detailed description of the illustrations and comparisons to other works by the illustrator. Recommended grade levels are given. Additional sources for further readings as well as a complete index are also provided. This work is highly recommended for all elementary, middle school, and public libraries.

MULTICULTURALISM; PICTURE BOOKS

C; A

293. **Multicultural Projects Index: Things to Make and Do to Celebrate Festivals, Cultures, and Holidays Around the World**. 2nd ed. By Mary Anne Pilger. Libraries Unlimited, 1998. In press. 0-87287-524-0.

At long last we have an index that provides teachers and librarians with sources of projects to make for festivals and holidays celebrated around the world and by the many ethnic groups in the United States. Pilger has done a tremendous job, and the list of more than 1,100 numbered titles from which the projects come is invaluable for collection development. The only real limitation to this gold mine is the fact that many of the sources may be out-of-print because they go back as far as the 1960s. Still, this work, along with Pilger's companion index, *Crafts Index for Young People*, should prove useful as a reference tool and selection guide for all libraries that serve teachers, librarians, and parents of young children.   *HANDICRAFTS; MULTICULTURALISM*

C

294. **Multicultural Voices in Contemporary Literature**. By Frances Ann Day. Heinemann, 1994. 344p. $20. 0-435-08826-2.

Day believes that teachers can use fine multicultural literature to deepen and broaden sensitivities in writing styles, language subtleties, and world views. She focuses on the work of only 39 authors and illustrators from 20 different cultures. Arranged by authors/illustrators, each section contains personal data, a biographical sketch, a list of works with a synopsis of major works, and their primary focus. Suggestions for use in the classroom are also given. Appendixes include additional multicultural authors and illustrators. Finally, illustrator, title, and subject indexes are provided. This bibliography, with its interesting approach to multiculturalism, is recommended for all libraries that serve children, but especially school libraries that support multicultural teaching programs.

AUTHORS; ILLUSTRATORS; MULTICULTURALISM

C

295. **Native Americans in Children's Literature**. By John C. Stott. Oryx, 1995. 264p. $24.50. 0-89774-782-8.

In the foreword of this well-written and well-researched series of bibliographic essays, Joseph Bruchac, a Native American storyteller, poet, and novelist, states: "Stott, a Canadian professor of children's literature, proceeds with admirable patience and careful scholarship . . . based not only on research but in listening to living Native voices." Stott spent 20 years studying native culture firsthand, reading the literature of Native authors, and talking to them about their work. In the first essay, "The Way It Wasn't," he attempts to dispel the stereotypes and misrepresentations about Native Americans. Other important essays include "Native Tricksters and Legendary Heroes in Children's Literature" and "Cultures in Conflict." Each chapter (essay) concludes with a relevant annotated bibliography. Only those books that are well written and present an honest portrayal of the cultures they represent are recommended. Each entry contains a plot summary, related reading, and suggestions on incorporating the title in classroom teaching. This valuable book, which is more than a bibliography, is highly recommended as a teaching tool and a selection aid for all libraries working with children.

NATIVE AMERICANS

C
296. **Rainbow Collection: Multicultural Children's Books**. Minneapolis Public Library, 1995. $3.50.

Intended for children of all ages, this fully annotated list, compiled by the children's services staff of the Minneapolis Public Library, contains about 200 multicultural titles published from 1991 to 1995. The entries are arranged under broad and popular themes or subject headings such as "People and Places," "Families Together," and "Seasons and Celebrations." For quantity discounts contact Kathleen Johnson (612-372-6532) or write to the address below. Make checks payable to the Minneapolis Public Library and send orders to: Children's Services, Minneapolis Public Library, 300 Nicollet Mall, Minneapolis, MN 55401-1992.

MULTICULTURALISM

Periodicals

C*
297. **Magazines for Children: A Guide for Parents, Teachers, and Librarians**. 2nd ed. By Selma K. Richardson. American Library Association, 1991. 139p. $25. 0-8389-0552-8.

This revised and updated edition includes 90 titles recommended for children in preschool through eighth grade. Nearly a third of the titles are new since the 1983 edition. Detailed annotations describe the contents, interests, and special features of each selected magazine. Each entry also includes where indexed, grade level, and full bibliographic information. Appendixes cover such areas as lists by age/grade level, magazines from religious affiliations, and editions for the visually impaired. The subject index is by very broad topic. This very selective aid may want to stand side-by-side with Bowker's *Magazines for Young People* (1991), which evaluates more than 1,000 for young people through high school. Both are recommended for reading guidance, advice to parents, and collection development and evaluation.

PERIODICALS

C*
298. **Magazines for Kids and Teens: A Resource for Parents, Teachers, Librarians, and Kids!** Ed. by Donald R. Stoll. Educational Press Association of America, 1994. 101p. $10. 0-87207-397-1.

This is an updated and expanded version of a title originally published in 1989 under the title *Magazines for Children*. Stoll has compiled an excellent list of more than 250 periodicals that earlier was published as a joint project of the prestigious International Reading Association and the Educational Press Association of America. Titles were selected from around the world and include such child-oriented topics as car racing, learning foreign languages, and wildlife. Each periodical entry includes a full description and adequate ordering information. Also appended is whether the editor accepts readers' work and if sample copies are available. Indexes provide access by age/grade level and subject. This outstanding source tends to focus on the more popular type of magazine, and it is quite current; therefore, it is highly recommended for use by parents, teachers, librarians, and kids. However, it does not supplant the very selective (only 90 titles) *Magazines for Children* or the very extensive (1,300 titles) *Magazines for Young People*, both of which have a different focus, and both of which were published in 1991 but still useful (see individual entries).

PERIODICALS

C*; A

299. **Primary Search**. CD-ROM. EBSCO, 1994– . quarterly. $549.

Intended to be used by children as well as adults, EBSCO's electronic database is more than a periodical index. This reference tool indexes and abstracts more than 100 titles with more than 25 percent containing full text. A number of periodical titles for teachers and librarians and a large number of full-text pamphlets are also included. The disc is both Macintosh and IBM/PC compatible. A list of magazine titles and pamphlets and a manual accompany the CD. However, the program is self-explanatory, and most children will be able to use it with little or no instruction. Coverage goes back to 1988 for most of the titles; for others it begins in 1994. Most of the titles listed are indexed in Bowker's *Children's Magazine Guide*, and a large number of the adult titles are listed in Wilson's *Readers' Guide*. A paper edition, *Primary Magazine Guide*, with limited coverage and without full text, is also available from EBSCO for $79. *Primary Search* can well serve as an introduction to electronic databases for young children. Highly recommended for all elementary school libraries and children's rooms of public libraries that can afford it (though when one considers the number of full-text titles, it is not an expensive reference tool). *PERIODICALS*

Picture Books and First Readers

C*

300. **A to Zoo: Subject Access to Children's Picture Books**. 4th ed. By Carolyn W. Lima and John A. Lima. Bowker, 1993. 1,158p. $55.95. 0-8352-3201-8.

This book is designed to help librarians, teachers, and parents find the right book for children preschool through second grade. This greatly expanded and updated edition indexes more than 15,000 fiction and nonfiction picture books (an increase of thousands of titles since the still-useful 1986 and 1989 editions) for youngsters in preschool through second grade. It has been chosen as an ALA Outstanding Reference Source. The selections are indexed under 700 subject, author, title, and illustrator entries. The preface describes the purpose and organization of the book. This is followed by a brief history of children's books, including a selected bibliography. The body of this useful index is divided into five parts: subject headings (with many cross-references); a subject guide; a useful bibliographic guide (arranged by authors in most cases and including title, illustrator, publisher, date, ISBN, and subjects); and complete title and illustrator indexes. Board books, popular books, and important out-of-print titles are included. The authors, who are practicing librarians, have personally read almost every title. This new edition is recommended for all public libraries and elementary school libraries for use by all individuals working with the very young. *PICTURE BOOKS*

C*; Y

301. **ABC Books and Activities: From Preschool to High School**. By Cathie Hilterbran Cooper. Scarecrow, 1996. 164p. $27.50 pap. 0-8108-3013-2.

More than 500 alphabet books are included in this list of more than 5,000 items that also includes creative activities, games, and projects. The books are arranged by subject in 10 areas; each area includes information about the subject, a fully annotated bibliography, and a variety of activities. Librarians, teachers, and others working with children from preschool into junior high school age will find this a useful resource. *ALPHABET BOOKS; GAMES*

C

302. **The Art of Children's Picture Books: A Selective Reference Guide**. 2nd ed. By Sylvia S. Marantz and Kenneth A. Marantz. Garland, 1995. 320p. (Garland Reference Library of the Humanities, 825). $43. 0-8240-2745-0.

This retrospective bibliography of 450 books, articles, theses, and media items about children's picture books is grouped into six broad areas, including the history, production, criticism, anthologizing, and further research of picture books. Each entry has a brief annotation and full bibliographic information. There are also artist, author, and title indexes. A major drawback in this otherwise useful bibliography is the lack of a subject index. Nonetheless, this relatively inexpensive book is recommended for elementary school and public libraries rounding out their collection of picture book bibliographies.

PICTURE BOOKS

C*

303. Beyond Picture Books: A Guide to First Readers. 2nd ed. By Barbara Barstow and Judith Riggle. Bowker, 1995. 450p. $49.95. 0-8352-3519-X.

Barstow and Riggle, two experienced children's librarians, have updated their popular 1989 edition and have added almost 900 more titles; many titles from the first edition were deleted. First readers are defined as "books intended for children at a first or second grade level . . . have a recognizable format and generally belong to a series." Most of the titles were published between 1951 and 1995 and include books in- and out-of-print and fiction and nonfiction. Entries are listed in alphabetical order by author and sequentially numbered. Each entry provides full bibliographic information, subject headings, reading level, and a brief annotation. A special feature of this work is the list of 200 in-print outstanding titles considered a core collection. The work concludes with five detailed indexes: subject, title, illustrator, readability, and series. This work continues to be a perfect complement to Bowker's *A to Zoo* and would be a welcome addition to all libraries serving young readers.

BOOKS FOR BEGINNING READERS

C; A

304. Books, Babies, and Libraries: Serving Infants, Toddlers, Their Parents, and Caregivers. By Ellin Greene. American Library Association, 1991. 186p. $25 pap. 0-8389-0572-2.

Based on her experience as a library educator and project director for the New York Public Library's Early Childhood Project, Greene found little in the field related to library work with the very young. She designed a graduate course to alleviate this problem. This book is based on topics covered in this course. In addition to a full text on the library's role in early learning and in parent education, book and nonprint collection recommendations are included. Also included are other bibliographies, a discography, and suitable toys. Appendixes include lists of professional articles and tools helpful in program planning.

LIBRARY PROGRAMS; PRESCHOOLERS

C

305. Choosing Your Children's Books: 2 to 5 Years Old. By Valerie White. Bayley and Musgrave, 1994. $13.95; $5.95 pap. 1-882726-15-4; 1-882726-10-3 pap.

In this briefly annotated, highly selective bibliography, about 150 recommended titles are included. They are arranged by subject and cover such genres as alphabet and counting books and such subjects as families and folklore. Similar in number of books included, treatment, and arrangement are the two other titles for parents by the same author in this series: *Choosing Your Children's Books: 5 to 8 Years Old* (Bayley and Musgrave, 1994. $13.95; $5.95 pap. 1-882726-13-8; 1-882726-11-1 pap.) and *Choosing Your Children's Books: 8 to 12 Years Old* (Bayley and Musgrave, 1994, $13.95; $5.95 pap. 1-882726-14-6; 1-882726-12-X pap.).

CHILDREN'S LITERATURE (GENERAL); PRESCHOOLERS; BOOKS FOR BEGINNING READERS

C

306. 450 More Story S-t-r-e-t-c-h-e-r-s for the Primary Grades: Activities to Expand Children's Favorite Books. By Shirley C. Raines. Gryphon House, 1994. $14.95 pap. 0-87659-167-5.

Like the author's earlier *Story Stretchers for the Primary Grades* (1992), this practical guide suggests popular children's books to enrich curriculum areas. In this volume are units in social studies, science, and literature, with individual chapters on such subjects as folktales, endangered species, and self-esteem. Each chapter highlights five picture books and suggests a variety of activities to enrich their use, such as art projects, writing, and creative dramatics. There are also many additional reading suggestions and references for further study. These two volumes are particularly useful in elementary school libraries.

LITERATURE—STUDY AND TEACHING; PICTURE BOOKS

C

307.   **Mother Goose Comes First: An Annotated Guide to the Best Books and Recordings for Your Preschool Child**. By Lois Winkel and Sue Kimmel. Holt, 1990. 174p. $14.95. 0-8050-1001-7.

Two well-known authorities in children's literature have pooled their knowledge and produced a handbook of highly selected and recommended titles for the preschooler. The titles are divided into general topics of interest (e.g., Mother Goose, stories about growing up and families). Each entry includes a bibliographic citation, a lively annotation, and an indication of age/grade level appeal. Their emphasis on phonorecordings is of some concern because this format seems to be in a state of transition. However, the list is solid and certainly recommended for all libraries serving children.

PHONORECORDINGS; PRESCHOOLERS; NURSERY RHYMES

C*

308.   **Picture Books for Children**. 4th ed. By Patricia J. Cianciolo. American Library Association, 1997. 288p. $38. 0-8389-0701-6.

This revised and updated edition of a work that is becoming a standard in its field reflects the tremendous growth of the children's literature publishing field. Most of the 268 titles chosen in this edition have been published recently. The stated purpose of this bibliography remains "to identify and describe picture books that will provide children with enjoyable, informative, and discriminating literary experiences." Titles chosen range from preschool to junior high school level. They are arranged by broad topical areas (e.g., "Other People," "The World I Live In," "The Imaginative World"). The titles are then arranged alphabetically by author. Entries include full bibliographic data, illustrator, intended age level, and an annotation that describes the illustrations and gives a story summary. This work is intended for a wide audience, including teachers, parents, and librarians. It is highly recommended for all libraries that serve children and adults that work with children.

PICTURE BOOKS

C; A

309.   **Picture Books for Looking and Learning: Awakening Visual Perceptions Through the Art of Children's Books**. By Sylvia S. Marantz. Oryx, 1992. 208p. $24.50. 0-89774-716-X.

Marantz, an experienced school media specialist, reviewer, writer, and art expert has given us a very detailed analysis of the picture book to foster a greater understanding and appreciation of the picture book as an art form. Focusing on 43 well-chosen picture books, she discusses all aspects of a book, especially the design techniques (e.g., shape, color, media, design). The chapters are arranged by age groups. Entries for each book analysis are about four pages long and include a discussion about the illustrator, dust covers, end papers, title page, publication and dedication page, and a page-by-page discussion. Also included are an activity and a list of other works by the illustrator. This fascinating book is recommended for all libraries serving children, with an extra copy for the professional collection.

PICTURE BOOKS

C*

310.   **Picture Books to Enhance the Curriculum**. By Jeanne McLain Harms and Lucille Lettow. H. W. Wilson, 1996. 496p. 0-8242-0867-6.

The purpose of this index is to identify and describe favorite and recent picture books that will be helpful in meeting the curricular and programming needs of teachers, librarians, and others working with children. Approximately 1,500 well-known picture books are included in this theme-organized volume compiled by two university professors (an authority in curriculum development and a professional youth collection librarian). The picture book titles are arranged under themes that link elementary school curriculum areas such as language arts, graphic and performing arts, social studies, science, and mathematics. The work is divided into four major sections: "A Key to the Themes," which lists all of the subject headings by which the titles are grouped; a theme index; an annotated picture book index that provides a description of every title; and an alphabetical list of book titles. The selected books had to meet the following criteria: literary and artistic quality, curriculum application, appeal to youth, and availability in most children's library collections. This interesting work is recommended for all libraries serving children as a reference tool and an aid for collection development. A copy should also be in the professional collection of all elementary schools.

PICTURE BOOKS

C

311. Play, Learn, and Grow: An Annotated Guide to the Best Books and Materials for Very Young Children. By James L. Thomas. Bowker, 1992. 439p. $30. 0-8352-3019-8.

Intended as a guide for working with the very young child up to age six, this annotated list contains a full range of resources, including books, videos, filmstrips, and audiocassettes. More than 1,100 items were chosen for inclusion from more than 5,000 print and nonprint materials considered by "a panel of knowledgeable, highly experienced specialists in child development who chose only those products judged to be the best in aiding the phases of child development." Each entry contains complete bibliographic information, age level, a brief annotation, and a "priority of purchase" ranking. This evaluative guide is recommended for all libraries that serve children and professionals who work with children. *PICTURE BOOKS; PRESCHOOLERS; AUDIOVISUAL MATERIALS*

C; Y

312. Pop-Up and Movable Books: A Bibliography. By Ann R. Montanaro. Scarecrow, 1993. 559p. $59.50. 0-8108-2650-X.

Montanaro has provided us with an unusual, extensive bibliography of books that literally have movable parts. More than 1,600 books published from the 1850s to the present are listed and described. An introduction traces the history of these fascinating books, which are literally centuries old. The selected entries are arranged alphabetically by author. Each citation has complete bibliographic information as well as a brief descriptive annotation. Thorough indexes are provided, including those for series, author/illustrator, paper engineers and designers, and titles. The lack of a subject index is unfortunate but does not limit the value of this worthwhile bibliography, which took a great deal of time and research to produce. It deserves a place in most libraries, especially those that serve children, historians, and bibliophiles. *POP-UP BOOKS*

C

313. The Preschool Resource Guide: Educating and Entertaining Children Aged Two Through Five. By Harriet Friedes. Plenum/Insight, 1993. 245p. $27.50. 0-303-44464-9.

This work includes a detailed account of child development as well as lists of useful resources for the preschool years. In addition to books, the author lists audio recordings, videocassettes, magazines, toys, games, and software. A directory of professional organizations is also appended. In addition to the interesting information for preschool children, the recommended lists will prove useful to libraries serving parents and teachers of the very young. *PRESCHOOLERS; CHILD DEVELOPMENT; INSTRUCTIONAL MATERIALS*

C

314. They're Never Too Young for Books: A Guide to Children's Books for Ages 1 to 8. By Edythe M. McGovern and Helen D. Muller. Prometheus Books, 1994. 342p. $14.95. 0-87975-858-9.

This newly revised list is becoming a standard for selecting books for preschoolers through the primary grades. Intended for parents, this fully annotated and inexpensive bibliography of hundreds of titles has a place as a reference tool and selection aid in every nursery school, elementary school, and children's department library. *CHILDREN'S LITERATURE (GENERAL); PRESCHOOLERS*

C

315. Wordless–Almost Wordless Picture Books: A Guide. By Virginia H. Ritchey and Katharyn E. Puckett. Libraries Unlimited, 1992. 223p. OP. 0-87287-878-3.

Ritchey and Puckett have compiled an extensive list of almost 700 wordless (or practically wordless) books intended for the very young. The titles are organized alphabetically by author. Each entry includes full bibliographic information, a short précis of the story, and descriptions of the illustrations. A special feature of this work is the inclusion of six indexes: title, format, use of print, series, illustrator, and subject. Another bonus is the resource list of articles and books that deal with wordless books intended for adults. Find a copy of this well-organized book for all libraries that serve the very young and those that work with this age group. *PICTURE BOOKS; STORIES WITHOUT WORDS*

Programs and Activities

General and Miscellaneous

C

316. **Beginning with Books: Library Programming for Infants, Toddlers, and Preschoolers**. By Nancy N. DeSalvo. Library Professional Publications/Shoe String Press, 1993. 186p. $29.50. 0-208-02318-6.

DeSalvo, a professional librarian, draws on her wide experience in library programming for preschoolers and shares many practical ideas and sample programming techniques for librarians working with parents. Each sample program includes many annotated suggestions of books, music, games, and the like. This brief account is an important addition for reference, programming ideas, and collection development for all libraries and centers that work with the very young.

PRESCHOOLERS; LIBRARY PROGRAMS

C*

317. **Bookplay: 101 Creative Themes to Share with Young Children**. By Margaret Read MacDonald. Library Professional Publications/Shoe String Press, 1995. 230p. $32.50. 0-208-02280-5.

MacDonald, the author of *Booksharing: 101 Programs to Use with Preschoolers*, compiled this sequel to help busy teachers and librarians develop theme-based story programs. The 100+ theme ideas involve the use of a full array of media including books, music and dramatic activities, films, videos, and poetry. The programs are arranged in 18 major categories. The titles listed in the bibliographies are useful for basic book purchasing as well as program use. There is also a list of professional resources. Recommended for elementary schools and children's rooms of public libraries.

LIBRARY PROGRAMS; STORYTELLING; PRESCHOOLERS

C*

318. **Booksharing: 101 Programs to Use with Preschoolers**. By Margaret Read MacDonald. Library Professional Publications/Shoe String Press, 1988. 236p. $35; $25 pap. 0-208-02159-0; 0-208-02314-3 pap.

MacDonald has provided us with this excellent handbook on library programming with two-and-a-half to five-year-olds. More importantly, added to this gem is a bibliography of titles to be used in the suggested programs and a film list. This essential book is recommended for all libraries where children's librarians need program ideas. A newer and complementary work by MacDonald, and one that takes a thematic approach, is *Bookplay: 101 Creative Themes to Share with Young Children* (1995). Both of these practical guides are highly recommended for all libraries where children's librarians need program help.

LIBRARY PROGRAMS; STORYTELLING; PRESCHOOLERS

C

319. **Children Talking About Books**. By Sarah G. Borders and Alice Phoebe Naylor. Oryx, 1993. 256p. $29.95 pap. 0-89774-737-2.

This is a collection of fascinating book discussions, led by adults, where children talk about books and what they mean to them. It covers a multitude of topics ranging from sibling rivalry to grief and moral reasoning. A total of 36 children's books are discussed. Many of these titles could be used as the basis of a book discussion group.

BOOK DISCUSSION GROUPS

C

320. **Creative Fingerplays and Action Rhymes: An Index and Guide to Their Use**. By Jeff Defty. Oryx, 1992. 255p. $29.50 pap. 0-89774-709-7.

Part 1 of this unique guide gives all sorts of background material that explains the history and use of fingerplays, plus ways of integrating these activities into various stages of childhood development, types of development, and special needs. Part 2 is an index by subject and first line to about 3,000 fingerplays and action rhymes found in 95 collections. Most of these sources are still in print and can be acquired by libraries needing them. This practical handbook is highly recommended for elementary schools, nursery schools, and children's rooms. *FINGERPLAYS*

C

321. More Creative Uses of Children's Literature. Volume 1: Introducing Books in All Kinds of Ways. By Mary Ann Paulin. Library Professional Publications/Shoe String Press, 1992. 619p. $35. 0-208-02202-3.

This update of Paulin's *Creative Uses of Children's Literature* (1982) focuses on titles published during the next 10 years, so consequently the vast majority of the titles listed are still readily available. In addition to many creative approaches to storytelling, booktalking, and multimedia presentations, the real value of this work is the many lists and annotated bibliographies arranged by subject and type. Almost half of the book is made up of bibliographic indexes. This creative volume is recommended for all libraries that work with children, especially those interested in a multimedia approach to using children's literature. *LIBRARY PROGRAMS*

C*

322. Read for the Fun of It: Active Programming with Books for Children. By Caroline Feller Bauer. H. W. Wilson, 1992. 372p. $45. 0-8242-0824-2.

This book of practical programming ideas aims to foster and support literature-based learning programs. It is intended for all who are interested in bringing books and children together—parents, librarians, and teachers. The strength of this book is the numerous lists arranged by age and interest. Additionally there are lists for reading aloud, storytelling, and professional reading. This bibliography is recommended for all school and public library collections for ready-reference, reading guidance, programming, and collection development. *READING GUIDANCE; LIBRARY PROGRAMS*

C

323. Storyteller's Research Guide: Folktales, Myths, and Legends. By Judy Sierra. Folkprint, 1996. 90p. $14.95 pap. 0-9636089-4-0.

In this handy, practical paperback guide, the author, a renowned folklorist, supplies information on bibliographies and research sources for folktales and how to get permission to use them. It will be very helpful in both libraries and classrooms. *FOLKLORE; STORYTELLING*

C

324. The Storytime Sourcebook: A Compendium of Ideas and Resources for Storytellers. By Carolyn N. Callum. Neal-Schuman, 1990. 177p. $24.95 pap. 1-55570-067-5.

Using a subject arrangement from alphabet to zoo, the author describes resources and activities for a variety of story hours. For each of the 100 topics this guide suggests filmstrips, films or videos, books, crafts, fingerplays, and other activities. Additional lists include a title guide to each of the recommended filmstrips and videos that gives bibliographic information and publishers' names; a directory of book publishers and media distributors; and indexes to recommended book titles, authors, crafts, and activities. For children's rooms and primary school libraries. *STORYTELLING*

C; A

325. Using Children's Books in Preschool Settings. By Steven Herb and Sara Willoughby-Herb. Neal-Schuman, 1994. 181p. $32.50. 1-55570-156-6.

The authors, experienced educators and librarians, have created a practical how-to resource for presenting books early in a child's life, based on the premise that literacy is the foundation upon which learning throughout life is based. Following an overview on child development, many activities using books are described. While the emphasis is on use, the extensive bibliographies and resource lists are helpful in creating programs and providing materials for a head start toward learning, literate adults. This practical guide is recommended for teachers, librarians, and parents working with preschoolers in day care centers, nursery schools, and public libraries. *PRESCHOOLERS; CHILD DEVELOPMENT*

Read-Aloud Programs

C*

326. **Books Kids Will Sit Still For: The Complete Read-Aloud Guide**. 2nd ed. By Judy Freeman. Bowker, 1990. 660p. $45. 0-8352-3010-4.

Freeman, a former elementary school librarian-turned-professor of children's literature, calls her new edition "a manual of ways to fool around with books." She could well have added "and to mix and match them with kids." This revised and updated edition is chock-full of ideas on using books in reading aloud, booktalking, and storytelling programs. The second half of the book lists more than 2,000 fiction and nonfiction titles from preschool to grade six. Each entry includes full bibliographic data and an annotation that lists titles of similar books and suggestions for activities. A bibliography of professional titles is an added bonus. The detailed index is divided by author, title, and subject. A newer, equally excellent book in this read-aloud series is *More Books Kids Will Sit Still For*. Both titles are highly recommended for all libraries offering services to young children. *READ-ALOUD PROGRAMS*

C*

327. **The Latest and Greatest Read-Alouds**. By Sharron L. McElmeel. Libraries Unlimited, 1994. 210p. $18.50. 1-56308-140-7.

McElmeel has compiled an exciting list of tested books appropriate for reading aloud to children of elementary through middle school age. It is meant for use by librarians, teachers, parents, and even older children reading to younger children. The books are arranged by general reading and listening level and age. Each entry is annotated with a plot summary and bibliographical information. Practical guidelines for reading aloud to both individuals and groups are included. This inexpensive work is highly recommended for all libraries serving youngsters in grades K–6. *READ-ALOUD PROGRAMS*

C*

328. **More Books Kids Will Sit Still For**. By Judy Freeman. Bowker, 1995. 869p. $45. 0-8352-3520-3.

Freeman designed this work to serve as a supplement to the popular and still useful *Books Kids Will Sit Still For* (contains more than 2,000 titles). More than 2,000 new titles have been added to the new edition. The lists follow three introductory sections that deal with the process of choosing and using exciting picture books, poetry, folklore, fiction, and nonfiction with young people ages 3 to 12. The selections are organized into four major categories: fiction, folk and fairy tales, myths, and legends. The fiction section makes up about 60 percent of the selection and is subdivided by grade level. Each entry contains a brief annotation, suggested activities, similar titles and subject headings, and full biblio-graphic data. An appended professional bibliography is followed by author, title, illustrator, and subject indexes. This cleverly titled book is highly recommended for all libraries that serve children. *CHILDREN'S LITERATURE (GENERAL); READ-ALOUD PROGRAMS*

C

329. **The Read-Aloud Handbook**. 4th ed. By Jim Trelease. Viking/Penguin, 1995. 368p. $12.95 pap. 0-14-046971-0.

This is an updated and expanded gold mine of more than 1,200 books that were chosen for their suitability or adaptability for reading aloud. Trelease also reviews the advantages of reading aloud. Though the lack of adequate annotations and other points about each title may be considered a shortcoming, this inexpensive book is recommended for all libraries that serve children. *READ-ALOUD PROGRAMS*

C

330. **Reading Rainbow Guide to Children's Books: The 101 Best Titles**. By Twila C. Liggett and Cynthia Mayer Benfield. Citadel, 1994. 288p. $19.95; $12.95 pap. 1-55972-222-3; 0-8065-1493-0 pap.

The 101 tried-and-true read-aloud books were selected from the 400 titles that appeared on the popular PBS TV show *Reading Rainbow* during its first 10 years of programming. Following an introduction that discusses the chosen books and the show, the titles are arranged alphabetically by popular subjects such as adventure, animals, sports, and science. The books are discussed in great detail; generally at least a full page is allotted each title. A bibliography of additional titles is included.

Librarians, teachers, and parents will welcome this handy, inexpensive list of best books which have received national attention. It is recommended for all libraries serving children as an aid in selection and reading guidance. *READ-ALOUD PROGRAMS*

C

331. **Reading Together Is Better**. Children's Services Division, Michigan Library Association, 1994. n.p.

Reading aloud to youngsters serves a dual role; it offers pleasure and promotes an interest in books and reading. This annotated list of 48 fiction titles is geared for young people in grades 4–6. There is also a brief bibliography of additional resources for identifying more books. Teachers, parents, and librarians will appreciate a copy of this inexpensive list, which is available from the Children's Services Division of the Michigan Library Association. Send $3 plus $1 for postage and handling for 25 copies (single copies not available). Order from and make checks payable to: Michigan Library Association, 1000 Long Blvd., Ste. 1, Lansing, MI 48911. *READ-ALOUD PROGRAMS*

C

332. **Story Hour: 55 Preschool Programs for Public Libraries**. By Jeri Kladder. McFarland, 1995. 231p. $38.50. 0-7864-0065-X.

Each of these audience-tested story hour programs for preschoolers are theme-based. They contain lists of books that have been used successfully and many tips on effective presentations.
STORYTELLING; READ-ALOUD PROGRAMS; PRESCHOOLERS

C

333. **Story Programs: A Source Book of Materials**. By Carolyn Sue Peterson and Ann Fenton. Scarecrow, 1994. 304p. $29.50. 0-8108-3207-0.

With divisions by age groups—toddler (ages 2–3), preschooler (ages 3–5), and primary (ages 6–8)—this resource provides lists of appropriate books and other printed resources, plus a variety of additional materials, all useful for story hours and their related activities. Included are instructions on making such props as puppets, suggestions for creative dramatics, and sample story programs. The bibliographies and lists of materials will be useful for collection development.
STORYTELLING; READ-ALOUD PROGRAMS

Reading Guidance

C; A

334. **Beyond Storybooks: Young Children and Shared Book Experience**. By Judith Pollard Slaughter. International Reading Association, 1993. 176p. $19.95. 0-87207-377-7.

Slaughter has designed a practical guide for parents, teachers, librarians, and others working with beginning or problem (at-risk) readers in preschool and primary grades. She offers many teaching ideas and suggestions that will aid and perhaps inspire teachers and librarians. Of particular interest is the list of more than 100 big book editions of favorite stories. Each title is fully annotated. More than a bibliography, this guide is recommended for all libraries dealing with youngsters that need motivational reading material, especially elementary school libraries; the list of recommended titles alone is worth the low cost. *READING GUIDANCE*

C*

335. **Books to Help Children Cope with Separation and Loss: An Annotated Bibliography**. 4th ed. By Masha Kabakow Rudman et al. Bowker, 1993. 514p. $57. 0-8352-3412-6.

This bibliography of about 750 "real-life situation books" serves as a companion volume to the 1989 3rd edition ($46. 0-8352-2510-0), which included about 600 titles and is still in print. The selections included fiction, nonfiction, poetry, and folklore and are targeted for youngsters ages 3–16. Each entry includes a detailed annotation and full bibliographic information; they are arranged under explicit and direct headings such as losing a friend, old age, prison, abuse, death, and suicide. A number of other recommended bibliographies include useful books for applying bibliotherapeutic procedures

and strategies; for example, see *Books That Heal*. This comprehensive bibliography should be added to the list for all libraries working with children and serving teachers, parents, librarians, and counselors.
BIBLIOTHERAPY

C

336. **Choices: A Core Collection for Young Reluctant Readers, Volume 3**. By Peg Glisson and Sharon Salluzo. John Gordon Burke Publisher, 1994. 272p. $45. 0-934272-30-1.

This continuation of the first volume of *Choices* (1984) and *Choices, Volume 2* (1990) covers material for second to sixth graders published between 1989 and 1993. Included are more than 200 titles that have appeal for the young reluctant reader and that can also be used effectively in literature-based curricula. The book is in two sections. In the first, each book is fully annotated under the author's name. In the second, a subject approach, the same annotations are repeated (sometimes several times) under a variety of subjects, including interest and reading levels, plus a heading for "Group 2," those youngsters who are able but unmotivated readers. In spite of the repetition and the book's price, it has many good choices and covers grade levels not usually included in bibliographies of high-low books.
HIGH INTEREST–LOW VOCABULARY BOOKS

C

337. **The Integrated Curriculum: Books for Reluctant Readers, Grades 2–5**. By Anthony D. Fredericks. Libraries Unlimited, 1992. 187p. $21. 0-87287-994-1.

Focusing on 40 children's books that have been found to interest even the most reluctant reader, the author discusses proven methods that motivate readers and suggests activities that challenge and fascinate youngsters. Links are suggested through these books to many curriculum areas such as math, social studies, health, and art.
RELUCTANT READERS

C; A

338. **Parents Who Love Reading, Kids Who Don't**. By Mary Leonhardt. Crown, 1993. 238p. $20. 0-517-59164-2.

Leonhardt offers many suggestions to parents on how to get young people to enjoy reading and to make reading a real part of their lives. The focus of her how-to approach is on the older student. Though this practical book is aimed at parents, teachers and librarians will also profit from its sound advice and nontraditional approach. Included is an extensive list of books (even comic books) and magazines, old standbys, and many based on recommendations of young people. Recommended for all elementary school and public libraries.
READING GUIDANCE

C*

339. **Primaryplots 2: A Book Talk Guide for Use with Readers Ages 4–8**. By Rebecca L. Thomas. Bowker, 1993. 431p. $42. 0-8352-3411-8.

This guide, by an elementary school librarian, is intended "to serve as a guide for booktalks, story programs and reading guidance." Like its earlier 1989 edition *Primaryplots* (which is still in print) it is geared to the very young. This fine work complements others in Bowker's series of guides for booktalks: *Introducing Bookplots 3, Middleplots 4, Juniorplots 4*, and *Seniorplots*. The 150 early reading and picture books chosen were published between 1988 and 1992. They are arranged in eight chapters under broad topics of literature (e.g., "Enjoying Family and Friends," "Developing a Positive Self-Image," "Finding Humor in Picture Books," "Focusing on Folk-tales"). Each entry includes full bibliographic information, reading level, a plot summary, notes on thematic material, suggested activities, audiovisual adaptations, and an annotated list of related titles. This guide is highly recommended for all libraries that serve the very young and people who work with the very young.   *PICTURE BOOKS; BOOKTALKS*

C; A

340. **Sensitive Issues: An Annotated Guide to Children's Literature, K–6**. By Timothy V. Rasinski and Cindy S. Gillespie. Oryx, 1992. 288p. $29.95 pap. 0-89774-777-1.

Intended for teachers and librarians, this work suggests titles that deal with current and sensitive issues such as divorce, substance abuse, death, child abuse, prejudice, nontraditional home environments, and cultural differences. All of the titles were published since 1975, and most are still in print.

Indexes by author, title, and subject facilitate use. Librarians might also want to consider the slightly more expensive but more comprehensive *The Best of Bookfinder* (1992). Most elementary school and public libraries will want both. *BIBLIOTHERAPY*

C*

341. **What Do Children Read Next? A Reader's Guide to Fiction for Children**. Ed. by Candy Colburn. Gale, 1994. 1,135p. $39.95. 0-8103-8886-3.

Similar in format and purpose to Gale's *What Do I Read Next?* and *What Do Young Adults Read Next?* this extensive bibliography has almost 2,000 entries. It covers books suitable for youngsters from first through eighth grade; therefore, there is some overlap with the young adult title. Entries are arranged alphabetically by author and contain publication data, title, characters, plot summary, and the like. A bit more attention is placed on the illustrator and illustrations. About half of the titles were published within the last five years; therefore, a greater emphasis is placed on the tried and true. This work is highly recommended for all elementary, middle/junior high, and public libraries. *READING GUIDANCE*

Reference Books

C

342. **Children's Book Review Index**. By Barbara Beach and Beverly Baer. Gale, annual. $114. 0-8103-5457-8 (1995 cumulation).

This annual volume lists about 25,000 review citations. It is not intended as a selection aid, but it can be vital in locating reviews and other evaluative information that will determine acquisition. Reviews for books, periodicals, books on tape, and electronic media in about 450 periodicals are tabulated in this spin-off from *Book Review Index*. Children's books are defined as those suitable for children ages 10 and under. A five-volume cumulation, *Children's Book Review Index: Master Cumulation, 1965–1984* (1985. $350. 0-8103-2046-0), and a later four-volume cumulation, *Children's Book Review Index, 1985–1994 Cumulation* (1996. $400. 0-8103-5457-8), are available. *BOOK REVIEWS*

C

343. **Children's Reference Plus: Complete Bibliographic, Review, and Qualitative Information on Books, Reference Books, Serials, Cassettes, Software, and Videos for Children and Young Adults**. Bowker. CD-ROM. One-year subscription, $595; three-year subscription, $1,695 (both MS-DOS versions).

This CD-ROM product includes a massive collection of Bowker's published works in the field of children's and young adult literature. The CD-ROM includes *Children's Books in Print*, *El-Hi Textbooks*, children's titles listed in *Bowker's Complete Video Directory*, and *Words on Cassette*, plus 24 more specialized publications such as *Best Books for Children*, *Primaryplots*, *Books for the Gifted Child*, *High-Low Handbook*, and *More Notes from a Different Drummer*. The disk is a companion to Bowker's *Books in Print Plus* and *Library Reference Plus*. *Children's Reference Plus*, though expensive, will find a place in very large collections where having all this material in a single database is a great convenience. *CHILDREN'S LITERATURE (GENERAL); CD-ROMS; REFERENCE BOOKS*

C

344. **The Children's Song Index, 1978–1993**. By Kay Laughlin et al. Libraries Unlimited, 1995. 153p. $37.50. 0-56308-332-9.

More than 2,500 songs found in 77 songbooks published between 1978 and 1993 are listed in this index, which allows users to access songs by title and first line or subject. Preceding these indexes is an alphabetical list, by author, of the works indexed, with complete bibliographical information. The latter can be helpful in collection building in this area. This work is a continuation of the out-of-print *Index to Children's Songs* (Wilson, 1979) by Peterson and Fenton. *SONGS; MUSIC*

C

345. **Reference Books for Children**. 4th ed. By Carolyn Sue Peterson and Ann D. Fenton. Scarecrow, 1992. 399p. $39.50. 0-8108-2543-0.

More than 1,000 annotated titles are included in this revised evaluative tool. All of the titles have been time-tested and have been culled from recommended sources. Nonprint media are not included. Each entry has full bibliographic data and a brief descriptive annotation (50–100 words). Author, title, and subject indexes aid in easy access to the entries. This work is intended as a guide to collection development; however, because the cutoff date is mid-1990, other sources may have to be checked for newer editions or new titles if used as a buying guide or evaluation checklist of an existing collection. Still, this guide, along with other sources such as *Children's Catalog*, will be useful for elementary school media centers and children's departments of public libraries.   *REFERENCE BOOKS*

C*

346. **Reference Books for Children's Collections**. 3rd ed. Comp. by the Children's Reference Committee. New York Public Library, 1996. 79p. $10. 0-87104-735-7.

This slim bibliography lists almost 400 reference book titles, ranging from the elementary level to adult materials used by children. The list includes 165 new titles published since the 1991 edition. The books are current and are arranged by broad subject area. Each entry contains a brief descriptive annotation and full bibliographic information. This list is recommended for all elementary schools and children's departments of public libraries. The price, in the bibliographic information, plus a $1 handling charge, is for one to five copies. Make checks payable to and send orders to: Office of Branch Libraries, New York Public Library, 455 Fifth Ave., New York, NY 10016.   *REFERENCE BOOKS*

Science and Mathematics

C

347. **Bringing the World Alive**. Orion Society, 1995. 48p. $6.

The Orion Society, a nonprofit educational/environmental organization dedicated to promoting a better understanding of the need to protect our wildlife and our global environment, has released its latest bibliography of nature stories for young children. Listed are 115 picture books that would appeal to preschoolers through the primary grades; they include old standards as well as new stories. Each entry includes full bibliographic data, a brief description, and a recommended age level. This handy and inexpensive booklet would be a worthwhile addition to all libraries working with the very young. It is available from: The Orion Society, 136 E. 64th St., New York, NY 10021.

          NATURE STUDY; PICTURE BOOKS

C; Y

348. **Children's Literature for Health Awareness**. By Anthony L. Manna and Cynthia Wolford Symons. Scarecrow, 1992. 678p. $55. 0-8108-2582-1.

The authors have compiled an unusual and useful bibliography that lists nonfiction and some fiction titles that deal with the health concerns, needs, and problems of children in kindergarten through eighth grade. This work shows how health education can be integrated into the language arts program. It is basically an annotated list, organized by subjects that cover a wide range of health-related topics.

          HEALTH

C

349. **Counting Your Way Through 1-2-3: Books and Activities**. By Cathie Hilterbran Cooper. Scarecrow, 1996. 224p. $33.50 pap. 0-8108-3125-2.

The 663 counting books for young children described in this annotated guide are divided into 10 subject areas. Each section includes a description of the subject area, an annotated bibliography of books related to this area, and a number of book-related activities. There is also a brief historical look at the background of counting books. This title will be valuable for classroom teachers and librarians building collections of counting books.   *COUNTING BOOKS; PICTURE BOOKS*

C

350. Guide to Math Materials: Resources to Support the NCTM Standards. By Phyllis J. Perry. Libraries Unlimited, 1997. 120p. $20 pap. 1-56308-491-0.

With this guide all types of math materials for the elementary grades can be located and investigated. Organized under such topics as problem-solving, number sense, and geometry, this guide lists all kinds of materials such as various kinds of blocks, clocks, scales, cubes, calculators, and sorting toys. Specialized math books, computer software, and other learning devices like activity cards, puzzles, and games are also included. Annotations include a description, grade levels, possible applications, and an indication of exceptional quality. Addresses of publishers and suppliers are also given.

MATHEMATICS

C

351. How to Use Children's Literature to Teach Mathematics. By Rosamond Welchman-Tischler. National Council of Teachers of Mathematics, 1992. 75p. $8.50. 0-87353-349-6.

Using standard children's books like *Caps for Sale* and *Stone Soup*, the author shows that concepts such as graphing and measuring can be taught through the use of picture books. There are illustrations from many of the books discussed. *MATHEMATICS; PICTURE BOOKS*

C

352. It's the Story That Counts: More Children's Books for Mathematical Learning, K–6. By David J. Whitin and Sandra Wilde. Heinemann, 1995. 224p. $21.50 pap. 0-435-08369-4.

A sequel to the authors' *Read Any Good Math Lately?*, this book provides additional ideas to encourage mathematical thinking and promote the teaching of math through literature. In a chatty style, reports are given on new techniques, responses of children, and the thoughts of some writers, like Tana Hoban, who write math books for youngsters. The second half discusses recent books in a series of thematically arranged chapters. There is even a chapter on multiculturalism in children's math books. Classroom teachers will get many teaching ideas from this book, and librarians will find it valuable as a selection aid. *MATHEMATICS*

C

353. Literature-Based Science Children's Books and Activities to Enrich the K–5 Curriculum. By Christine Roots Hefner and Kathryn Roots Lewis. Oryx, 1995. 186p. $29.95 pap. 0-89774-741-0.

Hefner and Lewis stress that because science is an integral part of our existence, literature and science go hand-in-hand. The book is organized by subject (thematic units) within grade levels. The subjects are those typically covered in most elementary school science curriculum areas: animals, plants, human body, Earth science, space, energy and motion, and ecology. Annotated bibliographies of recommended fiction and nonfiction books, audiovisual materials, and extensive activities are included for each grade level and theme. This book should be useful to teachers planning units of study and to librarians developing collections of science materials at the elementary school level. *SCIENCE*

C*

354. Outstanding Science Trade Books for Children in [year]. Children's Book Council, annual. Free.

This list, which has been issued annually since 1973, is a project of CBC's joint committee with the National Science Teachers Association (NSTA). Each year's list includes about 100 outstanding books written for youngsters in prekindergarten to eighth grade. They were chosen by science educators and librarians from the 5,000 to 6,000 children's books published each year. This list appeared originally in *Science and Children*. In addition to being of high literary quality, the selections emphasize accuracy, consistency with current scientific knowledge, and readability. Each entry includes a recommended grade level, an annotation, and bibliographic information. This list is highly recommended along with another fine list published by the CBC: *Notable [year] Children's Trade Books in the Field of Social Studies*. Single copies are available for a 6"x 9" envelope with $.75 postage; copies are also available in quantity. For more information and ordering write to: CBC, 568 Broadway, Ste. 404, New York, NY 10012. *CHILDREN'S LITERATURE; SCIENCE*

C

355. **Read Any Good Math Lately? Children's Books for Mathematical Learning K–6**. By David Whitin and Sandra Wilde. Heinemann, 1992. 206p. $21. 0-435-08334-1.

This bibliographic guide is intended to foster an understanding of a variety of mathematical concepts in elementary school children. Both children's fiction and nonfiction books are included. The basic mathematical operations (addition, subtraction, multiplication, and division) are treated in separate chapters. Other chapters deal with more complex concepts such as geometry and fractions. Each chapter discusses how children's books can be used to present a specific math topic. Many practical ideas are provided. This bibliography/handbook is highly recommended for every elementary school library and most children's departments of public libraries. *MATHEMATICS*

C; A

356. **Resources for Teaching Elementary School Science**. National Academy Press, 1996. 312p. $17.95. 0-309-05293-9.

Fully annotated curriculum packages are included in this valuable aid to teaching elementary school science. Included are lists of books about science and teaching, 600 science centers, zoos, museums, directories of science periodicals, and a list of organizations that provide additional resources. This handy and inexpensive guide is recommended for every elementary school library with a second copy in the professional collection. Public libraries will also want a copy in their children's room reference department as an aid to teachers and parents and as a tool for collection development. *SCIENCE*

C; A

357. **Teaching Science to Children**. 2nd ed. By Mary D. Iatridis. Garland, 1993. 216p. $35. 0-8153-0090-5.

The purpose of this bibliography is to provide all those involved in teaching science to children (preschool through grade 3) with awareness of and access to current theories, strategies, and instructional materials. Each chapter of this annotated bibliography has an introductory essay, followed by a list of materials or a bibliography of resources. The areas covered by the various chapters include a review of science textbooks, a rundown on science activities with books that help children learn scientific principles, a bibliography of science books for children, and a brief discussion of science education for the special child with a list of recommended titles. Because of the importance of the topic and the dearth of similar guides, this work is recommended for all libraries that serve those who teach science to children. *SCIENCE*

C

358. **The Wonderful World of Mathematics: A Critically Annotated List of Children's Books in Mathematics**. By Diane Thiessen and Margaret Matthias. National Council of Teachers of Mathematics, 1993. 241p. $17 pap. 0-87353-353-4.

About 500 trade books are reviewed in this excellent list, which has the full endorsement of the authoritative national organization of mathematics teachers. Entries are arranged by specific subjects, such as early number concepts, measurement, and spatial sense. The annotations are descriptive and evaluative and rate the books with stars. Also included are recommended grade levels and whether the books are single or multiconcept. Indexing is by author and title. A companion volume that covers the secondary school levels and is published by the same organization is *Mathematics Books: Recommendations for High School and Public Libraries*. Both volumes are highly recommended. *MATHEMATICS*

Social Studies

C; A

359.   **Children of Separation: An Annotated Bibliography for Professionals**. By Greta W. Stanton. Scarecrow, 1994. 358p. $42.50. 0-8108-2695-X.

In this bibliography, almost 1,000 annotated references spanning a period of 20 years can be used by adults to help children cope with loss of identity, maturation problems, foster care, adoption, and divorce, in addition to single-parent, extended family, and stepfamily living. Additionally included are about 85 resources for children, followed by author and subject indexes. This work can help identify materials for a professional collection.   *FAMILY LIFE*

C

360.   **Children's Books on Ancient Greek and Roman Mythology: An Annotated Bibliography**. By Antoinette Brazouski and Mary J. Katt. Greenwood, 1994. $49.50. 0-313-28973-5.

This bibliography lists 381 books published from the mid-nineteenth century through 1992 that deal with Greek and Roman mythology for children in grades 4 through 8. Also included are scholarly essays on the importance of the study of mythology, a history of children's books on mythologies, and how to introduce mythology to youngsters. The critically annotated bibliography is arranged by author and indicates grade level suitability. Unfortunately, most of the books listed are now out-of-print, which seriously limits this title as a collection development tool.   *MYTHOLOGY, CLASSICAL*

C*

361.   **Notable [year] Children's Trade Books in the Field of Social Studies**. Children's Book Council, annual. Free.

This list, which has been issued annually since 1972, is a project of CBC's joint committee with the National Council for the Social Studies (NCSS). About 150 notable books written for youngsters in grades K–8 are included each year. They are chosen by social studies educators and language arts specialists from almost 5,000 children's books published per year. This annual bibliography appears first in the journal *Social Education*. In addition to being of high literary quality, the selections "emphasize human relations, represent a diversity of groups and are sensitive to a broad range of cultural experiences." The list is divided into categories (e.g., world history, the American frontier, folktales, biography, peace). Full bibliographic data, recommended grade levels, and an annotation are provided for each entry. Single copies are available for a 6"x 9" SASE with $.75 postage; copies are also available in quantity. The CBC also has available for free (with a similar SASE) *Outstanding Science Trade Books for Children*. For more information or to order, write to: CBC, 568 Broadway, Ste. 404, New York, NY 10012.   *SOCIAL STUDIES*

C

362.   **Religious Books for Children: An Annotated Bibliography**. 3rd ed. By Patricia Pearl Dole. Church and Synagogue Library Association, 1993. 40p. $9.35. 0-915324-35-0.

Dole, a Presbyterian church librarian, has compiled this bibliography of 350 titles with the intention of having it serve "primarily as a guide for the selection of children's religious books and secondarily for the evaluation of this area in library collections." In other words, she has attempted to create a basic collection that would meet the needs of very diverse religious organizations, or perhaps even lay organizations with collections of religious materials. The emphasis here is the Judeo-Christian faith (only 3 of the 36 pages are devoted to Buddhism, Islam, Hinduism, Native American faith, and Sikhism). Every entry has a brief annotation, recommended age level (preschool through grade 6), and enough bibliographic information for ordering, including prices as of 1993. All entries are arranged by a specific subject, but author and title indexes are also provided. This slim, inexpensive, well-done bibliography is recommended for many types of religious libraries, especially Christian church libraries because of its emphasis.   *RELIGIOUS LITERATURE*

C

363. **Social Studies Through Children's Literature: An Integrated Approach**. By Anthony D. Fredericks. Libraries Unlimited, 1991. 192p. $24. 0-87287-970-4.

In this activity-centered approach to social studies in the elementary school, 32 instructional units are outlined. Each features picture books and story books that illustrate curriculum concepts and contain strong literary qualities. Summaries of books, topic areas, curriculum applications, activities, and critical thinking questions are included. An annotated bibliography and list of resources are also provided.

SOCIAL STUDIES

C; A

364. **Teaching Social Studies to the Young Child: A Research and Resource Guide**. By Blythe S. Farb Hinitz. Garland, 1992. 164p. $24. 0-8240-4439-8.

Hinitz has compiled an excellent sourcebook of current ideas and resources for the teaching of social studies to students from kindergarten to third grade. The book is in the form of a bibliographic essay and focuses on history, geography, and economics. Many relevant citations deal with how to present social studies skills, concepts, and principles. The work is intended for advanced education students and curriculum specialists as well as practicing elementary school classroom teachers. This brief resource guide is recommended for professional education libraries and academic libraries supporting courses in education. *SOCIAL STUDIES*

C

365. **Understanding American History Through Children's Literature: Instructional Units and Activities for Grades K–8**. By Maria A. Perez-Stable and Mary Hurlbut Cordier. Oryx, 1994. 328p. $24.95. 0-89774-795-X.

The authors feel that students can connect with Americans of the past through well-written works of fiction, nonfiction, biography, legends, and folktales. Through this connection, they can be made aware of the ethnic, racial, religious, political, and sociological diversity that is America. Based on this premise, the authors (an experienced librarian and a teacher and curriculum facilitator) have teamed up to create a series of developmentally appropriate activities to complement selected readings. The book is divided into two parts, first by grade levels (K–3 and 4–8) and then by units of study arranged chronologically by major periods or events, such as the colonial period and the Civil War. The readings contain descriptive annotations related to each unit of instruction that list objectives and detailed activities. This practical guide also includes tables, diagrams, and charts. An extensive bibliography and an index complete the volume, which is recommended for every elementary and middle school library.

U.S. HISTORY; HISTORICAL FICTION

C

366. **U.S. History Through Children's Literature**. By Wanda Miller. Libraries Unlimited, 1997, 240p. $25. 1 56308-440-6.

Miller, a reading specialist, has compiled a list of quality children's fiction and nonfiction titles recommended by reviewers and educators. These titles would enrich the study of U.S. history for students in grades 4–8. The book is arranged by broad topics reflecting phases or events of U.S. history, such as exploration, Native Americans, the American Revolution, the Industrial Revolution, the Civil War, and World War II. Two recommended book titles, and those that are closely related to the topic, are chosen for each area. One is for use with a whole class, and one is for use with an individual or a small group. Each title entry contains a detailed summary of the book, author information, suggested activities, topics for discussion, and further reading recommendations. This teaching guide, though it does not contain an extensive list of recommended book titles, has an important focus and would serve well as a selection aid and a device for librarians to work more closely with teachers. Therefore, it is recommended for all elementary, middle school, and public libraries.

U.S. HISTORY; HISTORICAL FICTION

C; A*
367. **Using Literature to Teach Middle Grades About War**. By Phyllis K. Kennemer. Oryx, 1992. 236p. $29.95. pap. 0-89774-778-X.

This book is undoubtedly one-of-a-kind. Kennemer has developed series of study units around six wars involving the United States: the Revolutionary and Civil wars, World Wars I and II, Vietnam, and the Persian Gulf. The plan for each unit is similar: a selected chronology, a list of recommended books, a sample lesson plan, suggested activities, and a glossary. The recommended books include classics as well as current fiction and nonfiction (including biography) and picture books. Most of the titles are for grades 6 through 8; however, a number of titles for more advanced readers and reluctant readers are included. Author and title indexes complete this interesting work, which is recommended for all school and public libraries.   *WAR; LITERATURE—STUDY AND TEACHING*

C
368. **A Window into History: Family Memory in Children's Literature**. By Eleanor Kay MacDonald. Oryx, 1996. 227p. $24.95. 0-89774-879-4.

The family is the foundation of the social studies curriculum in elementary schools and middle schools. MacDonald has compiled an interesting list of 203 fiction and nonfiction books and audiocassettes that focus on family memory as a source of historical accuracy in presenting a picture of American history. Titles chosen are personal narratives of family histories. The selected items include primary source material as well as fiction and picture books for elementary and middle school age children. Criteria applied in choosing the items include historically accurate, focused on the American experience, and considered essentially true with no major character or events altered. The entries are grouped under seven major topics such as the frontier experience, the immigrant experience, and the changing world of Native Americans. Each entry includes a detailed annotation, era, geographic location, and recommended grade level. Appended are books for further reading, oral history projects, and an index by ethnic origin, historical period, and location. This interesting volume should prove useful for both teachers and librarians and is recommended for all elementary, middle school, and public libraries.
                                    FAMILY LIFE; U.S. HISTORY

IV

Sources for
Young Adults
(Grades 7–12)

General and Miscellaneous

Y*

369. **Beacham's Guide to Literature for Young Adults, Volume 6, 7, 8**. Ed. by Kirk H. Beetz. Beacham Publishing, 1994. $189. Complete set (vols. 1–8) $434. 0-933833-32-6.

This is perhaps a first choice for young people when they need critical information on books they have read or help in choosing a book to read. These three new volumes which complete the set include more than 200 novels, short story collections, general nonfiction, and biographies published between 1980 and 1994. Previously published volumes 1–3 cover generally the same wide range of literary types; volume 4 covers science fiction, adventure novels, myths, epics, and mysteries through 1990; and volume 5 covers fantasy and gothic novels through 1991. All of the titles are fully described and analyzed. Books are arranged in alphabetical order by title, and each entry includes type of work, a brief summary, an assessment of literary quality, a brief biographical sketch of the author, suggestions for discussion or reports, and a list of criticism. All text is written on a level and style that would appeal to young adults. There is an author/title index. Though expensive, these readable guides are recommended for use by students, teachers, and librarians in school, academic, and public libraries. Beacham also publishes the 11-volume *Beacham's Encyclopedia of Popular Fiction* (1996. $550. 0-933833-38-5).

YOUNG ADULT LITERATURE (GENERAL)

Y*

370. **Best Books for Senior High Readers**. By John T. Gillespie. Bowker, 1991. 931p. $55. 0-8352-3021-X.

This latest addition to the Best Book series maintains the high standards set in the others. More than 10,000 recommended books of high quality geared to the 15–18 age group are included. Entries include full bibliographic data and a brief annotation. Titles are arranged by broad subject area and subdivided by specific topics (e.g., sports and games is followed by baseball, basketball, bowling, etc.). As with the previous volumes in this series, a detailed subject/grade level index and separate author and title indexes are included. This resource is an excellent aid for collection evaluation and development and reader guidance, and is highly recommended for all secondary school and public libraries. Continued in *Best Books for Young Adult Readers* (Bowker, 1997). *YOUNG ADULT LITERATURE (GENERAL)*

Y*

371. **Best Books for Young Adult Readers**. by Stephen J. Calvert. Bowker, 1996. $59.95. 0-8352-3832-6.

Calvert has compiled a continuation of the very popular *Best Books for Junior High Readers* and *Best Books for Senior High Readers* (see individual entries) into a comprehensive bibliography of more than 8,000 titles aimed at readers ages 12 to 18. Most of the selections included were published from 1990 to 1995 and were recommended by such reviewing sources as: *Booklist*, *Book Report*, VOYA, and

School Library Journal. The fully annotated titles are arranged by subject. This exhaustive list is recommended for all libraries that serve young adults, especially those that own the two other titles.

YOUNG ADULT LITERATURE (GENERAL)

Y*

372. **Best Books for Young Adults: The Selection, the History, the Romance**. By Betty Carter. American Library Association, 1994. 214p. $25. 0-8389-3439-0.

The author brings together in one volume more than 6,000 books, which include all of the books appearing in the annual list of Best Books for Young Adults selected by YALSA from 1966 to 1993. This valuable list of fiction and nonfiction titles covers a wide range of interests and levels (young people between the ages of 12–18) and includes many titles originally written for adults but of interest to young adults. The volume also includes a history of young adult literature. A bibliography of the works cited and an index are provided. This well-prepared bibliography is recommended for reader's advisory, selection, weeding, and collection evaluation for all libraries serving young adults.

YOUNG ADULT LITERATURE (GENERAL)

Y*

373. **The Book Scene . . . Especially for Teens**. Comp. by the Young Adult Services Department, Minneapolis Public Library, 1996. 60p. $5.

More than 500 recommended titles are listed in this attractive booklet. This annual list of fiction and nonfiction is aimed at young adult readers ages 12–18. Titles are arranged by subject in 40 areas that would appeal to young people: American history, contemporary issues, horror, poetry, celebrating diversity, science facts, science fiction and fantasy, women in the forefront, and more. Each entry includes some bibliographic information and a brief annotation. Copies are available by mail. Order from: Young Adult Services Department, Minneapolis Public Library, 300 Nicollet Mall, Minneapolis, MN 55401-1992.

YOUNG ADULT LITERATURE (GENERAL)

Y

374. **Books for Teens: Stressing the Higher Values**. By Edith S. Tyson. Church and Synagogue Library Association, 1993. 32p. $8.25. 0-915324-34-2.

Works that display positive values and promote a healthy self-image without being preachy or didactic are included in this annotated bibliography of recommended books for teenagers from grades 7 through 12. In addition to presenting a value or values beyond self, each book must be of proven popularity and available in paperback. The few that are included in hardback are still so current as to be unavailable in any other format. This list, though intended for volunteers working in church or synagogue libraries, can still be used as a checklist for acquisition activities or for reading guidance with young adult librarians. Copies are available by prepaying $10.35 and sending orders to: Church and Synagogue Library Association, Box 19357, Portland, OR 97280-0357.

YOUNG ADULT LITERATURE (GENERAL); VALUES

Y*

375. **Books for the Teenage 1996**. New York Public Library, annual. $6.00. 0-87104-734-9.

This venerable bibliography, published annually by the Office of Young Adult Services of the New York Public Library, is now in its 67th edition. As stated in the introduction, this "list has been especially prepared for teenagers in New York City since 1929." The current list has been completely redesigned into a slick magazine type; it includes more than 1,000 titles that would be appealing to teenagers throughout the country, especially urban youngsters. The titles are grouped into 70 broad subject categories and include a good mix of old time-tested titles and brand new 1990s titles. Each entry includes some bibliographic information (author, title, publisher) and a one-line catchy descriptive note. Copies are available free to teenagers at the various branches of the NYPL; copies are available to adults for $6. Additional charges for mailing and handling are: 1 to 5 copies, $1.00; 6 to 10 copies, $1.25; bulk orders, $1.50. Copies can be ordered by mail from: Office of Branch Libraries, New York Public Library, 455 5th Ave., New York, NY 10016.

YOUNG ADULT LITERATURE (GENERAL)

Y*

376. **Books for You: An Annotated Booklist for Senior High Students**. National Council of Teachers of English, 1995. 432p. $21.95. 0-8141-0367-7.

More than 1,000 books, selected for their appropriateness and appeal to teenage readers, are listed in this newest edition of *Books for You*, which has been prepared with the help of a committee of teachers, librarians, and school administrators appointed by the highly regarded NCTE. Each newly revised edition complements the older editions rather than replaces them. This edition includes titles published between 1988 and 1994 and is a good mix between fiction and nonfiction and adult and young adult. Titles are arranged by 35 popular subject categories ranging from adventure and computer technology through romance, war, and westerns. The annotations are written to appeal to young people. Another feature of this new edition is the more than 150 titles with a multicultural focus. Author and title indexes are included. There are enough differences between this list and the NYPL's *Books for the Teenage* that most libraries will want to use both for collection development, reading guidance, and booktalking. This time-tested bibliography is highly recommended for all libraries serving young adults.

YOUNG ADULT LITERATURE (GENERAL)

Y*

377. **Fiction for Youth: A Guide to Recommended Books**. 3rd ed. By Lillian Shapiro and Barbara Stein. Neal-Schuman, 1992. 264p. $35. 0-55570-113-2.

This outstanding bibliography of twentieth-century novels lists and annotates more than 600 challenging titles for young adult readers. Quality and appeal were two major criteria for inclusion. Most are adult novels, but a few of the better young adults titles are included. The books are arranged by authors, with 10- to 12-line annotations describing the book and giving brief critical remarks. There are subject and title indexes and a directory of publishers. This is a valuable tool for reader's guidance and collection development in senior high schools.   *YOUNG ADULT LITERATURE (GENERAL)*

Y*; A*

378. **Good Reading: A Guide for Serious Readers**. 23rd ed. By Arthur Walhorn et al. Bowker, 1990. 465p. $44. 0-8352-2707-3.

Since its first appearance in 1932, this guide to world literature from ancient times to the present has become a mainstay in high school and public libraries for reader's advisory work and collection building. There are now about 3,000 annotated titles included under five different sections: "Historical Periods," "Regional and Minority Cultures," "Literary Types," "Humanities and Social Sciences," and "Sciences," with many subdivisions in each section. Each division has an introductory essay. Special features of this edition include a core list of 101 significant books, a section on reference books, and separate lists of books to read before entering college, while on vacation, and after retiring. This work is updated regularly.   *ENGLISH LITERATURE; AMERICAN LITERATURE*

Y; A

379. **Great Books of the Christian Tradition and Other Books Which Have Shaped Our World**. By Terry W. Glaspey. Harvest House, 1996. $7.95 pap. 1-56507-356-9.

Arranged by chronological periods, this detailed bibliography introduces the great books of the past with annotations that are notable for their clarity and enthusiasm. Coverage for both classics and contemporary literature inspires one to read, and there is advice on establishing personal reading goals, setting up book discussion groups, and possible titles for such groups. Some suggestions for children's reading are also included. Though the bibliography is written from a Christian point of view, most of the books discussed are secular works although they usually express positive, traditional values.

CHRISTIAN LITERATURE

Y*

380. **Growing Up Is Hard to Do**. By Sally Estes. Booklist/American Library Association, 1994. 64p. $7.95 pap. 0-8389-7726-X.

Published by *Booklist*, this is a compilation of excellent bibliographies that first appeared in that periodical. Fiction and nonfiction titles are included under a wide variety of topics, like "Growing Up Male" and "Growing Up Religious." Other topics include growing up gay, as an outsider, during World

War II, as a jock, and in specific geographical areas (e.g., the South). A separate "Growing Up Listening" section features unabridged audiobooks. This is a suitable companion volume to the equally fine *Genre Favorites for Young Adults*.   *YOUNG ADULT LITERATURE (GENERAL)*

Y*; A*
381. **Guide to Popular U.S. Government Publications**. 4th ed. By Frank W. Hoffmann and Richard J. Wood. Libraries Unlimited, 1997. 275p. $35. 0-56308-462-7.

This is a continuation of the *Guide* by Leroy C. Schwarzkopf that first appeared in 1986. The present guide contains 1,400 titles, most of which were published between January 1993 and 1996. Some earlier publications, such as popular serial titles and government bestsellers, are also listed. An introduction on government documents and how to obtain them is followed by the main body of the book, in which titles are arranged under broad subject headings with some subdivisions. Entries include issuing agency, date, stock number, price, SuDocs number, and a brief annotation. The choices have been judiciously made and represent the needs of the general reader. There are title and subject indexes. This is a fine guide to free and inexpensive material for school, college, and public libraries.   *UNITES STATES—GOVERNMENT DOCUMENTS; FREE MATERIAL*

Y*
382. **Literature for Today's Young Adults**. 5th ed. By Alleen Pace Nilsen and Kenneth L. Donelson. HarperCollins, 1995. 620p. $43. 0-673-99737-5.

This updating of a basic study/textbook in young adult literature has placed a greater emphasis on adolescent psychology. The sections on short stories, television and movies, and YA magazines have been greatly expanded. In addition to many annotated lists of titles recommended especially for young people, there are excellent bibliographies of further reading for teachers and librarians. The selection of titles ranges from the stoical/classical to the very current and popular, and little distinction is made between books for the teenager and adult books suitable for young adults. Author, title, and subject indexes are included. While the earlier editions are still useful, this revised and expanded edition is recommended for secondary school and public libraries.   *YOUNG ADULT LITERATURE (GENERAL)*

Y*
383. **More Teens' Favorite Books: Young Adults' Choices 1993–1995**. International Reading Association, 1996. 76p. $9.95. 0-87207-149-9.

To select this list of just 30 favorite titles, more than 4,000 ballots were cast by teenagers from all parts of the United States to determine what young people consider enjoyable reading. The purpose of this annual project, as with a similar program with younger children, *More Kids' Favorite Books*, is to stimulate reading, especially with reluctant readers, by having young people themselves serve as the critics. Using peer promotion has evidently been successful. The titles contain brief annotations and adequate bibliographical information. This short and inexpensive list should be popular with teenagers and is recommended for all libraries serving that age group. Copies can be ordered directly by sending a check payable to the IRA and mailing it to: International Reading Association, Order Department, 800 Barksdale Rd., Box 8139, Newark, DE 19714-8139.   *YOUNG ADULT LITERATURE (GENERAL)*

Y*
384. **Nonfiction for Young Adults: From Delight to Wisdom**. By Betty Carter and Richard Abrahamson. Oryx, 1991. 233p. $29.50. 0-89774-555-8.

Carter and Abrahamson, two noted authorities in young adult literature, have provided an invaluable aid for teachers and librarians. They discuss the role of nonfiction in literature-based curricula and convincingly praise the merits of nonfiction: "We hope to show the literary qualities of nonfiction as well as define its importance for young adults. We suggest that the vital element nonfiction lacks is professional attention." Criteria for evaluating nonfiction are also elaborated. Finally, they include an extensive and excellent bibliography of nonfiction considered popular with young adults. This handbook, which will undoubtedly be used as a standard text for courses in young adult literature, is recommended for all libraries that serve young adults.   *YOUNG ADULT LITERATURE (GENERAL)*

Y*

385. **Popular Reading for Young Adults: A Collection of Booklist Columns**. Ed. by Sally Estes. American Library Association, 1996. 64p. $7.95. 0-8389-7835-5.

Lists recently published in *Booklist* (plus a few additions) make up this handy and inexpensive guide of young adult and adult fiction and nonfiction. The lists consist of subjects and genres that should whet the appetites of sophisticated young adults and include such thematic groupings as self-image, poetry, historical fiction, biography, disaster, and virtual reality. This list could be used in conjunction with its companion volume *Popular Reading for Children III*. This handy and inexpensive list of bibliographies would be useful for reading guidance and collection development and is recommended for all libraries serving young adults. *YOUNG ADULT LITERATURE (GENERAL)*

Y; A*

386. **Reader's Adviser**. 14th ed. Ed. by Marion Sader. Bowker, 1994. 6 vol. $500/set. 0-8352-3320-0.

Begun in 1921 as *Bookman's Manual*, this reference source has become a standard tool in almost all libraries and continues to be "a reflection of the current state of the best available books in print in the United States." It provides basic material for the nonspecialist, student, and librarian. It is updated approximately every five years. This greatly expanded edition provides profiles of its authors plus annotated bibliographies of selected in-print works by and about them. Each volume has its own editor and introduction that provides interesting background concerning the genre. The six volumes are available as a set or as individual volumes for $110 each. The titles of the six volumes are as follows:

386.1   Volume 1: **The Best in Reference Works, British Literature, and American Literature**. Ed. by David Scott Kastan and Emory Elliott. 1994. 1,512p. 0-8352-3321-9.

386.2   Volume 2: **The Best in World Literature**. Ed. by Robert DiYanni. 1994. 1,162p. 0-8352-3322-7.

386.3   Volume 3: **The Best in Social Sciences, History, and the Arts**. Ed. by John G. Sproat. 1994. 1,168p. 0-8352-3323-5.

386.4   Volume 4: **The Best in Philosophy and Religion**. Ed. by Robert S. Ellwood. 1994. 1,088p. 0-8352-3324-3.

386.5   Volume 5: **The Best in Science, Technology, and Medicine**. Ed. by Carl Mitcham and William F. Williams. 1994. 976p. 0-8352-3325-1.

386.6   Volume 6: **Indexes**. 1994. 840p. 0-8352-3326-X.

REFERENCE BOOKS; READING GUIDANCE

Y; A*

387. **The Reader's Adviser on CD-ROM**. Bowker/Reed Reference, 1994. $400 single user; $550 network use. 0-8352-3849-0.

This edition includes the entire 14th edition of *Reader's Adviser*; the power to view, download, and print; brief summaries of 58,000 titles by 120 authors; and 3,700 author biographies. This comprehensive electronic reference makes it possible to find information quickly and to make in-depth searches by author, title, subject, keyword, and ISBN. Annual updates are planned. All the power of Boolean searching is here for all libraries that can afford it, especially secondary schools with a large college-bound student body. *READING GUIDANCE; REFERENCE BOOKS*

Y; A

388. **The Reader's Catalog: An Annotated Selection of More Than 40,000 of the Best Books in Print. . . .** 2nd ed. Ed. by Geoffrey O'Brien. Random House, 1996. 1,500p. $34.95 pap. 0-924322-01-2.

More than 40,000 English-language titles appear in this one-volume list. The titles are arranged under 208 different subject areas. All of the titles were in print at the time of publication. Criteria for the inclusion of "best" books are not stated, and most annotations are very brief. Still, the price is right, and most public libraries and high school libraries will want this, if for no other reason than it will serve as a quick identifying checklist on so many subject areas. It would make a convenient first step in filling gaps in the collection. *READING GUIDANCE*

Y*

389.   **Senior High School Library Catalog**. 15th ed. H. W. Wilson, 1997. 1,500p. (Standard Catalog Series). $130. 0-8242-0921-4.

The 15th edition of this basic selection aid for senior high school libraries and young adult collections in public libraries is the same in scope and treatment as previous editions. The approximately 6,000 entries suitable for readers in grades 9 through 12 have been carefully chosen by practitioners from around the country. The nonfiction titles are arranged by Dewey Decimal numbers, and the fiction by author's last name. There is a separate section on short story collections. For each entry there is extensive bibliographic information, including complete cataloging information and subject headings. The annotations take the form of excerpts from reviews in reputable reviewing sources. There are usually two; the first is descriptive, the second critical. Professional tools are included. About half of the text consists of the single-alphabet index, which includes entries for author, titles, subjects, and more than 11,000 analytics. The last section consists of a directory of publishers and distributors. Purchase price also includes the supplements for 1998, 1999, 2000, and 2001. This is an indispensable tool for building core collections.   *YOUNG ADULT LITERATURE (GENERAL)*

Y*; A*

390.   **Subject Bibliographies**. Superintendent of Documents. U.S. Government Printing Office, various dates. Free.

The Government Printing Office publishes a number of pamphlets that list what are considered to be the most useful government documents available on a variety of subjects, including aging, accounting and auditing, economics, gardening, adult education, air pollution, poetry and literature, and transportation. They were once known as "Price Lists" and now total about 225 in number. They are revised periodically and usually include a listing of books, reports, and pamphlets that would be of general interest. These subject bibliographies are available free through the GPO, but first request a list of those that are available. The use of these pamphlets is a convenient way of building vertical file materials in public, high school, and college libraries with inexpensive authoritative material.

UNITED STATES—GOVERNMENT DOCUMENTS;
FREE MATERIALS; VERTICAL FILE MATERIALS

Y; A*

391.   **Tapping the Government Grapevine: The User-Friendly Guide to U.S. Government Information Sources**. 2nd ed. By Judith Schiek Robinson. Oryx, 1993. 227p. $34.50 pap. 0-89774-712-7.

This extensive bibliography updates the 1988 edition of a fine guide. It is intended to serve as a practical guide to locating federal, state, municipal, foreign, and international information sources. The book is arranged into chapters that each cover a broad topic. Some of the divisions focus on the distributors of information, such as the Government Printing Office; others focus on types of information, such as statistics and government regulations. The work is enhanced with detailed subject, title, and agency indexes. This work is recommended for purchase by most academic, public, special, and secondary school libraries where the subject coverage warrants.

UNITED STATES—GOVERNMENT DOCUMENTS

Y; A

392.   **University Press Books for Public and Secondary School Libraries**. Association of American University Presses, annual. 114p. Free. ISSN 1055-4173.

This new annual bibliography is a combination of the two AAUP annuals of recommended university press titles, one for public and one for school libraries, that were issued for many years. Because there was a certain amount of overlap, the combined catalog that lists more than 500 university press titles makes good sense. Journals and serials are excluded. Each annotated entry is arranged in Dewey Decimal number order; they are annotated with quotes from reviews. An author and title index is provided. Suggested for all public libraries and school libraries, especially smaller libraries that may need help in acquiring appropriate titles from the large output of the university presses. Free to librarians by writing on library's letterhead to: Association of American University Presses, Publications Department, 584 Broadway, Ste. 410, New York, NY 10012.   *UNIVERSITY PRESS BOOKS*

Y

393.   **Young Adult Annual Booklist** . Young Adult Services, Los Angeles Public Library, annual. $10.

This brief booklet, which has been published annually for the past seven or eight years, annotates and evaluates the fiction and nonfiction titles added to the young adult collection of the L.A. Public Library during the previous year. Also included is a list of "Adult Books Having YA Interest." An author and title index is provided. To order, send a check for $10 to: Attn: Betty Lunn, Young Adult Services, Los Angeles Public Library, 630 W. 5th St., Los Angeles, CA 90071.

YOUNG ADULT LITERATURE (GENERAL)

Y

394.   **Young Adult Literature and Nonprint Material: Resources for Selection**. By Millicent Lenz and Mary Meacham. Scarecrow, 1994. 336p. $37.50. 0-8108-2906-1.

Intended as a comprehensive selection aid for educators and librarians choosing young adult resources, this annotated bibliography includes critical and descriptive information on more than 600 books, magazines, audiovisuals, and electronic databases. Most of the entries were published or produced between 1988 and 1993. The entries are divided into seven major topics and subdivided by type of resource or specific subject. Cross-references handle items that fall under more than one area. Full bibliographic citations necessary for ordering are included. Annotations include an overview of contents, scope, arrangement, indexes, and any special features. Author, title, and subject indexes complete this extensive bibliography, which should prove extremely useful for middle/junior high school, senior high school, and public libraries as a current aid to selection and reference tool.

INSTRUCTIONAL MATERIALS; BIBLIOGRAPHIES

Y*

395.   **The Young Adult Reader's Adviser**. Bowker, 1992. 2 vol. $79.95. 0-8352-3068-6.

Modeled after Bowker's *Reader's Adviser*, this two-volume set was designed to help students, teachers, and librarians find recommended reading material on subjects and authors for varying age groups ranging from middle school through senior high. Included are more than 17,000 bibliographic entries and biographical profiles of more than 850 authors. Entries are arranged under four main subject categories reflecting the typical secondary school curricula: literature and language arts, mathematics and computer science, social science and history, and science and health. Noticeably missing from the main sections is the category for the fine and performing arts. Entries include full bibliographic data. Each of the two volumes contains the Profile Index, an alphabetical listing of all individuals highlighted; the Author Index, a list of the authors, editors, and translators of all books included; and the Title Index, a complete listing of all books cited. Bibliographies with annotations are found in the profiles section and in specific subject areas. This "book finder" for young adults is highly recommended for all secondary school libraries and public libraries serving young adults.

YOUNG ADULT LITERATURE (GENERAL); READING GUIDANCE

Y

396.   **Young Adult Reading Activities Library**. Ed. by Patricia S. Morris and Margaret A. Berry. Center for Applied Research in Education; distr. Prentice Hall, 1993. 6 vols. $16.95/vol.; $101.70/set. 0-87628-993-6; 0-87628-393-8/set.

Each of the volumes begins with a reading list of about 450 titles followed by activities to support reading programs. The books are arranged by subjects and are suitable for students in grades 6 through 12. Each entry is annotated and indicates a reading level. The six volumes are:

396.1   **Modern Realistic Fiction**. 0-87628-585-X.

396.2   **Historical Fiction**. 0-87628-393-8.

396.3   **Science Fiction**. 0-87628-856-5.

396.4   **Mystery and Suspense**. 0-87628-603-1.

396.5   **Biography and Autobiography**. 0-87628-190-0.

396.6   **Nonfiction**. 0-87628-612-0.

YOUNG ADULT LITERATURE (GENERAL)

Art and Music

Y

397. **Building a Classical Music Library**. 3rd ed. By Bill Parker. Jormax Publications, 1994. 286p. $14.95. 0-9641332-0-2.

More than 100 composers are represented in this discography chosen by Parker, who hopes to make composers come to life as real humans, and to recommend recordings (compact discs) that have wide consensus as to their merits. Entries are arranged alphabetically by composer within the major stylistic periods: Middle Ages and Renaissance; baroque; early, middle, and late romantic periods; and modern. Each entry contains a brief critique of the composer, a selected list of representative works, and recommended recordings of these works. This discography is recommended as a basic buying guide for all public libraries and for secondary school libraries within schools with a strong music department.

CLASSICAL MUSIC; COMPACT DISCS; DISCOGRAPHY

Y; A

398. **The Literature of Rock III, 1984–1990**. By Frank Hoffmann and B. Lee Cooper. Scarecrow, 1995. 2 vol. $99.50. 0-8108-2762-X.

This extensive bibliography updates and expands the earlier volume *The Literature of Rock II*, which covered 1979–1983 (1986. $85.50. 0-8108-1821-3). More than 10,000 entries from hundreds of books and periodicals are arranged under broad subject areas and further subdivided into more specific areas. Unfortunately, most citations are not annotated. A performers index lists identifying citation numbers. There are two useful appendixes; one lists books and periodicals indexed, and the other lists a core collection of rock records. This comprehensive work will be useful to rock fans as well as scholars of popular culture and is recommended for larger secondary school and most public libraries building a collection in this area.

ROCK MUSIC

Y; A

399. **National Gallery of Art Color Reproduction Catalog**. National Gallery of Art. Free.

This catalog of one of America's finest art museums lists postcards, plaques, and reprints of paintings in their large collection. Included are reproductions of many of the greatest, from Botticelli to Renoir to Whistler. Each painting is illustrated in color; each entry details what kind of reproductions are available. Recommended (along with catalogs of other famous museums, e.g., New York's Metropolitan Museum of Art) for school and public libraries to develop their collection of art reproductions.

ART

Y; A

400. **Rap Music in the 1980s: A Reference Guide**. By Judy McCoy. Scarecrow, 1992. 261p. $32.50. 0-8108-2649-6.

McCoy has compiled a bibliography/discography on one of the newest forms of music, which is very much related to Black oral tradition improvisation and the everyday experiences of Black youth. There are more than 1,000 entries on the literature of the field and entries for about 75 recordings. All of the entries contain bibliographic information and a brief annotation. Indexes by artists, album titles, and subjects are also included. This work may be considered for high school, academic, and public libraries that have collections or are building collections on popular culture, Black studies, or music.

RAP MUSIC; AFRICAN AMERICANS

Y; A

401. **Rockabilly: A Bibliographic Resource Guide**. By B. Lee Cooper and Wayne S. Haney. Scarecrow, 1990. 372p. $39.50. 0-8108-2386-1.

More than 35 years of rockabilly music are included in this extensive list of printed resources. Many well-known performers, such as Charlie Feathers, Carl Perkins, Jerry Lee Lewis, Elvis Presley, Shakin' Stevens, the Cramps, and the Stray Cats, are represented among the more than 220 rockabilly singers and instrumentalists listed. The bibliographic survey includes biographies, historical studies, concert and record reviews, discographies, and articles from magazines. Author and name indexes are provided. This bibliography is recommended as a reference aid and collection building guide for secondary school, academic, and public libraries supporting collections or programs in rock and country music, popular culture, and American studies.

ROCK MUSIC; COUNTRY MUSIC; POP CULTURE; DISCOGRAPHY

Y; A
402. **Twentieth-Century Choral Music: An Annotated Bibliography of Music Suitable for Use by High School Choirs.** 2nd ed. By J. Perry White. Scarecrow, 1990. 226p. $25. 0-8108-2394-2.

This is a critical, selective bibliography of twentieth-century choral compositions accessible to high school choirs. It represents major composers and stylistic trends during this century. Each of the 360 entries (120 new to this edition) include composer, title, voicing, accompaniment, text, range, difficulty, style, comments, publisher, usage, date, and level (junior high school through college). Appended is a list of major music publishers. A composer index and a title index are also provided. This valuable bibliographic guide is recommended for all music, high school, academic, and public libraries with strong music interests.

CHOIRS (MUSIC); CHORAL MUSIC

Audiovisual Materials

Audio

Y; A
403. **All-Music Guide: The Best CDs, Albums, & Tapes.** Ed. by Michael Erlewine. Miller Freeman; distr. Publishers Group West, 1992. 1,176p. $19.95 pap. 0-87930-264-X.

As the title implies, this extensive selection aid covers all types of music, including country, rock, rap, and classical. More than 23,000 recordings of more than 6,000 artists are included under 27 music subject categories, with a chapter devoted to each category. Entries within each chapter are arranged alphabetically by artist or composer; each entry includes title, recording company, year of distribution, and a brief annotation. A symbol designates those considered by the editor to be "landmarks, the best an artist has to offer." Indexing is minimal; however, an artist index is included for most popular works, and a composer index is included for most classical titles. Despite the editor's subjectivity, this comprehensive and inexpensive guide is recommended for most libraries developing a collection in this area.

AUDIOCASSETTES; COMPACT DISCS; PHONORECORDINGS

Y; A
404. **The Blackwell Guide to Recorded Jazz.** 2nd ed. By Barry Kernfeld. Basil Blackwell, 1995. 450p. $19.95. 0-631-19552-1.

This work identifies more than 125 jazz artists and highlights the single most important work of each. Jazz music from all genres and time periods are represented, from the birth of jazz through the early 1990s. The work is chronologically arranged in 11 chapters representing the major styles of jazz and spotlighting the most important artists within each category. Bibliographic data is provided for each format currently available: LP, cassette, or compact disc. All songs on the recording and all artists are listed. All names mentioned are included in the comprehensive index. This work will be of more than passing interest to all jazz fans and to all libraries building collections to satisfy these buffs.

JAZZ; DISCOGRAPHY

Y; A
405. **The Grove Press Guide to Blues on CD.** By Frank-John Hadley. Grove Press, 1993. 256p. $14.95 pap. 0-8021-3328-2.

Though somewhat specialized in subject matter, this inexpensive guide includes blues as it appears in various genres—traditional, rhythm and blues, country, rock, and jazz. About 700 albums are listed, arranged by performer. Each entry includes the album title, label and number, running time, a critical annotation, and a star rating (from one to five). The time span covered is impressive, from Bessie Smith to Wynton Marsalis. A separate 30-page section on compilations and anthologies is arranged under the title of the CD. There is a complete index of all the album titles.

BLUES (MUSIC); COMPACT DISCS; DISCOGRAPHY

Y; A
406.   **The Guide to Classic Recorded Jazz**. By Tom Piazza. University of Iowa, 1995. 391p. $22.95 pap. 0-87745-489-2.

Most of the 800 recordings discussed in this discography date from the 1920s through the 1960s, thus the title "classic jazz." The book is divided into two main sections: the first covers ensembles, the second soloists by the instrument each played. The annotations are interesting and informative. Compact disc numbers are included when the recording is available in that format. The arrangement is complicated, which makes use of the index necessary to locate individual artists and their albums.

JAZZ; COMPACT DISCS; DISCOGRAPHY

Y; A
407.   **Kliatt Audiobook Guide**. By Jean B. Palmer. Libraries Unlimited, 1994. 237p. $34. 1-56308-123-7.

In the introductory sections of this useful bibliography, the mechanics of organizing and using audiobooks in libraries, classrooms, and homes are discussed with practical tips on maintenance, repairs, examples of successful programs in schools, and criteria for evaluating audiobooks. The body of the work consists of reprints of more than 450 detailed, signed reviews that appeared in *Kliatt* magazine from 1990 through 1993. Both fiction and nonfiction titles that would appeal to young adults and adults are included. Each entry includes material on the listening level, narrator, technical quality, and packaging. Lists of audiobook sources are included in an appendix. Bowker's *Words on Cassette* is an annual nonevaluative listing of all the audiobooks "in print."

AUDIOBOOKS

Y
408.   **Listener's Guide to Audio Books**. By John Wynne. Fireside, 1995. 393p. $14. 0-684-80239-2.

Wynne, an experienced producer of audiobooks, has compiled a comprehensive guide to sound-recorded books. He has chosen titles that are readily available to the public in retail outlets (and thus available to the smaller libraries). The annotated titles are arranged by popular subject areas such as action and adventure; fiction is further subdivided into classic and contemporary. Each entry lists author, title, reader, and a rating based on a scale of 4 to 1 (indicating from highly recommended to below par; a bomb indicates totally unsatisfactory). Additional lists of audiobooks not reviewed are included in this extensive guide. Author and title indexes are also provided. Wynne's decision not to include two major producers of unabridged works—Recorded Books and Books on Tape—is a serious limitation, nor does the book serve as a substitute for the very exhaustive *Words on Cassette*, with its 50,000-plus titles. Nevertheless, this inexpensive title is recommended for secondary school and smaller public libraries beginning audiobook collections and as a guide to patrons wanting to identify and purchase such items.

AUDIOBOOKS

Y; A
409.   **Penguin Guide to Compact Discs**. Penguin, 1996. 1,600p. $23.95. 0-14-051367-1.

This edition updates and expands the earlier editions of the *Penguin Guide*. Not surprisingly, it drops cassettes and LPs and includes primarily new titles or titles that have been transferred to CDs. Preceding the listing is an excellent essay discussing the advantages and disadvantages of CDs. Entries are arranged by composer, followed by type of composition; they contain evaluations of performances and recording quality. This guide has a strong British bias; however, an attempt was made to include the most important U.S. discs. This inexpensive guide is recommended for all libraries building or maintaining collections of classical music.

COMPACT DISCS; MUSIC

Y; A
410.   **Rock & Roll Review: A Guide to Good Rock on CD**. By Bill Shapiro. Andrews & McMeel, 1991. 299p. $9.95 pap. 0-8362-6217-4.

This is the 2nd edition, under a new title, of Shapiro's *The CD Rock & Roll Library: 30 Years of Rock & Roll on Compact Disc*. More than 1,000 short reviews are cited in this edition. Each entry includes title, year of publication, label, catalog number, and a rating (A–F), with notes on the technical and aesthetic quality indicating the basis for the rating. There is some question on Shapiro's subjectivity in selecting both the artists and the reviews; however, the work does serve a useful reference purpose, and it is helpful in identifying many rock and roll selections that are currently on CD for collection building in this area. This inexpensive guide is recommended for most secondary school and public libraries.   *ROCK MUSIC; COMPACT DISCS*

Y; A

411.   **Schwann Artist Issue**. Schwann, annual. $19.95.

This publication is the artist index to the fall *Schwann Opus Guide*. It lists only compact discs and cassettes in six different sections. The first section is an alphabetical listing of orchestras and ensembles with further subdivisions by conductors, composers, and titles of works. Next is a listing of the record releases identified by label, number, analog or digital recording, and format (CD or cassette). A separate section on conductors gives only the name of their orchestras. The last four sections give full record listings under instrumental soloists (arranged by instrument, then by artist), choral groups, opera groups, and vocalists. *The Schwann Opus Guide* lists recorded classical music by composers' names. There are about 45,000 CDs, cassette tapes, and laserdiscs in each issue (quarterly, $39.95/yr.; Canada, $49.95). *Schwann Spectrum*, which listed jazz, pop, and rock, was discontinued as of 1997. Both *Schwann Opus* and *Schwann Artist Issue* are valuable reference and collection-building tools in public and academic libraries as well as high school libraries with large CD collections.
COMPACT DISCS; AUDIOCASSETTES

Y; A

412.   **Words on Cassette**. Bowker, 1996. 1,500p. $149.95. 0-8352-3765-6.

Words on Cassette made its debut in January 1992 with the merger of Bowker's *On Cassette* with the recently acquired Meckler publication *Words on Tape*. The new publication is the most comprehensive guide to commercially available spoken-word audiocassettes, which is one of the fastest growing segments in the publishing/media production industry. Titles on spoken-word cassettes currently are available on every conceivable topic and audience level, covering fiction and nonfiction, contemporary works and classics, entertainment, education, and business in more than 30 languages. This edition provides easy access to information on more than 50,000 audiocassettes from more than 1,500 producers. There are five indexes: title, author, reader/performer, subject, and producer/distributor. Recommended for all academic and public libraries with audiocassette collections as well as school district libraries that can afford it.
AUDIOBOOKS

Video and Films

Y; A*

413.   **Halliwell's Film and Video Guide, 1997**. By Leslie Halliwell. HarperCollins, 1996. 1,312p. $22.50 pap. 0-06-273432-6.

Most of this volume is taken up with brief reports on more than 13,000 motion pictures (with an indication if they are available on videocassette). As in previous editions, the films are arranged in alphabetical order by title. Entries include title, country of origin, running time, color or black-and-white, director, principal cast members, and awards. Films are given one to four stars. The annotations are brief but pithy and critical. There are lists of alternate titles, English-language titles of foreign films, and original titles of foreign films. This work is considered the standard film guide in print although libraries will probably want quite a number of different titles.   *MOTION PICTURES; VIDEOCASSETTES*

Y; A

414.   **Picture This! A Guide to Over 300 Environmentally, Socially, and Politically Relevant Films and Videos**. By Sky Hiatt. Noble Press, 1992. 389p. $12.95. 1-879360-05-5.

Hiatt has compiled an extensive list of activist films on such topics as poverty, race, war, and gay rights. Many, though not all, are readily available in video format. This timely list can serve as a companion to Kevin Brownlow's *Behind the Mask of Innocence* . . . (University of California Press, 1992. $25 pap. 0-520-07626-5). Recommended for those libraries having a large film/video collection or special collections in the topics cited in the subtitle; this includes public, academic, and school district-wide libraries.
MOTION PICTURES; VIDEOCASSETTES

Y; A

415.   **Roger Ebert's Movie Home Companion, [year]**. By Roger Ebert. Andrews, McMeel & Parker, annual. 1998 edition. $17.95. 0-8362-3688-2.

Reviewing hundreds of films, each edition grows about 50 percent larger as the popularity of videocassettes has soared since Ebert compiled his first *Companion* in 1986. Ebert lists each film's title, rating, running time, year of release, and a personal rating from one to four stars. The index highlights the year's ten best movies. Another useful title is Lynn Minton's *Movie Guide for Puzzled Parents* (Delacorte, 1984. $12.95. 0-385-29284-8). The big difference is that Minton evaluates films for suitability for children, whereas Ebert highlights films suitable for parents. Obviously, most libraries will want to have both guides side-by-side. Ebert's guide is recommended for all high schools and public libraries having videocassette collections for home viewing.   *MOTION PICTURES; VIDEOCASSETTES*

Y; A

416.   **The Third World in Film and Video, 1984–1990**. By Helen W. Cyr. Scarecrow, 1991. 256p. $29.50. 0-8108-2380-2.

This is Cyr's 3rd in a series of filmographies on the Third World. The earlier two, titled *Filmography of the Third World*, were published in 1976 (o.p.) and 1985 ($25. 0-8108-1783-3). The latest edition, renamed to reflect the fact that videocassettes have been added, lists more than 1,100 titles (not included in the earlier editions) that relate to Third World countries and what Cyr calls "the Third World in our midst," the major ethnic minorities in North America. Entries are arranged geographically by region and country. Annotations and full bibliographic information are provided, including distributors' names and addresses. This guide will be well-used in most secondary school and public libraries for reference, library programming, and collection development.

DEVELOPING COUNTRIES; MOTION PICTURES; VIDEOCASSETTES

Y; A

417.   **Safe Planet: The Guide to Environmental Film and Video**. Alternative Media Information Center, 1991. 40p. $13.50; $9.50 individuals (both pap.).

This booklet lists and provides descriptive annotations on more than 80 films and videos dealing with the environment. Information on how to rent or purchase is given with appropriate addresses. Copies are available from Alternative Media Information Center, 121 Fulton St., 5th Flr., New York, NY 10038.   *ENVIRONMENT; MOTION PICTURES; VIDEOCASSETTES*

Y; A

418.   **Seen That, Now What? The Ultimate Guide to Finding the Video You Really Want to Watch**. By Andrea Shaw. Fireside, 1996. 573p. $14.95 pap. 0-684-80011-X.

More than 5,400 films released through 1994 are arranged by broad headings such as action, comedy, and drama that are further subdivided by narrower subjects. Entries give year, running time, a quality rating (A through F), a brief plot summary, the director, and cast. There are title, director, and actor indexes. This subject approach makes it relatively easy to locate movies on individual topics.

VIDEOCASSETTES

Y

419.   **Selected Videos and Films for Young Adults, [year]**. Young Adult Services Division, American Library Association, annual.

This is an annotated, illustrated color brochure of recommended videos and films released in the United States in a given year that are recommended for use in programs for young adults. The films were chosen on the basis of appeal, technical quality, contents, and use possibilities by a committee appointed by the Young Adult Services Division of ALA. It is compiled annually. Single copies are available for a stamped self-addressed envelope. In quantity the price is $20 per 100. Write to: ALA Publishing Services, Order Department, 50 E. Huron St., Chicago, IL 60611.

VIDEOCASSETTES; MOTION PICTURES

Y; A

420. **Shakespeare Films in the Classroom**. By Jo McMurtry. Archon, 1994. 249p. $39.50. 0-208-02369-0.

More than 100 videos of Shakespeare's plays are discussed and analyzed in this guide to cassettes suitable for classroom use. There are 35 sections, each devoted to a single play. For each video, bibliographic information is given, including year, color or black-and-white, running time, producer, and director. Major characters and their actors are listed, and an extensive critical annotation covers text modifications, interpretations, settings, and costumes. There is also a bibliography of reviews and sources for rental or purchase. This is a useful bibliography in high school, college, and public libraries. See also the more extensive *Shakespeare on Screen*.   *SHAKESPEARE, WILLIAM*

Y; A

421. **The Ultimate Movie Thesaurus**. By Christopher Case. Holt, 1996. 1,076p. $19.95 pap. 0-8050-3496-X.

Case, a professor of film at the University of Arkansas, has compiled an extensive and recommended list of about 8,000 feature films arranged by title. Each entry contains a lot of data including a short plot summary, year, running time, rating in number of stars (his own judgment), MPAA (Motion Picture Association of America) rating, cast characters, genre and subject category, and more. Appended are a subject listing under broad subject, box office hits arranged chronologically by year, and a list of three- and four-star films. Though titled "Ultimate," this list is not as extensive as *Bowker's Complete Video Directory* (Bowker, 1995, 3v. $229.95. 0-8352-3586-6) or Gale's *Video Source Book*, but because Case is selective and only a fraction of the cost of the other works, it is worth considering as a reference tool and selection aid for school and public libraries with video collections.   *VIDEOCASSETTES*

Y; A

422. **The Video Source Book, 1994**. 15th ed. Ed. by Julia C. Furtaw. Gale, 1994. 2 vols. $260. 0-8103-5408-X.

With the rapid growth of the video industry has come the need for a comprehensive listing of what is available. *The Video Source Book*, with 91,000 entries that describe 130,000 currently available titles, is the most comprehensive of several lists available. All areas of entertainment, education, culture, medicine, and business are included. The set is designed to aid in both evaluation and acquisition. Entries contain full information needed for acquisition as well as other valuable facts such as running time, date of release, subject category, and age suitability. A list of names, addresses, and phone numbers of almost 2,500 distributors is provided in a separate section. Additionally, there are extensive indexes by titles, subjects, close caption, casts, and more. A similar work is *Bowker's Complete Video Directory*, which is less expensive but not as comprehensive and does not include thousands of technical, scientific, and medical titles. Libraries developing and maintaining video collections will want one or the other of these comprehensive sources but probably not both.   *VIDEOCASSETTES*

Y; A

423. **Videos for Understanding Diversity: A Core Selection and Evaluative Guide**. By Gregory I. Stevens. American Library Association, 1993. 217p. $31.50. 0-8389-0612-5.

The importance of a greater understanding of the diversity in our society, and the role of audiovisuals (in this case videos) as motivational and informational tools, is generally accepted today. The author, with the assistance of faculty members at the State University of New York at Albany, has evaluated feature and documentary videos that have a multicultural theme. He has selected and compiled a list of 126 videos that will have a positive effect on the acceptance and tolerance of diversity. Included are videos on race relations, politics, gender issues, social relationships, and social stereotypes. The videos are arranged alphabetically by title. Each lengthy evaluation includes content summary, suggestions for use in the classroom, and critical comments. Full bibliographic information, such as series, producer/distributor, date, technical information, and availability of study guides, is also included. In some cases suggested readings are provided. A category and title index and a directory of distributors complete the work. This core list should prove useful for all secondary school, academic, and many public libraries.   *MULTICULTURALISM; VIDEOCASSETTES*

Y; A

424.   **Western Civilization: A Critical Guide to Documentary Films**. By Neil M. Heyman. Greenwood, 1996. 244p. $59.95. 0-313-28438-5.

Heyman has compiled a bibliography of critical reviews of more than 173 documentaries representing many periods of history and suitable for use in Western Civilization courses in secondary schools and colleges (or perhaps used in library programming). Entries are arranged in chronological order. Each title entry includes length, year of production, color or black-and-white, producer or distributor, a series note if applicable, a one- or two-line annotation, and a longer critical essay. A letter grade from A to D is assigned to each film. In this age of the videocassette, a current filmography of this scope is welcome. Despite the fact that video availability is not indicated, this bibliography is recommended for school district-wide, academic, and public libraries as a reference tool, and for libraries maintaining film collections as a selection aid.   *MOTION PICTURES; HISTORY*

Authors and Illustrators

Y; A

425.   **African American Writers**. Ed. by Valerie Smith et al. Scribner's, 1991. 544p. $90. 0-684-19058-3.

This is a collection of well-written and scholarly essays on well-known African American writers. The presentation of each author includes a brief biographical sketch, a list of major writings with an appraisal, and a bibliography of books and articles for further study. Though limited to only 34 writers, this complement to the basic *American Writers* (Scribner's. 8 vols. $499. 0-684-17332-0) is recommended for most secondary school, undergraduate college, and public libraries.

AFRICAN AMERICANS; AUTHORS

Y

426.   **Authors and Artists for Young Adults**. Gale. $72/vol. 0-8103-7584-2.

This bio-bibliography, which now numbers approximately 20 volumes, maintains the level of excellence and bridges the gap between Gale's *Something About the Author* for children and *Contemporary Authors*, which is designed for adults. New volumes usually appear two times a year. Each volume includes material on 20–25 individuals that covers personal and professional biographical information, a portrait, a bibliography of writings and adaptations, a secondary bibliography, and sources for additional information. This is an important reference/selection source for school and public libraries serving young adults at the junior and senior high school levels. Highly recommended.   *AUTHORS*

Y; A

427.   **Concise Dictionary of American Literary Biography**. Gale, 1987–1989. 6 vols. $380. 0-8103-1818-0.

This set is a spinoff from the massive *Dictionary of American Literary Biography*, which contains entries for 2,300 American writers of fiction, poetry, and plays. The present set is limited to about 200 major writers. In addition to biographical information and critical analyses, entries include awards and prizes, a chronological list of works, and an extensive secondary bibliography of such works involving the author as books, articles, letters, interviews, papers, and locations of manuscripts. This set is intended for purchase by high school, junior college, and public libraries. There is also an eight-volume companion set, *Concise Dictionary of British Literary Biography* (1991–1992. $410. 0-8103-7980-5).

AMERICAN LITERATURE; ENGLISH LITERATURE; AUTHORS

Y; A

428.   **Contemporary American Dramatists**. St. James Press, 1994. 768p. $55. 1-55862-214-4.

This spinoff from *Contemporary Dramatists* (described below) profiles about 200 American dramatists since the end of World War II, from Eugene O'Neill to Tony Kushner. Included are writers for the stage, screen, radio, and television. As well as biographical information, there are a signed critical essay for each author, a full bibliography of written works, and a listing of critical sources. The latter two sections can be helpful in collection development. A companion volume is *Contemporary British Dramatists* (Gale, 1994. $55. 1-55862-213-6). *DRAMATISTS*

Y; A
429.   **Contemporary Dramatists**. 5th ed. St. James Press, 1993. 857p. $140. 1-55862-185-7.

This is a completely revised edition of a standard reference source. For each of the 450 dramatists included there are a biography, critical essay, and lists of materials by and about the writer. Information is given on other important bibliographies and locations of manuscript collections. As well as an important reference work, this volume can be a fine selection aid in larger collections for young adults. *DRAMATISTS*

Y; A
430.   **Contemporary Novelists**. 6th ed. By Susan W. Brown. St. James Press, 1996. 1,173p. $140. 1-55862-189-X.

This volume supplies information on more than 600 contemporary novelists published in English. Each entry includes biographical material about the author, a bibliographical listing of the author's writing, and a selection of secondary sources about the author and his or her work. Public and some high school libraries will find this work valuable. *NOVELISTS*

Y; A
431.   **Contemporary Poets**. 6th ed. By Tracy Chevalier. St. James Press, 1996. 1,336p. $160. 1-55862-191-1.

There are entries for about 800 living poets in this edition of a standard work. In addition to biographical material, each entry contains a signed critical essay and, as a help in collection development, a complete list of separately published books and a list of works about the poet. This will be of value in most medium and large public libraries and, perhaps, in high schools with advanced English classes. *POETS*

Y; A
432.   **Contemporary Popular Writers**. By David Mote. St. James Press, 1996. 500p. $130. 1-55862-216-0.

In this collection of critical essays, 300 of today's most popular and best-known novelists, playwrights, poets, and nonfiction writers are highlighted. Authors include many popular with young adult readers, like Stephen King, Agatha Christie, Michael Crichton, Danielle Steel, Toni Morrison, and Alex Haley. For each author are given personal information, a bibliography of works, a critical essay, and a list of works about the author. There are indexes by author, nationality, genre, and title. This is both a fine reference source and a good checklist for collection building in high school and young adult collections. *AUTHORS*

Y; A
433.   **Contemporary World Writers**. St. James Press, 1993. $140. 750p. 1-55862-200-4.

This update of the 1984 volume *Contemporary Foreign-Language Writers* profiles 358 important living writers of fiction, drama, and poetry who write in languages other than English and whose works have been translated into English. Each entry contains a who's who–style biography, a complete bibliography citing English translations of the works, a list of critical studies, and a critical essay of up to 1,000 words. This will be a valuable asset in some high school libraries as well as public and college libraries. *AUTHORS*

Y; A
434.   **Dictionary of Literary Biography**. Gale, 1978– . $108/vol.

This extensive set now totals more than 100 volumes and covers American writers, British writers, Canadian writers, Austrian writers, French writers, German writers, and Spanish writers. These books are not intended for selection purposes, but each entry in every volume contains extensive listings of primary and secondary sources on the author being highlighted. These lists can be helpful for identifying materials for interlibrary loans. From the many volumes in the parent set that deal with American authors, there is a six-volume abridgment that covers writers from the colonial period to the present: *Concise Dictionary of American Literary Biography* ($350. 0-8103-1818-0). *AUTHORS*

Y; A

435. **Great Woman Writers**. By Frank N. Magill. Holt, 1994. 611p. $40. 0-8050-2932-X.

One hundred thirty-five female authors are included in this bio-bibliographic dictionary that covers writers from antiquity to the present. More than half are American; the rest are chiefly European. After biographical material and a critical analysis of each author's work are bibliographies of her principal works and listings of important biographies and criticism. *WOMEN WRITERS; AUTHORS, WOMEN*

Y; A

436. **Major Twentieth-Century Writers**. Ed. by Bryan Ryan. Gale, 1991. 4 vol. $295/set. 0-8103-7766-7.

This reference work includes novelists, poets, playwrights, and other authors of the twentieth century who are most often studied in high schools and colleges (according to a survey of librarians and educators in the United States and Great Britain). This reference set is designed for the smaller library that doesn't really need (or is unable to afford) the more extensive *Contemporary Authors*. While this set is international in scope, authors chosen for inclusion have written in English, or their works have been translated into English. All sketches taken from *Contemporary Authors* have been reviewed and updated. All entries follow the familiar CA format and include personal biographical facts, a bibliography of complete works by the author, and a bibliography of biographical/critical sources for more extensive research. This bio-bibliographic set is recommended for all secondary school, academic, and public libraries that do not presently hold *Contemporary Authors*. *AUTHORS*

Y; A*

437. **Masterpieces of African-American Literature**. Ed. by Frank N. Magill. HarperCollins, 1992. 608p. $45. 0-06-270066-9.

This guide to about 150 titles represents the works of more than 90 African American writers (37 of whom are women) and includes novels, plays, autobiographies, and poetry. It serves as a companion volume to the many other titles in the *Masterpieces Series* edited by Magill. The entries are organized alphabetically by title. Each entry includes full bibliographic data as well as other important information such as principal characters, plot, analysis, and critical comment. Descriptions of standard works covering more than 200 years and a number of young adult titles are included. Author and title indexes complete the volume. Although only 150 titles are dealt with, this convenient collection is highly recommended as a reference tool and selection guide for high school, public, and undergraduate college libraries. *AFRICAN AMERICAN LITERATURE; AUTHORS, AFRICAN AMERICAN*

Y; A

438. **Modern American Novel: An Annotated Bibliography**. By Steven G. Kellman. Salem Press, 1991. 162p. (Magill Bibliographies). $40. 0-8108-2798-0.

This slim volume is designed to be a beginning guide to accessible materials about major modern novelists. Kellman has selected for inclusion 16 novelists of the first half of the twentieth century, including Cather, Dreiser, Faulkner, Fitzgerald, Hemingway, Lewis, London, Steinbeck, Wilder, and Wolfe. Entries are arranged alphabetically by author. General studies about each author are followed by entries on individual works. Full bibliographic information and a brief annotation are included with each entry. This is part of the Magill Bibliographies series, which also includes Taylor's *Restoration Drama* and Aubrey's *English Romantic Poetry*. This brief, well-focused volume is recommended for many high school and public and all undergraduate academic libraries for general reference and collection development. *AUTHORS, AMERICAN; FICTION*

Y; A

439.   **Modern American Women Writers**. Ed. by Elaine Showalter et al. Scribner's, 1991. 583p. $85. 0-684-19057-5.

This volume and *African American Writers* complement the well-known older parent set *American Writers*, also published by Scribner's. In an attempt to update the parent set, there is some inevitable duplication of women covered (e.g., of the 41 women included in this volume, 22 are also included in *American Writers*). Long biographical and critical essays are followed by detailed references to complete works by and selected works about each writer. This scholarly bio-bibliography is recommended for most academic and public and many secondary school libraries for general reference, interloans, and collection building.   *AUTHORS, WOMEN; AUTHORS, AMERICAN*

Y; A

440.   **Nobel Laureates in Literature: A Biographical Dictionary**. Ed. by Rado Pribic. Garland, 1990. 497p. (Garland Reference Library of the Humanities, 849). $25. 0-8240-7541-4.

Nobel winners in literature are arranged in alphabetical order, which makes this handy reference source easy to use. There is also a chronological list of those receiving awards. Each entry includes a biographical sketch and a select bibliography. An appendix includes a list of secondary sources. Much of the information in this bio-bibliography is found elsewhere, but it will be convenient for students and others working specifically on Nobel winners in literature. Recommended for most academic and large public libraries and some high school libraries needing resources in this area.   *NOBEL PRIZES*

Y; A*

441.   **Research Guide to Biography and Criticism: Volumes 5 and 6**. Ed. by Walton Beacham et al. Beacham Publishing, 1991. 914p. $125. 0-933833-27-X.

Nearly 130 English-language (mainly contemporary American, Canadian, and British) authors have been added to the 325 authors included in the base set and 1990 update. The format and purpose of volumes 5 and 6 are similar to the set; each presents a chronology of the author's life; a selected list of the author's works; evaluative annotations of selected criticism; an overview of biographical, autobiographical, and critical sources; and citations to treatments in other reference books. These two volumes are recommended for all secondary school, undergraduate academic, and public libraries, and are a must for all libraries having the earlier volumes.   *AUTHORS*

Y

442.   **Speaking for Ourselves: Autobiographical Sketches by Notable Authors of Books for Young Adults**. Ed. by Donald R. Gallo. National Council of Teachers of English, 1990. 231p. $14.95.

This is a collection of fascinating autobiographical sketches of 87 of the most popular writers of fiction for young adults. Popularity was determined by a poll administered to past and present officers of the Assembly on Literature for Adolescents of the NCTE. Many of the authors describe how they became writers and how they regard their work. For each, there are a portrait and a selective bibliography of the major works with publication dates. The latter is a fine checklist for collection development. This is a useful item for any library that serves young adults. There is a sequel by the same author, *Speaking for Ourselves, Too* (1993. 235p. $14.95 pap. 0-8141-4623-6). In the companion volume, *Speaking of Poets: Interviews with Poets Who Write for Children and Young Adults* by Jeffrey S. Copeland (1993. 127p. $12.95. 0-8141-4622-8), 16 important poets discuss their work.   *POETS; AUTHORS*

Y; A

443.   **Twentieth-Century African-American Writers and Artists**. By Chester Hedgepeth. American Library Association, 1991. 323p. $42. 0-8389-0534-X.

Almost 250 African-American artists, musicians, and writers are profiled in this bio-bibliography. Each entry includes a short biography, a critique of the individual's work, a selected list of works, and a selected bibliography of titles about the person. The volume is organized alphabetically by biographee. The annotations are generally well written. Many of the individuals included in this volume are not cited in standard biographical sources. This is an important acquisition for secondary school, academic, and public libraries.   *AUTHORS, AFRICAN AMERICAN; ARTISTS, AFRICAN AMERICAN; MUSICIANS, AFRICAN AMERICAN*

Y*; A*

444.   **Wilson Author Series**. H. W. Wilson. 1938–1991.

This time-tested bio-bibliographic series now consists of more than a dozen volumes covering writers from 800 BC into the mid-1990s. Earlier volumes, which have not been revised, are still useful. Each volume follows a similar pattern: "Sketches describe their subjects' lives and careers, literary significance, and critical evaluations, and include lists of the author's principal works with date first published, lists of major critical works, and a portrait or photograph, where available." This series is highly recommended for all secondary school libraries. Titles currently available in this bio-bibliographic series include:

444.1   **American Authors, 1600–1900**. Ed. by Stanley J. Kunitz and Howard Haycraft. 1938. $65. 0-8242-0001-2.

444.2   **British Authors Before 1800**. Ed. by Stanley J. Kunitz and Howard Haycraft. 1952. $53. 0-8242-0006-3.

444.3   **British Authors of the Nineteenth Century**. Ed. by Stanley J. Kunitz and Howard Haycraft. 1936. $55. 0-8242-0007-1.

444.4   **European Authors, 1000–1900**. Ed. by Stanley J. Kunitz and Vineta Colby. 1967. $68. 0-8242-0013-6.

444.5   **Greek and Latin Authors, 800 BC–AD 1000**. By Michael Grant. 1980. $60. 0-8242-0640-1.

444.6   **Twentieth Century Authors**. Ed. by Stanley J. Kunitz and Howard Haycraft. 1942. $85. 0-8242-0049-7.

444.7   **Twentieth Century Authors: First Supplement**. Ed. by Stanley J Kunitz and Howard Haycraft. 1955. $75. 0-8242-0050-0.

444.8   **World Authors, 1950–1970**. Ed. by John Wakeman. 1975. $95. 0-8242-0429-0.

444.9   **World Authors, 1970–1975**. Ed. by John Wakeman. 1980. $78. 0-8242-0641-X.

444.10   **World Authors. 1975–1980**. Ed. by Vineta Colby. 1985. $80. 0-8242-0715-7.

444.11   **World Authors. 1980–1985**. Ed. by Vineta Colby. 1991. $90. 0-8242-0797-1.

444.12   **World Authors. 1985–1990**. Ed. by Vineta Colby. 1995. $95. 0-8242-0875-7.

444.13   **Index to the Wilson Author Series**. Revised 1991. $25. 0-8242-0820-0.

AUTHORS

Y; A

445.   **World Literature Criticism, 1500 to the Present: A Selection of Major Authors from Gale's Literary Criticism Series**. Ed. by James Draper. Gale, 1992. 6 vol. $360. 0-8103-8361-6.

This work contains lists of about 225 authors, "specially compiled to meet the needs of high school and college students." The selected titles represent many nations and a broad selection from 1500 to the present. This work is intended to serve those libraries unable to afford or that are overwhelmed by the huge Gale Literary series, "and most of the sources cited are available in typical small and medium-sized libraries." Each entry contains a biographical sketch, excerpts of selected criticism, and a short bibliography of secondary sources. Author, nationality, and title indexes complete the volumes. This "one-stop" guide is recommended for all libraries, especially smaller libraries with tight budgets or smaller collections.   *LITERATURE; AUTHORS*

Biographical Sources

Y; A*

446.   **Biography Index.** . . . H. W. Wilson, current. Subscription that includes four quarterly paperbound issues and a hardcover annual cumulation, $190; online and on CD-ROM, inquire for prices. ISSN 0006-3053.

This basic reference tool has been published since 1946. It indexes biographical material that has been published in more than 2,700 periodicals, more than 2,000 English-language books of individual and collective biographies, memoirs, obituaries, fiction, juvenile literature, and biographical material from otherwise nonbiographical sources. Biographical material is accessed in two ways. The name index is arranged alphabetically by the name of the biographee and includes date of birth and death, nationality, profession, and full bibliographic citation. The index to professions and occupations has names of the biographees covered in that particular issue. The sources indexed become a recommended selection list for purchase or interlibrary loans. *Biography Index* is recommended for all secondary school, academic, public, and other libraries that offer general reference services.   *BIOGRAPHY*

Y* ; A*
447. **Research Guide to American Historical Biography**. Ed. by Suzanne Niemeyer. Beacham Publishing, 1991. 5 vol. $63/vol.; $315/set. 0-933833-24-5.

Another biographical dictionary? This set not only has complete biographical coverage of prominent Americans, but for each entry there are extensive and diverse bibliographic sources for additional information (from very basic to quite specialized). The work was designed for secondary school and undergraduate students working on papers, as well as graduate students and faculty doing research. Further and most important, it was also designed to serve librarians as both a ready-reference and an acquisitions checklist. Volumes 1 through 3 include individuals in a wide range of fields (e.g., politics, business and labor, education, religion). Volume 4 emphasizes women, Native Americans, and minorities, and volume 5 concentrates on entertainers, Civil War personalities, and additional minorities. Each volume, especially 4 and 5, stands alone and can be purchased separately. In addition to biographies and autobiographies, many primary sources are cited. A section titled "Fiction and Adaptations" describes novels, films, plays, and other creative works about the individual. A cumulative index to all five volumes is included in volume 5. This excellent resource is recommended for all secondary school, academic, and public libraries.   *BIOGRAPHY*

Careers and
Vocational Guidance

Y; A
448. **Chronicle Career Index, 1996–97**. Ed. by Nancy Kehoe. Chronicle Career Publications, 1996. 84p. $14.25. 1-55631-254-7.

This bibliography on occupational and educational guidance materials includes hundreds of books, pamphlets, documents, and audiovisual materials listed in groups according to producer, publisher, or sponsor. Many but not all are annotated. There are subject and keyword indexes, but unfortunately the work is awkward to use.   *OCCUPATIONS; EDUCATIONAL COUNSELING; VOCATIONAL GUIDANCE*

Y*; A*
449. **The Encyclopedia of Careers and Vocational Guidance**. 10th ed. By William E. Hopke. Rosen, 1996. 4 vols. $149.95. 0-8239-2532-3.

This work contains a great deal of information on careers. For each career it supplies a bibliography of additional sources that in libraries can be of help in building both regular and vertical file collections. The set reviews major industries such as apparel, computers, and teaching; gives overviews about jobs, training required, and future possibilities; and lists sources for additional information. It also provides information on hundreds on specific careers. In the overview articles, there is material on job outlook, training, working conditions, and salaries, plus other related information, including lists of further sources.   *OCCUPATIONS; VOCATIONAL GUIDANCE*

Y; A
450. **Exploring Tech Careers**. By Hollie R. Cosgrove. Ferguson, 1995. 2 vols. $89.95. 0-89434-161-8.

One hundred eight different technical occupations are described in this volume, including library technician, embalmer, licensed practical nurse, paralegal, and special effects specialist. For each entry a variety of descriptive material is given, including job definition, typical duties, salaries, educational requirements, availability outlook, and working conditions. There is also a section on sources of additional information that includes listings of professional organizations, books, and periodicals. This section can be helpful in building vocational guidance collections in high schools and public libraries. (See also *The Encyclopedia of Careers and Vocational Guidance*, entry 449.)

OCCUPATIONS; VOCATIONAL GUIDANCE

Y; A

451.   **Free and Inexpensive Career Materials: A Resource Directory**. By Cheryl S. Hecht. Garrett Park Press, 1995. unpaged. $19.95 pap. 1-880774-09-7.

This work lists 821 organizations and agencies that supply career information in the form of pamphlets and leaflets for $5 or under. They include trade and professional organizations, federal and state agencies, academic departments, foundations, companies, and publishers. Each entry includes an address, telephone number, titles of materials, any cost, and, in many cases, a brief description of the item. Preceding this list is an index of 250 occupations and subjects with references to the organizations that supply useful materials on that topic. Unfortunately, this index could be more thorough. Nevertheless, this inexpensive guide will be helpful in building vertical file collections of career materials.

OCCUPATIONS; VOCATIONAL GUIDANCE; VERTICAL FILE MATERIALS; FREE MATERIALS

Y*; A*

452.   **How to Find Out About Financial Aid**. 1996–1998 ed. By Gail Ann Schlachter. Reference Service Press, 1995. 334p. $37.50. 0-918276-26-8.

This is a bibliography of more than 700 commercially available directories of financial aid. Entries for each directory contain full bibliographic material plus annotations about the aid's purpose, arrangement, limitations, and special features. There are separate chapters on scholarships, fellowships, grants, awards, loans, internships, databases, and search services, with subdivisions by disciplines (e.g., social science), by special populations (e.g., ethnic groups), and by geographical areas. Addresses and telephone numbers of publishers are given, and there are indexes by name, title, place, and subject. This thorough work will be of great value in developing financial aid collections in high school, college, and public libraries.   *FINANCIAL AID; SCHOLARSHIPS, FELLOWSHIPS, ETC.*

Y; A

453.   **Job Hunter's Sourcebook**. 2nd ed. By Michelle LeCompte. Gale, 1993. 1,106p. $65. 0-8103-8201-6.

The main body of this work contains sources of job hunting information for 155 alphabetically arranged professions and occupations. Resources include help wanted ads, employer directories, employment agencies, placement services, handbooks and manuals, and network lists. Another section discusses general employment topics, such as how to use the library for job hunting and how to identify and use general employment information. There is an general index to sources cited. This hefty volume combines the "how to" aspects of job hunting with directory information. The latter will be of value in helping public, academic, and high school libraries in developing their career collections.

OCCUPATIONS; VOCATIONAL GUIDANCE

Y*; A

454.   **Planning Your Future: Resources on Careers and Higher Education**. Ed. by Juleann Fallgatter et al. Amideast, 1995. 349p. $29.95. 0-913957-13-5.

More than 1,000 free or inexpensive publications are listed in this expanded update of *Guide to Educational Advising Resources*. Major career fields are covered, including biological, agricultural, and environmental sciences; communications; design; engineering; philosophy and religion; and public service. Chapter 1 lists college guides, financial aid sources, and guides to specific careers and majors. Books and pamphlets are arranged alphabetically by title in each section. Other chapters list software, including CD-ROM and video resources, and sources for disabled individuals and student athletes. Publisher, subject, and title indexes simplify the process of accessing the valuable resources. Most of the material is aimed at high school students; however, some graduate school–level material is included. This guide is recommended for high school, public, and college libraries.

EDUCATIONAL COUNSELING; OCCUPATIONS; VOCATIONAL GUIDANCE

Y*; A*

455. **Professional Careers Sourcebook: Where to Find Help Planning Careers That Require College or Technical Degrees**. 4th ed. By Sara Bernstein and Kathleen M. Savage. Gale, 1995. 875p. $95. 0-8103-8915-0.

This up-to-date career planning sourcebook provides a wealth of current information. It serves as a companion volume to *Vocational Careers Sourcebook*, which includes 125 careers not requiring a four-year degree. The careers in this profession-oriented volume are arranged in career clusters such as writers, artists, and engineers. Individual career profiles include a brief abstract taken from the well-known *Occupational Outlook Handbook*. Each career entry also includes information on general career guides and audiovisual materials, professional associations, standards and certification, basic reference handbooks related to the profession, professional and trade periodicals, and more. A master alphabetical index to all publications and other information sources is a gold mine for collection development. This sourcebook will be much used by high school and college students as well as professionals involved in career planning. The cost of this work (which can quickly become outdated) is of some concern; however, it appears that it will be revised regularly. Recommended for all secondary school and public libraries. *OCCUPATIONS; PROFESSIONS; VOCATIONAL GUIDANCE*

Y; A

456. **VGM's Careers Encyclopedia**. 3rd ed. Ed. by Craig T. Norback. National Textbook/VGM Career Books, 1995. 500p. $39.95. 0-8442-8692-3.

More than 180 careers are included in this one-volume guide. Careers are listed in alphabetical order for quick reference. Following a brief description of the career, each entry contains detailed information on places of employment, working conditions, education, training, expected income, and additional sources of information. An index is provided. This guide contains more information on fewer careers than the similar work edited by William E. Hopke, *The Encyclopedia of Careers and Vocational Guidance*. Both volumes are recommended for high school, academic, and public libraries. *OCCUPATIONS; VOCATIONAL GUIDANCE*

Y; A

457. **Vocational and Technical Resources for Community College Libraries: Selected Materials, 1988–1994**. Ed. by Mary Ann Laun. American Library Association, 1995. 622p. $95. 0-8389-7775-8.

Designed primarily for the community college library, this collection of annotated bibliographies covers 58 vocational fields. The print and nonprint bibliographies are organized into 10 chapters covering general categories, including allied health, building and construction trades, business, communications, production technologies, criminal justice and law, education, engineering and technology, graphic and apparel arts, sciences, and social sciences. Each list was compiled by a librarian experienced with that particular field. Each bibliography is preceded by an introduction that presents an overview of that area of study and includes related professional journals. Each entry contains an annotation and bibliographic information helpful for ordering. Most of the material was published between 1988 and 1994. An author and a title index complete the work. In addition to community colleges and technical institutes, this bibliography will be useful for all vocational-technical high schools. *VOCATIONAL GUIDANCE; OCCUPATIONS; PROFESSIONS*

Y*; A*

458. **Vocational Careers Sourcebook: Where to Find Help Planning Careers in Skilled, Trade, and Nontechnical Vocations**. 3rd ed. Ed. by Kathleen M. Savage and Karen Hill. Gale, 1997. 1,129p. $79. 0-8103-6470-0.

This new career planning sourcebook provides information on about 125 careers listed in the well-known *Occupational Outlook Handbook* that do not require a four-year college degree. It serves as a companion volume to the *Professional Careers Sourcebook*, which relates to 111 careers requiring a degree. Each career entry listed includes brief information such as training and working conditions, followed by guides for additional information. This sourcebook will be much used by high school students and adults involved in career planning. Highly recommended for all secondary school and public libraries. *OCCUPATIONS; VOCATIONAL GUIDANCE*

Y; A

459. Where to Start Career Planning: Essential Resource Guide for Career Planning and Job Hunting. 8th ed. By Pamela L. Feodoroff and Carolyn Lloyd Lindquist. Cornell University; distr. Peterson's Guides, 1991. 299p. $17.95. 1-56079-056-3.

This edition of this useful guide updates its predecessors and, like the earlier editions, is based on the career planning library at Cornell University's Career Center. Introductory information includes a great deal of valuable data on financial aid, planning a career, internships, and more. This is followed by a listing of more than 2,000 publications described and arranged under 21 broad career fields such as agriculture, biological science, education, engineering, and health services. The appendix includes a list of audiovisual materials, periodicals that list job offerings, and periodicals related to careers. The quality of the annotations, and low price make this a wise purchase for high school, college, and public libraries for developing or maintaining a career collection.

OCCUPATIONS; VOCATIONAL GUIDANCE

Computer Technology

Internet and Online Services

Y; A

460. CyberHound's Guide to Internet Databases. Gale, 1997. 1,250p. $99. 0-7876-1163-8.

With about 1,000 more listings than the previous edition (then known as *Gale Guide to Internet Databases*), this directory identifies and tells how to access and retrieve about 5,000 Internet databases. Though the *Guide* focuses on major government, academic, research, and educational databases, there is also coverage of pop culture and trivia. Databases are described and rated for content, design, and ease of use. In addition to a master index, there are four separate indexes by host/provider, subject, white pages, and alternate formats. This is only one of the seven *CyberHound's Guide to Internet . . .* published by Gale. There are separate volumes on locating specific discussion groups, companies, nonprofit organizations, libraries, and people. Of particular interest to collection development is *CyberHound's Guide to Publications on the Internet* (1996. $79 pap. 0-7876-1025-9). *INTERNET; DATABASES*

Y; A

461. The Internet Compendium: Guides to Resources by Subject. By Louis Rosenfeld et al. Neal-Schuman, 1995. 3 vols. $175. 1-55570-188-4.

Using hundreds of subjects as access points, this index and directory is a guide to more than 10,000 resources on the Internet. As well as telling exactly how to find each resource, there is a critical analysis of each site. Each of the three volumes also includes a special introductory section on how to get started, searching techniques, and exploring with gopher, the World Wide Web, and more. If desired, the volumes can be purchased individually at $75 each. The volumes are:

461.1 **The Internet Compendium: Subject Guides to Health and Science Resources** (1-55570-219-8).
Thousands of annotated Internet sites are listed, covering all branches of scientific study and their applications.

461.2 **The Internet Compendium: Subject Guides to the Humanities** (1-55570-218-X).
Some of the areas covered are art, authors and literature, music, performers, religion, and philosophy. There is also coverage of full reference texts and even games.

461.3 **The Internet Collection: Subject Guides to Social Science, Business, and Law** (1-55570-220-1).
Hundreds of topics in the social sciences are covered, including up-to-the-minute information on trade and commerce, law and government, and current job listings. Internet addresses for nearly all government agencies and departments are included.

INTERNET

Y, A

462.   **The Online 100: Online Magazine's Field Guide to the 100 Most Important Online Databases**. By Mick O'Leary. Pemberton Press, 1996. 256p. $22.95. 0-910965-14-5.

According to O'Leary, who is a regular contributor to the column "Consumer Online," which appears in *Online Magazine*, the main purpose of this paperback is to identify the most important databases in the most important subjects rather than the most heavily used or the largest. O'Leary had an advisory board select the most important (though they did not have concrete criteria for selection). Nevertheless, this guide, which contains approximately two pages of description on each database, should prove helpful. Each entry gives guidelines for selecting, an indication of costs online, and accessibility on the Internet. This aid is recommended for large public and academic libraries; however, it may well be considered for school district-wide centers.   *ONLINE DATABASES*

Y; A

463.   **OPAC Directory: An Annual Guide to Online Public Access Catalogs and Databases**. Comp. by Regina Rega. Meckler, 1993. 309p. $60. 0-88736-883-2.

As more and more libraries convert their card catalogs to online databases, librarians need to be kept informed of developments. The current technology and trend is for schools (even elementary schools) to have ready access to the catalog of their local and regional public libraries, even if their own catalogs are not yet online. This directory, which has been published since 1990 (previously under the title *Dial In*), describes in detail almost 300 academic and public library online catalogs. It offers guidance on how to access them from remote locations via a computer equipped with a modem. All libraries serving young people should acquire the latest issues of this annual in order to keep abreast of current developments.   *ONLINE LIBRARY CATALOGS*

Y*

464.   **Using the Internet, Online Services, and CD-ROMs for Writing Research and Term Papers**. Ed. by Charles Harmon. Neal-Schuman, 1996. 168p. $29.95. 1-55570-138-4.

Most of the first half of this handbook covers writing a term or research paper. While this is helpful information, most of this information is readily available in other sources. The second half of the work, however, is a gold mine of information on technological resources currently available, such as the Internet, online services, and CD-ROMs. The descriptions, definitions, and list of WWW sites alone make this readable, timely book a must purchase. Two copies are recommended for most secondary school and public libraries, the first for reference and collection development, the second for circulating to patrons.   *ONLINE DATABASES; INTERNET; CD-ROMS*

Software

Y; A

465.   **CD-ROM Buyer's Guide and Handbook**. 3rd ed. By Paul T. Nicholls. Pemberton Press, 1993. $44.50. 0-910-96508-0.

The purpose of this guide is to help first buyers of CD-ROM hardware and software. In its 15 chapters are covered such subjects as an industry overview, explanations of hardware and software (including topics like drives, interface cards, retrieval software, and workstations), and multimedia standards. There is also an evaluation and review of 200 basic core products plus a glossary of terms and a directory of published reviews. This work is limited in use as a collection development tool, but it is a fine background book.   *CD-ROMS; COMPUTER SOFTWARE*

Y; A

466.   **CD-ROMs in Print**. Gale, annual. 1,232p (1996 ed.). $139. 0-7876-0803-3.

This annual guide lists commercially available CD-ROMS from around the world on every topic, with about 9,000 titles arranged by title from about 3,700 publishing and distributing companies. For each entry, information is given on such topics as coverage and scope, demonstration discs available, cost, hardware and software, updates, and equivalent publications in other media. All available formats— DOS, Windows, Mac, 3D0, Sega, CD, and others—are listed. There are several indexes and directories appended: one by subject, others by audience level, format, and purpose. Other indexes are for geography and distributors and publishers. Though not evaluative, this is a fine listing of CD-ROMs currently available. Librarians should be aware of its existence, but its price will preclude purchase except in large public library and district-wide curriculum collections. Another directory with similar coverage originates in England: *The CD-ROM Directory, 1996* (Multimedia, 1996. $155. 1-56159-185-8).

COMPUTER SOFTWARE; CD-ROMS

Y; A
467.   **CD-ROMs Rated: A Guide to the Best and Worst CD-ROMs and Multimedia Titles**. By Les Krantz. McGraw-Hill, 1995. $19.95 pap. 0-07-912052-0.

This is a fascinating paperback in which the author evaluates a number of CD-ROMs in the areas of reference work, education, and entertainment. Various formats (e.g., Windows, Mac) are represented. The credentials of the evaluators, their criteria, and the rating system are explained prior to the annotated listings. A demonstration CD-ROM is included. The book is interesting to browse through for tips on possible purchases.   *CD-ROMS; COMPUTER SOFTWARE*

Y; A
468.   **Guide to Selecting and Acquiring CD-ROMs, Software, and Other Electronic Publications**. By Stephen Bosch et al. American Library Association, 1994. 48p. $15 pap. 0-8389-0629-X.

Though not a bibliography of recommended CD-ROMs, this handy guide provides directions and guidelines for librarians to select and acquire materials in various electronic formats. Types of materials are defined, criteria are outlined, and steps in acquiring these products are provided. There are also a glossary, sources of further information, and an index.   *CD-ROMS; COMPUTER SOFTWARE*

Y; A
469.   **303 CD-ROMs to Use in Your Library: Descriptions, Evaluations, and Practical Advice**. By Patrick R. Dewey. American Library Association, 1995. 238p. $30. 0-8389-0666-4.

Dewey reviews nearly 270 CD-ROM programs and series in detail and cites references to many more titles. All were selected for their suitability for libraries. Arranged by subject, each entry contains evaluations, price, platform and hardware requirements, and network availability. Additional data regarding content, searching features, and user levels are also included. The diverse range of subjects covered is noteworthy, including: art and music; education and careers; health, medicine, and nutrition; literature and religion; and U.S. information and statistics. As more and more libraries develop CD-ROM collections, aids such as this are needed and welcome. This bibliography is recommended for all academic public libraries and some high school libraries.   *CD-ROMS*

Free and Inexpensive Materials

Y; A
470.   **Consumer Information Catalog: An Index of Selected Federal Publications of Consumer Interest**. Consumer Information Center, quarterly. Free.

In each of these pamphlets are about 200 free or inexpensive government booklets and other publications covering such topics of interest to consumers as employment, safety, health, nutrition, housing, ways to save money, and federal benefits. Each is also a valuable source for building the vertical file collections in libraries serving both adults and young adults. Copies are available free from: Consumer Information Center, Department LL, Pueblo, CO 81009.

VERTICAL FILE MATERIALS; FREE MATERIALS; CONSUMER EDUCATION

Y; A
471.   **Free Magazines for Libraries**. 4th ed. By Diane Jones Langston and Adeline Mercer Smith. McFarland, 1994. 303p. $28.50 pap. 0-89950-947-9.

This bibliography describes 700 free periodicals available from various private companies and agencies. Each publication meets basic standards of suitability and usefulness in libraries. They are arranged alphabetically by title under 62 topics such as folklore, forestry, law, geography, and sociology. Bibliographic material is complete for each entry, which also includes an evaluative annotation and information on subscribing. Appendixes include magazines suitable for small and medium-sized libraries, and a list of where (if anyplace) they are indexed. This is a valuable resource for both public and high school libraries.   *PERIODICALS; FREE MATERIALS*

Y; A
472.   **Free Resource Builder for Librarians and Teachers**. 2nd ed. By Carol Smallwood. McFarland, 1992. 352p. $27.50. 0-89950-685-2.
        This excellent guide to free library materials covers such formats as pamphlets, booklets, fliers, maps, and charts that are available from businesses, government agencies, and nonprofit organizations. About 3,000 sources are identified. The book is divided into six large sections covering business and finance, consumer affairs, government and legal affairs, health, library and archive usage, and travel and geography. Each has many subdivisions. There are additional sections on multiresource agencies where databases and clearinghouses are listed; another on special aids like film catalogs and curriculum guides; and "Resource Management," which gives explicit directions on how to organize a vertical file, with suggested subject headings. The listing of agency addresses is extremely valuable because, though many of the listed free materials may go out-of-print, these sources can be contacted for new publications. This work is a valuable resource for public, college, and high school libraries, but it is in need of an update.   *VERTICAL FILE MATERIALS; FREE MATERIALS*

Y; A
473.   **Lesko's Info-Power**. 3rd ed. By Matthew Lesko. Visible Ink Press, 1996. 1,600p. $29.95. 0-7876-0880-7.
        More than 30,000 free and low-cost sources of information are listed in this book. Although many of the items are readily available (e.g., from your congressperson), this is a handy compilation that is ideal for building up the vertical file. If one is selective, it can be useful for most school and public libraries.   *FREE MATERIALS; VERTICAL FILE MATERIALS*

Language and Literature

General and Miscellaneous

Y; A
474.   **The Classic Epic: An Annotated Bibliography**. By Thomas J. Sienkewicz. Salem Press, 1991. 265p. (Magill Bibliographies). $40. 0-8108-2811-1.
        This bibliography is intended for the nonscholar and the high school or college student approaching the reading and study of the *Iliad*, *Odyssey*, or *Aeneid* for the first time. It includes books, chapters in books, periodical articles, plot summaries, literary studies, and related material on each of these epics, plus listings of material on their authors. This work will be useful in public, college, and some large high school libraries.   *ROMAN LITERATURE; GREEK LITERATURE; CLASSICAL LITERATURE*

Y; A
475.   **Essay and General Literature Index**. H. W. Wilson, annual (including one June paperbound issue). $125.
        This comprehensive index to English-language books of essays and general nonfiction has covered these areas from 1900 to the present. Each issue is arranged in a single alphabet with entries for authors and subjects. Although a wide range of subjects is coverage the emphasis is on the humanities and social sciences. Issues appear with one paperbound issue in June, followed by annual volumes and five-year cumulations. Because this is used not just for reference but also for collection development, monthly

lists of new titles selected for indexing in the next issue are sent to subscribers. This allows adequate time for acquisition librarians to place orders before books go out-of-print. Recommended for high school, academic, and public libraries. *ESSAYS*

Y; A*

476. **Fiction Catalog**. 13th ed. H. W. Wilson, 1996. 1,000p. $115. 0-8242-0854-3.

This standard reference and bibliographic tool now lists more than 5,400 of the best English language in-print (and a few out-of-print) fiction titles. They are chosen by a select committee of librarians from across the United States and include books from different periods and languages (if translated into English). The main section is arranged by author and gives plot summaries, often a short critical annotation for each book, and a list of contents for each story collection. There is a title/thematic/subject index. Subscribers to the main volume also will get annual paperback updates (covering 1997, 1998, 1999, and 2000) that will usually contain an additional listing of 500 books each. This is a basic selection aid in academic and public libraries and can also be used in many high schools.

AMERICAN LITERATURE; ENGLISH LITERATURE; FICTION

Y; A

477. **Folklore of American Holidays**. By Hennig Cohen and Tristram Potter Coffin. Gale, 1991. 509p. $89. 0-8103-7602-4.

For more than 125 American religious and secular festivals, extensive information is provided, including a description of origins, general background, and methods of observation. Also included is a bibliography of readings for each holiday. A companion volume with similar coverage is *Folklore of World Holidays* by Margaret Read MacDonald (Gale, 1992. 739p. $89. 0-8103-7577-X).   *HOLIDAYS*

Y

478. **From Hinton to Hamlet: Building Bridges Between Young Adult Literature and the Classics**. By Sarah K. Herz and Donald R. Gallo. Greenwood, 1996. 128p. $29.50. 0-313-28636-1.

Designed to help teachers bridge the gap between the classics and young adult literature, this book is a practical, useful source for English teachers and librarians. After a brief history of young adult literature and its characteristics, the authors discuss the methods of teaching literature, levels of appreciation, and how to encourage literature's use with youngsters. The heart of the volume is the section where connections are made between the 12 most-taught classics and thematically related young adult novels. There are also chapters using young adult literature in other curricular areas like art, health, journalism, and dance, and a chapter on sources of information on young adult literature.

LITERATURE—STUDY AND TEACHING

Y; A

479. **Graphic Novels: A Bibliographic Guide to Book-Length Comics**. By D. Aviva Rothschild. Libraries Unlimited, 1995. 245p. $30. 1-56308-089-9.

Reviews of more than 400 trade comics and graphic novels published in English are included in this annotated guide. For each entry there is material on the quality of the graphics, characterization, story line, dialogue, and intended audience. Classics in the field are identified.

COMICS; GRAPHIC NOVELS

Y; A

480. **Popular World Fiction, 1900–Present**. Ed. by Walton Beacham and Suzanne Niemeyer. Beacham Publishing, 1988. 4 vols. $250. 0-933833-08-3.

This work serves as a companion volume to *Beacham's Popular Fiction in America* (Beacham, 1986). Included in this volume are 176 world authors whose work has been translated into English, and British and American writers whose reputations were established from 1900 to 1987. The vast majority of the authors included are American. "This set provides information on authors and novels not found in standard reference works such as *Masterplots*." Examples of this eclectic group of world authors include Edgar Rice Burroughs, Joseph Conrad, Elie Wiesel, William Faulkner, Margaret Mitchell, and

Sidney Sheldon. Most entries are more than seven pages long and include publishing histories, critical reception, and analyses of selected titles. Each entry includes two bibliographies, one for additional works by the author and the other for secondary sources about the author with a very brief note. Author and title indexes appear in the 4th volume. This set is recommended for high school, academic, and public libraries where additional information on popular fiction is needed; it would be helpful for both reference and collection development. *FICTION*

Y; A

481.   **Resources for Writers: An Annotated Bibliography**. By R. Baird Shuman. Salem Press, 1992. 167p. (Magill Bibliographies). $40. 0-89356-673-X.

Shuman, a professor of English, provides us with a bibliography of more than 530 titles. The entries are arranged into a number of major chapters covering various types of writing, such as plays and poetry; writing for commercial publication, for juveniles, and for magazines and journals; and preparing and marketing manuscripts. Most of the entries are for monographs or parts of books, and the vast majority were published from 1930 to the 1990s. As with other titles in the series, entries are arranged alphabetically by author. Each has full bibliographical data and a brief annotation of about 50 to 100 words. An author and title index concludes the volume. This bibliographic guide is recommended for academic and public libraries. Large secondary school libraries may also want to consider its purchase. *WRITING*

Y; A*

482.   **Short Story Index, 1989–1993**. H. W. Wilson, 1994. 1,071 pages. $135. (Annual subscriptions, $95).

This is the latest cumulation of this invaluable annual work that indexes stories published as part of collections of books or separately in magazines. The basic volume covers 1900–1949, and the subsequent continuations cover about five years of publications. This volume offers, in one alphabet, author, title, and subject access to about 20,000 stories published in approximately 1,000 anthologies and collections plus hundreds of periodicals. The list of collections analyzed is useful for collection development and interlibrary loans. There are also a separate directory of periodicals and a list of collections indexed. A separate volume, *Short Story Index: Collections Indexed 1900–1978* (1979. $45), is also valuable for these purposes. *SHORT STORIES*

Y; A

483.   **Supplementing Literature Programs: Selected Titles**. By Mary M. Eble and Jeanne L. Renton. Scarecrow, 1993. 287p. $42.50. 0-8108-2658-5.

A number of programs and young adult books that would be useful in developing writing and reading abilities in junior high school students were outlined in the authors' earlier *New Dimensions in School Library Media Service* (1988. 486p. $52.50. 0-8108-2115-X). This continuation offers a variety of books published in the late 1980s and early 1990s. The book is divided into six sections. In one, selected contemporary fiction is presented with plot summaries and suggested uses; in another, more challenging titles are given. Other sections discuss teaching contemporary and classic novels, suggestions for videos, and lists of neglected books that should be promoted in libraries. This is a good resource for developing units of literature study and identifying materials worth purchasing.

LITERATURE—STUDY AND TEACHING

Y; A*

484.   **To Be Continued**. By Merle L. Jacob and Hope Apple. Oryx, 1995. 376p. $43.50. 0-89774-842-5.

The authors have created a comprehensive guide to sequels. More than 1,300 entries are arranged alphabetically by author, followed by title of series and titles listed chronologically by date of the fictional event or by suggested reading order. Also included is an annotation that describes the narrative threads that link the various novels together. Bibliographic information and in-print and out-of-print status are provided. Indexes by title, genre, subject and literary forms, and time and place complete the work. This is an invaluable resource for reader's advisory work and helpful in collection development for all public libraries and many high school libraries. *SEQUELS*

Y; A

485. **The Whole Story: 3000 Years of Series & Sequences**. Ed. by John E. Simkin. D. W. Thorpe, 1996. 2 vols. $135. 1-875589-26-0.

Undoubtedly, this is the most exhaustive listing of series, sequences, and sequels. The volumes contain more than 85,000 English-language entries. The first volume has a list of series titles; volume 2 lists authors and individual titles. Access is possible by series title, author, or individual book title. While all levels are included, the preponderance of titles are on the adult level. For a listing of sequels on a children's or young adult level, one may want to consider Anderson's *Fiction Sequels for Readers 10 to 16* (McFarland, 1990. 150p. $19.95 pap. 0-89950-519-8). Nonetheless, *The Whole Story* is a recommended purchase for libraries that can afford it. *SEQUELS; SERIES*

Y; A

486. **World Mythology: An Annotated Guide to Collections and Anthologies**. By Thomas J. Sienkewicz. Scarecrow, 1996. 480p. $49.50. 0-8108-3154-6.

Myths from around the world are collected in this handy bibliography of English-language translations, retellings, and summaries. In addition to the familiar Greek, Roman, Norse, and Arthurian myths, this guide surveys less-familiar myths from Africa, Asia, Oceania, and the Americas. The entries are arranged geographically; each is fully annotated. Additional information includes comparative studies and collections of myths. Author, illustrator, and subject indexes complete this guide, which is recommended for all school and public libraries. *MYTHOLOGY*

Y

487. **Young Adult Fiction by African American Writers, 1968–1993**. By Deborah Kutenplon and Ellen Olmstead. Garland, 1996. 367p. $50. 0-8153-0873-6.

Almost 200 titles by about 50 African American authors are analyzed in this critical survey. Both major and lesser-known (or new) writers are included in this timely guide. The critical reviews, the most important part of this work, follow an introduction that traces the publishing trends of young adult literature by and about African Americans. Entries are arranged alphabetically by author. Extensive annotations contain a summary of the work and detailed critical evaluation. The authors achieve comprehensiveness, currentness, and extensive criticism of the chosen titles, which, though subjective, reflect the African American experience of almost a 30-year period. This well-written guide should serve as a valuable tool for young adults, teachers, and librarians and others interested in young adult literature generally or African American literature specifically.
AFRICAN AMERICAN LITERATURE; AUTHORS, AFRICAN AMERICAN

Drama

Y; A

488. **American Theater and Drama Research: An Annotated Guide to Information Sources, 1945–1990**. By Irene Shaland. McFarland, 1991. 168p. $36.50. 0-89950-626-7.

More than 500 sources are listed in this well-developed guide to American theater and drama since World War II. The emphasis is on the history of American theater and drama. All of the entries listed were published since 1965. Entries are listed under five major sections that include most aspects of the subject. The first two sections list general and specialized reference sources. Each entry includes author, title, publication information and date, and pagination. Annotations range from one line to a paragraph and are both descriptive and critical. An author index is provided. The strength of this work is the currentness of most of the entries; its limitations are the lack of a subject index and the lack of indication of in-print status. Despite these minor flaws, this work is recommended for most high school, academic, and public libraries. *THEATER—UNITED STATES; DRAMA*

Y; A
489.   **Classical Greek and Roman Drama: An Annotated Bibliography**. By Robert J. Forman. Salem Press, 1989. 239p. (Magill's Bibliographies). $40. 0-89356-659-4.

After an overview of Greek and Roman drama that lists general works, there are individual chapters on nine playwrights, including Aeschylus, Aristophanes, Euripides, Seneca, Sophocles, and Terence. There are three sections in each chapter. The first lists various editions of the writer's work, and the second and third cover recommended criticism and general criticism. All the titles listed are recommended and annotated. As well as a tool to identify critical studies, this work can be used as a collection-building source in public libraries and high school libraries where material on classical drama is needed. Also in the same series is *The Classic Epic*.

GREEK LITERATURE; CLASSICAL LITERATURE; ROMAN LITERATURE; DRAMA

Y*; A*
490.   **1/2/3/4 for the Show: A Guide to Small-Cast One-Act Plays**. By Lewis W. Heniford. Scarecrow, 1995. 273p. $39.50. 0-8108-2985-1.

Heniford has compiled an interesting and possibly one-of-a-kind list, and one that will be welcomed by speech and drama teachers and others involved with school or community theater. The compilation consists of often hard-to-locate plays with casts of four or fewer characters and written by authors such as O'Neill, Skinner, and de Maupassant. They range from classic selections to contemporary and experimental. *Play Index* does of course indicate cast size in its author entry; however, no index exists to access this feature. Heniford arranges the plays by title according to size of cast (e.g., one male, two females). In addition to basic bibliographic information, these primary entries include genre and provide suggestions of other pieces that might be used with them in a theater production. They also include information on how to get the script if it is out-of-print. There are also a complete author index, a glossary of terms, addresses of publishers, and a special section on suggestions for 25 theme productions. This excellent guide is recommended for any collection that supports a drama program or community theater, including high school, public, and academic libraries.   *DRAMA*

Y*; A*
491.   **Play Index 1988–1992**. Ed. by Juliette Yaakov and John Greenfieldt. H. W. Wilson, 1993. 542p. $80. 0-685-70308-8.

This basic index has been a standard reference tool for nearly 40 years for students, teachers, librarians, and those involved with theater and drama. This new 1988–1992 volume indexes 4,397 new and previously published plays appearing in new collections published during this five-year period. All plays have been written in or translated into English. The word "plays" is interpreted broadly; also included are puppet plays and TV and radio plays. The standard format, familiar to all librarians, is used in this work (i.e., plays can be accessed by author, title, subject, or dramatic style). However, only the author entry provides a full bibliographic citation, a descriptive annotation, and makeup of the cast; symbols are used to indicate suitability for children or young people. The list of collections indexed is an invaluable bibliography useful for collection development. All eight volumes (from 1949–1952 to the present) are still available, with prices ranging from $20 to $80; they index more than 30,000 plays published over more than 44 years. *Play Index* is recommended as a reference tool and aid for collection building for all school, academic, public, and special libraries involved in theater/drama.   *DRAMA*

Y; A
492.   **Shakespeare: An Annotated Bibliography**. Ed. by Joseph Rosenblum. Salem Press, 1992. 307p. $40. 0-8108-2802-2.

This annotated bibliography of Shakespeare criticism emphasizes books published in the twentieth century. It is organized in a series of subject-oriented chapters that cover such things as bibliographies, reference works, biographies, the Shakespearean stage, comedies, histories, and tragedies. There are also separate chapters for each of the plays. Each entry is annotated, and there is an author index. This basic, practical bibliography should be useful in public and college libraries as well as some high schools. Of a similar scope is *Shakespeare: A Bibliographic Guide* by Stanley Wells (Oxford, 1990. $65.00; $19.95 pap. 0-19-871036-4; 0-19-811213-0 pap.).   *SHAKESPEARE, WILLIAM*

Literary Criticism

Y; A

493. **Chelsea House Library of Literary Criticism**. By Harold Bloom. Chelsea House, 1985–1987. 37 vols. $55 and $60/vol.

This extensive series is not a selection aid per se. However, each of the author entries contains a bibliography of critical writings that could be checked for possible acquisitions. The series is divided into five sets that cover various literary periods: *The Critical Perspective* (10 volumes), *The Major Authors Edition of the New Moulton's Library of Literary Criticism* (5 volumes), *The New Moulton's Library of Literary Criticism* (10 volumes), *Twentieth-Century American Literature* (5 volumes), and *Twentieth-Century British Literature* (7 volumes). Collectively the sets cover about 2,000 major authors and give often lengthy excerpts from critical works. A typical entry is two pages in length, but for very important writers, like Chaucer, they are frequently around 100 pages. This work is chiefly for public libraries; however, some of the sets might be of value in large high school libraries with strong literature programs.   *AMERICAN LITERATURE; ENGLISH LITERATURE*

Y; A

494. **Facts on File Bibliography of American Fiction Series**. Ed. by Matthew Bruccoli. Facts on File, 1991–1994.

The volumes in this series are arranged by period and genre, including fiction, nonfiction, poetry, and drama. The three titles are: *Facts on File Bibliography of American Fiction Through 1865* (1994. $95. 0-8160-2115-5), *Facts on File Bibliography of American Fiction: 1866–1918* (1992. $95. 0-8160-2116-3), and *Facts on File Bibliography of American Fiction: 1919–1988* (1991. 2 vols. $145. 0-8160-2674-2). The latter is representative in scope and treatment of the other volumes. It begins with two bibliographies: one on 100 basic references sources and 10 essential periodicals for the study of American literature, and the other a list of important general, historical, and critical sources on this topic. There follows entries for 219 writers born prior to 1941 whose first significant works were published after World War I. Representative writers include Faulkner, Mailer, Steinbeck, Updike, and Cheever. For each author there is a brief biography, followed by a listing of published bibliographies of the author's works (separately published bibliographies and those appearing as periodical articles or parts of books). All of the author's works are arranged chronologically under type of publication like books or letters. The location of manuscript and archival collections related to the author are noted.

Secondary works of significance are listed by type, beginning with biographies and continuing with interviews and critical studies found in entire books, parts of books, essays, special journals, and articles. Indexes include a chronology of noteworthy fiction and events. This significant new bibliographic tool will be used in academic and public libraries as well as high schools with advanced literature programs.   *AMERICAN LITERATURE*

Y; A

495. **Masterplots**. Ed. by Frank N. Magill. Salem Press, various dates. 12 vols. $600. 0-89356-084-7.

The original *Masterplots* began in the late 1940s and has been constantly updated. The latest edition, in 12 volumes, was published in 1996. There are now 1,800 plot summaries and critical essays arranged alphabetically by title. Entries average three to five pages in length and include fiction, poetry, drama, essays, short stories, and nonfiction. Volume 12 has indexes by author, title, geography, and chronology. The *Masterplots II* series and the *Critical Survey* series are both still available. Each of the *Masterplots II* series consists of four to six volumes covering from about 300 to 500 titles (except the short story series, which has six volumes and includes more than 700 stories). This massive, long-standing publishing enterprise has become a mainstay in libraries for reference, reader's advisory work, and collection evaluation and development. The sets are recommended for most academic, secondary school, and public libraries. The *Masterplots II* series currently available are listed below in chronological order by publication date; they are all edited by Frank N. Magill and published by Salem Press.

495.1   **Masterplots II**
    495.1.1   **American Fiction Series**. 1986. 4 vols. $365. 0-89356-456-7.
    495.1.2   **Short Story Series**. 1986. 6 vols. $425. 0-89356-461-3.
    495.1.3   **American Fiction Supplement**. 1994. 2 vols. $185. 0-89356-719-1.
    495.1.4   **British and Commonwealth Fiction Series**. 1987. 4 vols. $350. 0-89356-468-0.
    495.1.5   **World Fiction Series**. 1988. 4 vols. $350. 0-89356-473-7.
    495.1.6   **Nonfiction Series**. 1989. YA. 4 vols. $350. 0-89356-478-8.
    495.1.7   **Drama Series**. 1990. 4 vols. $350. 0-89356-491-5.
    495.1.8   **Juvenile and Young Adult Literature Series**. 1991. 4 vols. $350. 0-89356-579-2.
    495.1.9   **Poetry Series**. 1992. 6 vols. $425. 0-89356-584-9.
    495.1.10 **Juvenile and Young Adult Biography Series**. 1993. 4 vols. $365. 0-89356-700-0.
    495.1.11 **African American Literature Series**. 1994. 3 vols. $275. 0-89356-594-6.
    495.1.12 **Women's Literature Series**. 1995. 6 vols. $500. 0-89356-898-8.

All of the above series plus *Cyclopedia of World Authors* I and II and *Cyclopedia of Literary Characters* I and II are available on CD-ROM for $750.   *LITERATURE*

Y; A
496.   **The New Moulton's Library of Literary Criticism: British and American Literature to 1904**. Ed. by Harold Bloom. Chelsea House, 1985–1988. 11 vols. $70/vol.; $770/set. 0-87754-778-5.
    The original work of this standard biographical work has been updated by the addition of some authors and the deletion of others who were not considered relevant by Bloom. Coverage begins with Beowulf and concludes with Kate Chopin. The last volume of this set (and other sets in the Moulton series) includes an extensive bibliography and an index; it may be purchased separately and would serve well for reference, interloans, and collection development. Most academic and public libraries would consider the entire set; secondary schools and smaller public libraries might consider only volume 11.
AMERICAN LITERATURE; ENGLISH LITERATURE

Y; A
497.   **Nineteenth-Century Literature Criticism**. Ed. by Laurie DiMauro. Gale. 41 vols. in print. $134/vol.
    This set, published since the early 1980s, fills the need for a source of critical comment on those authors who died during the nineteenth century. About three or four new volumes are published each year. This series provides extensive excerpts from published criticism of the major novelists, poets, playwrights, and other writers during the period. Each volume is about 500 pages in length and covers about 10 authors. Entries contain biographical information, bibliographies for the critical selections, and sources of additional information. This set is recommended for all academic libraries and for those public and secondary school libraries that can afford it.   *LITERATURE—HISTORY AND CRITICISM*

Y
498.   **Reference Guide to Short Fiction**. Ed. by Noelle Watson. St. James Press, 1994. 1,052p. $130. 1-55862-334-5.
    Watson has compiled, identified, and described in detail 400 short fiction titles of 325 writers of the nineteenth and twentieth centuries. The preface indicates that the most significant writers were determined by noted advisers, who are listed in the preface. Emphasis is placed on writers of the past rather than contemporary ones, and both foreign and English-language literature is included. Entries are arranged alphabetically by writer. Each entry has three major parts: a biographical sketch; a complete bibliography of the writer's published works, including novels, verse, plays, and the like; and an essay on selected important short fiction. Short fiction are generally under 1,000 words. Several authors are represented by more than one title. Similar works are Magill's *Critical Survey of Short Fiction* and *Masterplots II: Short Stories Series*. Both of these major works include critical analysis; however, Watson's work has more biographical information on the writers and contains more extensive bibliographies. It is also less expensive. Smaller libraries may not want to consider all the works. This title is recommended for high school, public, and academic libraries.   *SHORT STORIES*

Y; A

499. Teaching Guides for 50 Young Adult Novels. By Roberta Gail Shipley. Neal-Schuman, 1995. 131p. $34.95. 1-55570-193-0.

The author has selected 50 outstanding young adult novels that would be useful for English teachers to use in place of basal readers. An introduction outlines the steps needed to implement the program and cites the criteria applied to select the novels, which had to be well-written, to lend themselves to discussion, and to be relevant to today's teenagers. The novels are arranged alphabetically by author. Each entry contains a brief summary of the story, subjects included in the story, hints for the teacher, and questions for discussion or writing. An asterisk indicates those most suitable for writing activities. A list of the novels included and a subject index complete the volume. This short, highly selective list is recommended for middle or junior high schools. *LITERATURE—STUDY AND TEACHING*

Poetry

Y; A

500. The Columbia Granger's Index to Poetry. 10th ed. By Edith P. Hazen. Columbia, 1994. 2,150p. $199. 0-231-08408-0.

There are 79,000 poems by 11,000 authors found in 386 anthologies indexed in this volume, the main section of which is the title–first line–last line index. As well as being an important tool for reference purposes, the list of collections analyzed will be valuable in collection development in large young adult libraries and high schools. *POETRY*

Y; A

501. Nineteenth Century American Poetry: An Annotated Bibliography. By Philip K. Jason. Salem Press, 1990. 257p. (Magill Bibliographies). $40. 0-89356-651-9.

This work contains citations to criticism in general and on selected works of 16 well-known nineteenth-century American poets, including Bryant, Emerson, Longfellow, Whittier, Poe, Whitman, and Dickinson. After biographical information and criticism of each poet's work as a whole, Jason provides a 21-page bibliography of "general treatments of the period." Sources are from books, parts of books, and some periodical articles. The annotations are descriptive and critical. This bibliography is an important purchase for all academic and public libraries maintaining a collection of American poetry. *AMERICAN POETRY*

Y; A

502. Poetry Criticism. Ed. by Robyn V. Young. Gale, 1991– . 5 vols. $92/vol. 0-8103-5450-0 (vol. 1); 0-8103-5539-6 (vol. 2); 0-8103-5440-X (vol. 3); 0-8103-5541-8 (vol. 4); 0-8103-8333-0 (vol. 5).

Poetry Criticism is the newest addition to Gale's highly regarded series on literary criticism sources. Each volume of this fully illustrated guide to poets contains critical excerpts on 12 to 15 major poets—those most frequently studied in high schools and undergraduate college courses. Added volumes are tentatively planned to be issued biannually. Entries are arranged in alphabetical order by poet. Each entry contains a biographical sketch, excerpts of critical analyses, and sources of additional readings. Author, title, and subject indexes are provided. This bio-bibliographical source is recommended for reference and collection development in secondary school, academic, and public libraries. *POETRY*

Specific Genres

General and Miscellaneous

Y; A

503. Classic Cult Fiction: A Companion to Popular Cult Literature. By Thomas Reed Whissen. Greenwood, 1992. 360p. $69.50. 0-313-26550-X.

This work consists of essays on 50 books, each of which the author feels "touches the nerve of its time with uncanny accuracy." It begins with *The Sorrows of Young Werther* (1774) and ends with Douglas

Adams's *The Hitchhiker's Guide to the Galaxy* (1979). More than half have been published since 1960. Each essay contains a brief bibliography, and there are lists of other cult titles and of books for further reading. Though many may disagree with some of the inclusions and wonder why other titles have not been included, this is an interesting book for browsing and for ideas related to collection development in large high school and public libraries. *CULT FICTION*

Y*

504. **Genre Favorites for Young Adults**. Ed. by Sally Estes. American Library Association, 1993. 63p. $7.95 pap. 0-8389-5755-2.

This paperback lists surefire reading hits with a young adult audience under reading interest categories like mysteries, science fiction, and supernatural. The choices have been made judiciously; many are based on previously published bibliographies that have appeared from time to time in *Booklist*. This title will be useful for reading guidance and collection building in young adult collections as well as junior and senior high schools. Inquiries or purchase should be addressed to: ALA Publishing Order Dept., 50 E. Huron St., Chicago, IL 60611. *YOUNG ADULT LITERATURE (GENERAL)*

Y; A

505. **Genreflecting: A Guide to Reading Interests in Genre Fiction**. 4th ed. By Diana Tixier Herald. Libraries Unlimited, 1995. 367p. $38. 0-56308-354-X.

After an introduction on the nature of genre fiction, the author deals with such major areas as Westerns, thrillers, romance, science fiction, fantasy, and supernatural/horror. Each is broken down into subdivisions (e.g., the Westerns section contains subheadings such as mountain men, mining, the Indian, and railroads). This work is not intended to be an exhaustive bibliography but instead gives a few sample titles representing those currently available and popular authors. For each genre there is a selective annotated bibliography on its history and criticism plus material on bibliographies, book clubs, associations, and conventions. There are indexes by author and themes. Although the lack of annotations somewhat limits this work's value in book selection, it is still useful to familiarize librarians with popular reading tastes and to supply them with guidance for collection building. Young adult titles are not included, but its coverage of adult material will make it valuable in senior high schools as well as public libraries. *AMERICAN LITERATURE; ENGLISH LITERATURE*

Y*

506. **Teen Genreflecting**. By Diana Tixier Herald. Libraries Unlimited, 1997. 120p. $23.50. 1-56308-287-X.

Patterned after Herald's *Genreflecting*, which is aimed at adults (though it is also useful with young adults), this volume highlights why it is important for teachers and librarians to pursue teens' interests in genre literature to promote reading and broaden reading interests. This new guide focuses on teens in grades 6–12 and includes historical novels, science fiction, fantasy, mystery, suspense, horror, adventure, sports, romance, and contemporary novels (which deal with such topics as death, pregnancy, and suicide). This should be a very useful guide for reading guidance and selection. It is recommended for all secondary schools and public library young adult departments. *FICTION; READING GUIDANCE*

Adventure and Mystery

Y; A

507. **Cloak and Dagger Fiction: An Annotated Guide to Spy Thrillers**. 3rd ed. By Myron J. Smith and Terry White. Greenwood, 1995. 849p. $95. 0-313-27700-1.

5,807 spy thrillers are listed in this annotated bibliography, which is arranged by author. Most of the titles were published after 1940. Although the annotations are not evaluative, symbols are used to indicate such characteristics as absence of sex, use of a historical plot, and (most important for young adult librarians) whether the title is suitable for young adults. Introductory material includes a history of the genre and a bibliography of materials (chiefly books) on espionage. There are several interesting appendixes, including guides to pseudonyms and characters in series, plus author and title indexes. *SPY FICTION*

Historical Fiction

Y*
508.   America as Story: Historical Fiction for Secondary Schools. 2nd ed. By Rosemary K. Coffey and Elizabeth F. Howard. American Library Association, 1997. 240p. $25. 0-8389-0702-4.

More than 200 fiction works (84 are new to this edition) on American history are included in this highly selected bibliography useful for teachers and students in grades 7–12. Thirty-eight titles are recommended for advanced readers. The fully annotated titles are arranged in chronological order under broad topics from colonial America to America in the modern world. The titles were selected for literary quality and historical accuracy by Howard and a panel of curriculum specialists. Each annotation gives a plot summary, suggestions for follow-up activities, and recommended reading level. This well-developed bibliography is recommended as an important selection guide for all secondary school and public libraries.   *UNITED STATES—HISTORY—FICTION; HISTORICAL FICTION*

Y
509.   World Historical Fiction Guide for Young Adults. By Lee Gordon and Cheryl Tanaka. Highsmith, 1995. 381p. $30. 0-917846-41-9.

A high school librarian and a former English teacher team up to compile this bibliography of about 800 historical fiction titles. The title may be slightly misleading; this bibliography does not include the United States. However, the work is arranged first by continent or region, then subdivided by country or subregion. Under each heading the entries are listed alphabetically by author. Each entry provides full bibliographic information, a brief descriptive annotation, a list of review citations, suggested reading level, and a time period. Each of the works included received at least two positive reviews from a standard reviewing source. Books with more than one negative review were excluded. Further, all books were published since 1970, and though many may be out-of-print, they should be readily available in libraries. VanMeter's *World History for Children and Young Adults* covers some of the same ground (and the United States). However, Gordon and Tanaka have many more titles for other areas of the world, are more current, and limit their titles to those specifically for young adults. Despite its shortcomings, this work is recommended for all libraries serving young adults, even those that may presently own the VanMeter work.   *HISTORICAL FICTION*

Science Fiction, Fantasy, and Horror

Y; A
510.   Best in Science Fiction: Winners and Nominees of the Major Awards in Science Fiction. By Aurel Guillemette. Ashgate, 1993. 396p. $39.50. 1-85928-005-6.

Winners and nominees of 117 science fiction awards such as the Arthur C. Clarke, Locus, World Fantasy, and British Science Fiction are listed in this work of many charts but little text. The awards listed are those that are presented at least once in a five-year period and selected by experts in the field. The books are arranged in six sections: by award, author, title, year, and best of the best, and the "best" listed in chronological order. Unfortunately, full bibliographic citations are not included. Libraries with a similar work that also lists science fiction awards, *Reginald's Science Fiction and Fantasy Awards* (Borgo Press, 1993. $21. 0-8095-1200-9), need not purchase both. Either may be useful to libraries with large science fiction collections or many science fiction buffs.   *SCIENCE FICTION*

Y; A
511.   Encyclopedia of Science Fiction. By John Clute and Peter Nicholls. St. Martin's Griffin, 1995. $29.95 pap. 0-312-13486-X.

Included in the 4,360 articles in this oversized volume are articles on science fiction writers, illustrators, awards, subjects (e.g., time travel, children's science fiction), movies, television shows, countries, and terms. Along with the survey articles there are critical bibliographic essays on individual authors that can be helpful in collection development. Coverage ends at 1992. This is a fascinating paperback that covers its subject thoroughly.   *SCIENCE FICTION*

Y; A

512. **Fantasy: The 100 Best Books**. By James Cawthorn and Michael Moorcock. Carroll and Graf, 1991. 216p. $8.95 pap. 0-88184-708-9.

This highly selective list of fantasy fiction begins with *Gulliver's Travels* (1726) and continues chronologically to contemporary works. The lengthy annotations are both witty and erudite. This book will interest fantasy fans and librarians who can use it for reader's guidance and as a checklist for possible collection development. *FANTASY*

Y; A

513. **Fantasy Literature: A Reader's Guide**. By Neil Barron. Garland, 1990. 586p. $55. 0-8240-3148-2.

This excellent guide to fantasy literature is divided into two sections: a survey of the genre and a survey of research aids about the genre. Each section contains individual chapters written by subject specialists that consist of an overview essay and a critically annotated bibliography. These are selective, with important works starred. The second section includes material on reference works, history and criticism, library resources, films, awards, art and illustration, periodicals, and related topics. There are author, title, and theme indexes. This volume can be used in public libraries and in some high schools for research and collection development purposes. Its companion is *Horror Literature*. There is some overlapping of material (about 10 percent of the same text appears in both volumes), but both are valuable for acquisition purposes. *FANTASY; HORROR LITERATURE*

Y; A

514. **Grolier Science Fiction: The Multimedia Encyclopedia of Science Fiction**. Grolier, 1995. CD-ROM. $59.95. 0-7172-3999-3 (Windows version); 0-7172-3998-5 (Macintosh version).

Based on John Clute's *Encyclopedia of Science Fiction* and his *Science Fiction: The Illustrated Encyclopedia* (both have separate entries), this CD-ROM includes more than 6,000 entries ranging from 1 to 10 screens. Search categories include authors, films and TV, publications, art, and terms. Major themes like time, space, and life forms can also be searched. "Time Machine," "Gallery," and "Book Browser" are three other search options. "Time Machine" gives a history of science fiction by decades; "Gallery" leads to pictures, covers, theme essays, short interviews with authors, and clips of movies; and "Book Browser" provides access to lists of books by authors and by searching subjects like time travel, classics, and cyberpunk. There are 300 plot summaries, most of which are illustrated with cover art. "Book Browser" is particularly useful for collection evaluation and development. *SCIENCE FICTION*

Y; A*

515. **Horror Literature: A Reader's Guide**. By Neil Barron. Garland, 1990. 596p. $20. 0-8240-4347-2.

This book is divided into two main sections. The first surveys the genre, with chapters on such aspects of horror literature as Gothic romance and contemporary horror fiction. The second is a survey of research aids like reference works, history and criticism, and films and television programs. Each of the chapters is written by an expert and begins with a critical essay and ends with an extensive annotated bibliography with recommended titles starred. This is a companion piece to *Fantasy Literature: A Reader's Guide*, and there is a certain amount of overlap in material that involves 6 of the 13 chapters, or about 10 percent of the text. Both books have author, title, and theme indexes. Both books will be useful for research, reader's advising, and collection development in medium and large public libraries and many colleges and high schools. *HORROR—FICTION*

Y; A

516. **Horror: 100 Best Books**. By Stephen Jones and Kim Newman. Carroll and Graf, 1990. 256p. $8.95 pap. 0-88184-594-9.

A number of authors have contributed to this survey of the best in horror literature from 1592 (*Doctor Faustus* by Christopher Marlowe) to the mid-1980s. For each book there are a summary and a review essay. Appendixes include biographies of contributors and a bibliography of important readings about horror fiction. *HORROR—FICTION*

Y; A

517. **Magill's Guide to Science Fiction and Fantasy Literature**. By T. A. Shipped and A. J. Sobcsak. Salem Press, 1996. 4 vols. $300. 0-89356-906-2.

These four volumes cover 791 books or series of importance in the field of science fiction and fantasy. About one-third of them were published in the 1980s and 1990s. For each work there are a lengthy plot summary, character analysis, and useful critical remarks. The fourth volume has an extensive bibliography of critical works on both these genres, lists of award winners, and subject, title, and author indexes. This set is valuable for reference purposes as well as for collection development. In spite of its high price, it is recommended for all young adult collections.   *SCIENCE FICTION; FANTASY*

Y; A

518. **Presenting Young Adult Horror Fiction**. By Cosette N. Kies. Twayne, 1992. 203p. $19.95. 0-8057-8217-6.

Kies, the compiler of a number of bibliographies on the occult and the supernatural has added this collection by authors of horror literature to her fascinating list. She has selected authors that should appeal to young adult readers of horror stories, including V. C. Andrews, John Saul, Anne Rice, Robert Bloch, Dean R. Koontz, and Stephen King. Each chapter deals with a specific element of horror or a subgenre of horror such as gothic, scientific creations, monsters, cults, Satanism, criminal acts, dark fantasy, and the struggle between good and evil. Along with a chronology of each author's life and works, critical comments, and analyses, themes, plots, and characters of major works are discussed in depth. A selected bibliography and filmography are appended. This enjoyable and readable bio-bibliography will be of interest to many adults as well as young adults, especially horror fans. It is recommended for all libraries serving such an audience.   *HORROR—FICTION*

Y*; A*

519. **Reference Guide to Science Fiction, Fantasy, and Horror**. By Michael Burgess. Libraries Unlimited, 1992. 403p. $45. 0-87287-611-X.

Burgess has provided us with one of the best and most complete guides to the popular genres of science fiction, fantasy, and horror. A wide variety of reference sources are cited, such as encyclopedias and dictionaries, yearbooks, reader's guides, atlases, magazine and anthology indexes, and bibliographies of all types. Full bibliographic data, included with each entry, are followed by an extensive annotation in most cases. An added bonus is the section on core collections, which will be useful in building or evaluating an existing collection for any type of library. This inexpensive guide is highly recommended for all libraries serving science fiction, fantasy, or horror buffs.   *FANTASY; HORROR; SCIENCE FICTION*

Y; A

520. **Science Fiction: The Illustrated Encyclopedia**. By John Clute. Dorling Kindersley, 1995. 312p. $39.95. 0-7894-0185-1.

This beautifully illustrated encyclopedia is divided into subject-oriented chapters that cover such areas as the history of science fiction, magazines, major authors, classic titles, films, and television. It concludes with a glossary and an extensive index. The section on major authors is particularly interesting. Illustrated with portraits, movie stills, and dust jackets, the text gives biographical and critical material on each author (the entries for major writers are about two pages each) plus thorough bibliographies. This attractive work is useful for browsing as well as reference work. John Clute coauthored with Peter Nicholls the award-winning, more detailed and scholarly *Encyclopedia of Science Fiction*. Both of these works served as a basis for the *Grolier Science Fiction* CD-ROM (1995).   *SCIENCE FICTION*

Y; A

521. **St. James Guide to Fantasy Writers**. By David Pringle. St. James Press, 1996. 711p. $95. 1-55862-205-5.

Almost 500 fantasy writers past and present are included in this oversized biographical dictionary. The majority of writers are English-speaking but some foreign-language authors like Hans Christian Andersen are included. Historical figures like J. M. Barrie, Rudyard Kipling, Mark Twain, and Edgar

Rice Burroughs appear along with popular authors for adults (e.g., Terry Brooks, Jack Chalker, Roger Zelazny) and such writers for young people as Brian Jacques, Lloyd Alexander, Susan Cooper, and E. B. White. Each author receives a lengthy, critical biography; a full list of fantasy publications; and bibliographies of works in other genres and critical and biographical works. Only pure fantasy is included; a second volume on horror and gothic writers is planned. There is a companion volume: *St. James Guide to Science Fiction Writers*. Both will be useful for research and collection building in high schools and public libraries. *FANTASY*

Y; A

522. **St. James Guide to Science Fiction Writers**. 4th ed. St. James Press, 1996. 1,175p. $135. 1-55862-179-2.

    Formerly titled *Twentieth-Century Science Fiction Writers*, this hefty volume has entries for more than 600 of the world's most prominent writers of science fiction, past and present, for juveniles and adults. From traditional favorites like H. G. Wells and Robert Heinlein to more contemporary writers who have significantly changed the genre, like Doris Lessing and Michael Moorcock, this work gives lengthy biographical material that concentrates on a critical analysis along with thorough bibliographies by and about the author. This fascinating work will be of great value for young researchers as well as librarians. *SCIENCE FICTION*

Y*

523. **Supernatural Fiction for Teens: More Than 1300 Good Paperbacks to Read for Wonderment, Fear, and Fun**. 2nd ed. By Cosette N. Kies. Libraries Unlimited, 1992. 267p. $25 pap. 0-87287-940-2.

    The 1,300 paperbacks recommended in this bibliography are arranged alphabetically by author. Full bibliographic information and an interest-catching annotation are given for each title. Each entry is coded: A) written for teens, B) written for younger teens, C) written for adults, and D) a classic. There are subject and authors indexes. This is a valuable source for purchasing books as well as giving reader's guidance and preparing bibliographies and booktalks.
SUPERNATURAL—FICTION; HORROR—FICTION; PAPERBACK BOOKS

Y; A

524. **The Ultimate Guide to Science Fiction**. By David Pringle. Pharos/World Almanac, 1991. 407p. $24.50; $14.95 pap. 0-88687-537-4; 0-88687-536-6 pap.

    Pringle, in consultation with other science fiction authorities, has compiled a list of 3,000 novels, anthologies, and collections. Excluded are children's titles, fantasy, non-English books, and works published prior to 1970. The entries are alphabetically arranged by title, necessitating the use of the author index to access all listings by a given author. Each title is rated by Pringle from 0 to 4. Each entry has a three- or four-line story summary and evaluation. Also noted are date of first publication, type of work, sequels, related titles, and film adaptations. A similar critical guide with almost as many entries is Barron's *Anatomy of Wonder* (Bowker, 1995. $52. 0-8352-3288-3). Pringle's guide may not be the "ultimate guide"; however, it is useful for collection development and reference work and is recommended for most public, school, and academic libraries where there are science fiction fans. *SCIENCE FICTION*

Multiculturalism

General and Miscellaneous

Y*; A*

525. **American Ethnic Literatures: Native American, African American, Chicano/Latino, and Asian American Writers and Their Backgrounds**. By David R. Peck. Salem Press, 1992. 218p. $40. 0-89356-684-5.

    Peck has compiled a bibliography of writers of the four major ethnic groups in the United States: Native American, African American, Latino, and Asian. The first four chapters serve as an overview and general picture of ethnicity with an indication of availability of resources. Chapter 1 is an annotated listing of important reference works for ethnic studies. Chapter 2 presents major studies that deal with the social and historical aspects of a diverse society. Chapter 3 deals with teaching ethnic literature. Chapter 4 lists general studies of ethnic literature and is subdivided into sections on biography, fiction, and theater. The main body of the volume consists of the remaining chapters, with a chapter on each major ethnic group. Each of these chapters includes an introductory section dealing with the history and background of the ethnic group, followed by lists of resources and major critical studies. Peck's work is a real contribution to the field of multicultural materials. It is recommended for reference and as a buying guide to all secondary school, academic, and public libraries.

MULTICULTURALISM; AFRICAN AMERICANS; NATIVE AMERICANS; HISPANIC AMERICANS; ASIAN AMERICANS

Y; A*
526.   Asian Americans Information Directory: A Guide to Organizations, Agencies, Institutions, Programs, Publications, and Services Concerned with Asian American Nationalities and Ethnic Groups in the United States. Ed. by Karen Backus and Julia C. Furtaw, Gale, 1992. 461p. $75. 0-8103-8332-2.

This excellent directory of almost 5,000 listings deals with more than 20 Asian nationalities and ethnic groups in the United States. Within these nationality divisions, complete contact information and often descriptive annotations are provided for associations, museums, cultural organizations, embassies, consulates, government agencies, and much more, including publications. This directory does for Asian Americans what two other Gale publications do for two other major American minority groups: *Black Americans Information Directory* (see entry 536) and *Hispanic Americans Information Directory 1994–95* (1994. 490p. $85. 0-8103-7840-X). This excellent tool is highly recommended for reference, interlibrary loan, and collection development in most libraries, especially those serving a large Asian American community. *ASIAN AMERICANS*

Y; A
527.   Black Literature Criticism: Excerpts from Criticism of the Most Significant Works of Black Authors over the Past 200 Years. 2nd ed. Ed. by James P. Draper. Gale, 1992. 3 vols. $275. 0-8103-7929-5.

This latest addition to Gale's Literary Criticism Series follows the same general format as others in the series. More than 150 Black writers of the eighteenth, nineteenth, and twentieth centuries from the United States, Nigeria, South Africa, Jamaica, "and over a dozen other nations" are included. Each author entry consists of a biographical/critical introduction that concludes with references to other Gale works. Also included are a list of principal works and excerpts from criticism that present an overview of critical commentary on the author. Finally, each entry contains a bibliography of additional sources. Author, nationality, and title indexes for the whole set are included in volume 3. This set, while relatively expensive, is recommended for public, academic, and high school libraries. This title's overlap with Gale's Literary Criticism series will have to be considered, especially for smaller libraries.

AUTHORS, AFRICAN AMERICAN; AFRICAN AMERICANS

Y*
528.   Global Beat: A List of Multi-Cultural Books for Teenagers. Office of Young Adult Services, New York Public Library. 1992. 34p. $5. 0-87104-715-2.

This pamphlet lists multicultural books for teens under 10 main headings such as "The Far East," "Latin America and The Caribbean," "Native Americans," and "Coming to the U.S.A." Each is annotated with the teenager in mind. Copies are available for $5 plus mailing charges of $1 from: Office of Branch Libraries, New York Public Library, 455 Fifth Ave., New York, NY 10016. *MULTICULTURALISM*

Y; A
529.   Global Voices, Global Visions: A Core Collection of Multicultural Books. By Lyn Miller-Lachmann. Bowker, 1995. 590p. $52. 0-8352-3291-3.

Though intended for an adult audience, this companion to *Our Family, Our Friends, Our World* (1992) contains a great deal of material that can be used in young adult collections where advanced material is required. The 1,600 titles cover ethnic groups from all regions of the world. They are arranged into 15 chapters, each containing a map and an introduction to the literature of the region. The detailed annotations describe the contents of the work, its importance, and related works by the same author. Fiction, drama, poetry, nonfiction, essays, and biographies are included. The first four chapters cover minority groups in the United States: African Americans, Asian Americans, Latinos, and Native Americans. The contributors include subject specialists, librarians, and academics. There are useful author, title, and subject indexes. *MULTICULTURALISM*

Y; A

530. **New Immigrant Literatures in the United States: A Sourcebook to Our Multicultural Literary Heritage**. Ed. by Alpana Sharma Knippling. Greenwood, 1996. 386p. $65. 0-313-28968-9.

Knippling has pulled together a historical overview of post-World War II literatures dealing with immigrants and immigration to the United States. The work contains 22 chapters (essays) divided into four main sections: Asian American, Caribbean American, European American, and Mexican American literatures. African American literature was deliberately omitted because the author felt it deserved a separate study. Following a historical cultural introduction, each chapter includes sections dealing with the following topics: literary-cultural history, dominant concerns, major authors, early and recent efforts, and prevailing genres. This well-written collection of bibliographic essays on an important current topic is intended for both the scholar-researcher and general reader. Recommended for every high school, public, and academic library. *IMMIGRATION; MULTICULTURALISM*

Y; A

531. **The Schocken Guide to Jewish Books: Where to Start Reading About Jewish History, Literature, Culture, and Religion**. Ed. by Barry W. Holz. Schocken Books, 1992. 357p. $25. 0-8052-4108-6.

This book consists of 15 bibliographic essays intended to serve as a guide to the basic books on Jewish life, history, and culture. Some of the subjects dealt with in these chapters are the Bible, the Talmud, the Jewish Middle Ages, philosophy, women's studies, Israel and Zionism, the Holocaust, and books for young readers. Each topic is written by a subject specialist. This bibliography can help in readers' guidance and in collection building in the area of Jewish studies. *JEWS*

Y

532. **Writers of Multicultural Fiction for Young Adults: A Bio-Critical Sourcebook**. Ed. by Daphne Kutzer. Greenwood, 1996. 496p. $75.

In this bio-bibliography of multicultural fiction, Kutzer identifies 51 writers who have written books appropriate for young adults about ethnic groups: African American, Jewish, Native American, and Asian American. Many of the writers are themselves members of one of the groups. Each entry contains biographical information, a commentary on the major works and themes, critical reception, and a bibliography by and about the writer. A general bibliography on multicultural literature completes the work. This guide helps teachers, librarians, and young adult readers select important works and provides guidance in dealing with multicultural issues considered in young adult fiction. While there are many bibliographies on multicultural literature, Kutzer limits her list to those works specifically for young adults. She also identifies many authors who were virtually unknown. This work is recommended for all libraries that serve young adults as a reference tool and aid in collection development. *MULTICULTURALISM*

African Americans

Y; A

533. **The African American Resource Guide**. By Anita Doreen Diggs. Barricade Books, 1994. 224p. $12.99 pap. 1-56980-006-5.

Many areas are covered in this brief guide, including African American literature, colleges and universities, and cultural organizations. A major flaw is its lack of comprehensiveness; for example, dramatist August Wilson is not included in the list of writers; *Eye on the Prize* is not among the popular videos listed; and some major African American organizations, such as the Greek letter organizations, are not on the meager list of only 34 organizations. However, despite this limitation, the book is still useful and may be considered as an additional resource for small secondary schools or public libraries. The price is right. *AFRICAN AMERICANS*

Y; A
534.   **African-American Voices in Young Adult Literature**. By Karen P. Smith. Scarecrow, 1994. $45. 405p. 0-8108-2907-X.
      Smith explores a variety of genres in 14 original essays on African American authors, including poetry, horror, science fiction, and biography. Though not a bibliography per se, this interesting work includes many authors and mentions many titles that could be considered in young adult literature selection. Therefore, this professional source should prove useful to librarians and teachers exploring works written by and for African Americans. *AFRICAN AMERICANS*

Y; A
535.   **Black Adolescence: Current Issues and Annotated Bibliography**. By the Consortium for Research on Black Adolescence. Prentice Hall, 1990. $40. 168p. 0-8161-9080-1.
      This survey of the issues and problems involved with Black adolescence is divided into separate subject-oriented chapters, each written by a different person. Topics covered are psychosocial development, psychological health, physical health, drug abuse, suicide, academic performance, education and occupational choice, employment, family, adolescent relationships, sexuality and contraception, and teen parenting. Each chapter begins with a summary of the research and findings in the area and a fine annotated bibliography of basic readings in books and periodicals on the subject. This book will be of value in high schools and public libraries that serve a substantial African American population.
ADOLESCENCE—AFRICAN AMERICAN; AFRICAN AMERICANS

Y; A*
536.   **Black Americans Information Directory: A Guide to Approximately 4,500 Organizations, Agencies, Institutions, Programs, and Publications**. 3rd ed. Ed. by Darren L. Smith. Gale, 1993. 424p. $125. 0-8103-8082-X.
      This excellent directory is really a complete African American sourcebook and many reference works under one cover. One may well consider acquiring this title simply for the publications that are listed and consider all the other lists (i.e., organizations, agencies, institutions, and programs) as bonuses. This is an excellent tool for reference, interlibrary loan, and collection development. It is highly recommended for most libraries, especially for those serving a sizable African American community.
AFRICAN AMERICANS

C; Y; A
537.   **Celebrating Women's History: A Women's History Month Resource Book**. By Mary Ellen Snodgrass. Gale, 1996. 517p. $44.95. 0-7876-0605-7.
      More than 300 activities and projects, from games to arts and crafts activities, display ideas, and tributes to various individuals, highlight this resource book on creative ways to celebrate Woman's History Month in March. These activities are arranged in 29 subject chapters like art, geography, literature, and science. In addition to age/grade level, budget, and procedures, each entry has a list of sources, mostly books and videos. For collection development, an appendix lists museums, newsletters, publishers, and sources of various media. *WOMEN'S HISTORY MONTH; WOMEN*

Y; A
538.   **The Schomburg Center Guide to Black Literature: From the Eighteenth Century to the Present**. By Roger M. Valade and Denise Kasinec. Gale, 1996. 545p. $75. 0-7876-0289-2.
      Written under the auspices of the New York Public Library's esteemed Schomburg Center for Research in Black Culture, this useful reference work is an alphabetically arranged guide to authors, works, characters, themes, and topics associated with U.S. and international Black literature. Biographies of more than 500 writers and summaries of 460 major works are included. There are also 68 entries on related topics and terms. Additional features include chronologies on Black history and literature, dates of major literary awards won by Black authors, a history of the Schomberg Center, and extensive

indexes. Although coverage extends into the eighteenth century, emphasis is on the late twentieth century. This is a fine reference for high school and public libraries.

AFRICAN AMERICAN LITERATURE

Y*; A*

539. **Voices of the Spirit: Sources for Interpreting the African American Experience**. By Denise M. Glover. American Library Association, 1994. 211p. $25. 0-8389-0639-7.

The wish of the author of this carefully researched bibliography is to help transform historical events, laws, movements, statistics, and facts into personal experiences that are relevant and significant to our present lives . A variety of resources, such as general reference books, primary sources, traveling exhibits, biographies, photo books, and videos, are included in this annotated bibliography. Arrangement is by genre and historical period, beginning with the nineteenth century and extending to the present. Each chapter has an introductory statement that presents an overview of its contents. The entries are alphabetically arranged by author or producer. Each entry includes a lengthy (many are longer than a page) and evaluative annotation and suggested nonannotated additional works. Entries also contain complete bibliographic data. Suggestions for using the materials are provided in many cases. Author/title and subject indexes complete this excellent bibliography, which is recommended for all libraries.

AFRICAN AMERICANS

Hispanic Americans

Y; A

540. **Dictionary of Hispanic Biography**. Ed. by Joseph C. Tariff and L. Mpho Mabunda. Gale, 1995. 1,011p. $120. 0-8103-8302-0.

Of the 470 people included in this biographical dictionary of famous people from Latin America, the United States, and Spain, about 70 percent lived in the twentieth century. In addition to biographical information, each entry includes a list of selected materials by the subject (books, films, recordings, etc.) and works about that person. Included are prominent figures from all fields of endeavor with an emphasis on contemporary personalities. There are more than 200 portraits and an appended list of additional sources. The various bibliographies will be of some value in collection building in high schools with a large Hispanic American population.

HISPANIC AMERICANS

Y; A

541. **U.S. Latino Literature: An Essay and Annotated Bibliography**. By Marc Zimmerman. MARCH/Abrazo Press; distr. Independent Literary Publishers Association, 1992. 156p. $10.95 pap. 1-877636-01-0.

This work deals with important U.S. Latino writers and their literature. The major groups considered are Mexican Americans (Chicanos), Cubans, and Puerto Ricans. The first part of the book consists of an extensive essay describing Latinos and their cultural contributions, especially literary ones. The last two-thirds of the work consists of the annotated bibliography, which is also divided into the three main groups. The dates of the items range from the 1970s to the 1990s. Each entry contains full bibliographic data. The descriptive annotations vary in length. This inexpensive work is recommended for all academic and public libraries, especially those supporting a Hispanic studies program or serving a large Hispanic population.

AUTHORS, HISPANIC AMERICAN; HISPANIC AMERICANS

Native Americans

Y; A

542. **Dictionary of Native American Literature**. Ed. by Andrew Wiget. Garland, 1994. 5,987p. $95. 0-8153-1560-0.

Arranged chronologically, this collection of 70 essays by 52 members of the Association for the Study of American Indian Literature surveys both the oral and written literary heritage of Native Americans. Each of the signed, readable articles is well researched and contains a useful bibliography of primary and secondary sources. In a final section are essays on topics like teaching Native American literature and articles on such prominent writers as Vine Deloria and Louise Erdich. Though scholarly in tone, this work will be particularly useful in high schools with programs in Native American studies.

AUTHORS, NATIVE AMERICAN

Y; A

543. **The Native American in Long Fiction**. By Joan Beam and Barbara Branstad. Scarecrow, 1996. 384p. $56. 0-8108-3016-7.

Beam and Branstad have compiled a comprehensive bibliography of novels by and about Native Americans published during the last century (between the 1890s and the 1990s). All types of novels are included, such as science fiction, romances, Westerns, mysteries, and contemporary fiction. Adult and young adult novels are included. Native American authors are identified as to their tribe. Annotations are both descriptive and critical. The bibliography also contains indexes and appendixes of criticism and sources consulted. This interesting work is recommended for secondary school, public, and college libraries.

NATIVE AMERICANS

Y; A

544. **Reference Encyclopedia of the American Indian**. 6th ed. By Barry Klein. Todd Publications; distr. ABC-Clio, 1992. 1,100p. $125. 0-915344-30-0.

This hefty volume is newly revised and updated. Actually, there are three distinct volumes in one: a directory of reservations in the United States and Canada, associations, Native American centers, and the like; a biographical dictionary of prominent American Indians and others related to Indians; and the section most pertinent to this guide, an expanded bibliography of thousands of titles, with more than 500 new ones added to this edition. The subject listing and the audiovisual lists make this extensive bibliography particularly useful. This important reference source is recommended for most academic and public libraries. Unfortunately, most school libraries, where it would be used extensively, might have difficulty with the steep price.

NATIVE AMERICANS

Reading Guidance
and Library Programs

Y*; A*

545. **Adolescents at Risk: A Guide to Fiction and Nonfiction for Young Adults, Parents, and Professionals**. By Joan F. Kaywell. Greenwood, 1993. 269p. $45. 0-313-29039-3.

Kaywell has produced a fully annotated bibliography of more than 900 fiction and nonfiction books. The works were published through 1992 and focus on the psychological, social, and physical problems facing teens; they provide information for teens and the adults working with them. The works are arranged into 14 specific problem areas such as alienation and identity, eating disorders, abuse, homosexuality, death and dying, alcohol and drugs, divorced and single parents, adopted and foster families, and stress and suicide. Each chapter has background information on the subject, where to go for help, annotated fiction and nonfiction titles for teens, and professional reading. The annotations are written at a junior high school reading level. They vary in length from a single line to a brief paragraph and are primarily descriptive. Author and title indexes are provided. This work is highly recommended as a selection tool and bibliotherapy aid for school and public libraries.

ADOLESCENCE; BIBLIOTHERAPY

Y*

546. **Connecting Young Adults and Libraries: A How-to-Do-It Manual**. By Patrick Jones. Neal-Schuman, 1992. 278p. $42.50. 1-55570-108-6.

This is an extremely valuable guide to programming in libraries to attract young adult patrons. It is aimed at the thousands of public libraries that do not have a young adult librarian and includes ideas for promoting volunteerism, connecting with other groups, booktalking, program suggestions, censorship, and more. For the purposes of collection development there are a YA core collection, lists of popular magazines, and addresses of major publishers. The book's overall contents make it a must for school and public libraries; its bibliographies are an added bonus (although much of this material appears elsewhere). *YOUNG ADULT LITERATURE (GENERAL); LIBRARY PROGRAMS*

Y

547. **High-Interest Books for Teens: A Guide to Book Reviews and Biographical Sources**. 3rd ed. By Joyce Nakamura. Gale, 1996. 539p. $99. 0-8103-6925-7.

In an alphabetical listing by author, more than 3,500 young adult and adult books that Nakamura believes appeal to adolescents are included, with biographical sources given for the author and review citations given for each book. Both fiction and nonfiction titles are included, but there is no indication of interest or reading levels. There are both title and subject indexes. A number of factors limit the use of this book: its lack of consistent criteria for inclusion, its price, the lack of interest and reading levels, and the fact that many of the titles included are now out-of-print. Nevertheless, large collections that need material on high-interest books will find some value here. *HIGH INTEREST–LOW VOCABULARY BOOKS*

Y*

548. **High Interest–Easy Reading: An Annotated Booklist for Middle School and Senior High School**. 7th ed. By Patricia Phelan. National Council of Teachers of English, 1996. 115p. $11.95 pap. 0-8141-2098-9.

This bibliography contains about 300 fiction and nonfiction titles arranged by author under such broad topics as adventure, death, historical fiction, love and friendship, sports, and mystery. Each entry gives bibliographical information and an interest-provoking annotation aimed at the teenager. The choices are well made. A subject index allows finding works under specific topics like Vietnam War and AIDS. Only recently published books are included; librarians should continue to use earlier volumes (now unfortunately out-of-print) to supplement the present volume. One of the best titles on books for reluctant teenage readers. *HIGH INTEREST–LOW VOCABULARY BOOKS*

Y

549. **High/Low Handbook: Encouraging Literacy in the 1990s**. 3rd ed. By Ellen V. Libretto. Bowker, 1990. 304p. (Serving Special Needs Series). $43. 0-8352-2804-5.

This standard work on dealing with poor or reluctant readers is in three parts. The first part is a series of essays on writing, publishing, and working with these special populations. The second part, "Selecting and Evaluating High/Low Materials," deals with computers and reading, readability factors, and methods of determining reading levels. The third part, "The Core Collection," is an annotated bibliography of 312 high-low books that were published after 1985. Most are fiction, but there are some biographies and general nonfiction, and all are for students reading at first to fifth grade reading levels. There is an additional bibliography of about 100 titles suitable for youngsters at the fourth to eighth grade reading level. In appendixes there are annotated lists of other bibliographies and magazine sources, a directory of publishers and authors, and title and subject indexes. An extremely useful book for junior and senior high school libraries and public libraries, but in need of an update. *HIGH INTEREST–LOW VOCABULARY BOOKS*

Y*

550. **Juniorplots 4: A Book Talk Guide for Use with Readers Ages 12–16**. By John T. Gillespie and Corinne J. Naden. Bowker, 1993. 450p. $42. 0-8352-3167-4.

Although this is primarily intended as a manual to help librarians and teachers introduce books to junior-high-age students, it can also be used for collection building in libraries serving this age group. The 80 basic titles included are arranged under such topics as "Teenage Life and Concerns," "Adventure and Mystery Stories," "Biography and True Adventure" and "Guidance and Health." For each title are given a detailed plot summary, material on thematic content and methods of presenting the book, and an annotated bibliography of about 8 to 10 additional recommended titles that are related in theme or content. All 700-odd titles are listed in the author and title indexes, but only the main titles are analyzed in the subject index. This volume was preceded by *Juniorplots* (1967. $25.45. 0-8352-0063-9), *More Juniorplots* (1977. $25.45. 0-8352-1002-2), and *Juniorplots 3* (1987. $28.90. 0-8352-2367-1). Each of

these titles deals with different books but are essentially the same in arrangement and treatment. *Juniorplots 4* contains a cumulative index. This series is recommended for public and school libraries.
YOUNG ADULT LITERATURE; BOOK TALKS

Y; A
551.   **Light 'n Lively Reads for ESL, Adult, and Teen Readers**. By La Vergne Rosow. Libraries Unlimited, 1996. 300p. $40. 1-56308-365-5.

Designed to be used with remedial or reluctant older teens and adults involved in English as a Second Language (ESL) or adult literacy programs, this annotated bibliography of high-low books would also be of interest to the general reader who needs motivation. The books are arranged in 17 different high-interest units such as arts, sports, parenting, sickness/death, and science. Each section is subdivided into various levels designated as first readers and picture books, thin books, challenging books, book chapters, strong passages, newspaper and magazine articles, and suggested writing or dialogue activities. The lengthy annotations describe the book or article and offer suggestions on usefulness. Librarians, ESL and remedial reading teachers, parents, and adult literacy teachers will find this bibliography very useful. Highly recommended for all school and public libraries.
ENGLISH AS A SECOND LANGUAGE;
HIGH INTEREST-LOW VOCABULARY BOOKS; LITERACY

Y*; A
552.   **Outstanding Books for the College Bound: Choices for a Generation**. Young Adult Services Division, American Library Association, 1996. 200p. $22. 0-8389-3456-0.

More than 1,000 books are listed in this list of books compiled by YALSA'S Outstanding Books for the College Bound committee. The titles include all of the works chosen between 1959 and 1994 (1996 marks the 38th edition of this well-known bibliography) and cover a large variety of subjects and literary styles. Most of the titles listed are readily available in school and public libraries. Following an introductory essay that states the criteria used for selection and an overview of the process, the titles are arranged under six genres: the arts, biography, fiction, nonfiction, poetry, and books for the times. Each entry contains a brief annotation and year of selection. Full bibliographic information is not cited; however, it is not needed because many titles have a large variety of editions. A section lists all of the titles in chronological order, covering the last four decades. This revised and updated work is highly recommended as a reading guidance aid to young people planning on college and as an overall tool for evaluation and development of collections.
YOUNG ADULT LITERATURE (GENERAL); READING GUIDANCE

Y
553.   **Quick Picks for Great Reading, [year]**. Young Adult Services Division, American Library Association, annual.

Included in this brochure are 65 annotated titles intended to stimulate interest in reluctant teenage readers. All titles are at the sixth grade reading level or below but have high-interest appeal in terms of content, format, and artwork. All books have been published since 1989. The list is available annually. Copies are available at $24 for 100 copies from: ALA Graphics, 50 E. Huron St., Chicago, IL 60611.
HIGH INTEREST-LOW VOCABULARY BOOKS

Y; A
554.   **Reading Lists for College-Bound Students**. 2nd ed. By Doug Estell et al. Arco/Prentice Hall, 1993. 255p. $10. 0-671-84712-0.

This is a compilation of about 100 lists of books recommended by various colleges. The purpose is to give college-bound students a head start on their reading as they prepare for college. The editors have compiled a composite list of "100 Most-Often-Recommended Works." This list is annotated, and each entry contains full bibliographic data. Perhaps high school and public libraries would want to check their holdings against this list.   *YOUNG ADULT LITERATURE (GENERAL); READING GUIDANCE*

Y*

555. **Rip-Roaring Reads for Reluctant Teen Readers**. By Gale W. Sherman and Bette D. Ammon. Libraries Unlimited, 1993. 164p. $22.50. 1-56308-094-X.

The authors have identified 40 contemporary, high-interest, spellbinding books—rip-roaring books that they feel will appeal to even the most reluctant teen reader. The work is divided into two equal sections, with 20 titles for grades 5–8 and 20 titles for grades 9–12. The criteria applied for selection of titles were: recent publication date, short length, appealing format, eye-catching book jacket or cover, high interest, meaningful subject matter, well-known author, appropriate reading level, realistic characters, and gripping plots. Each title entry contains review citations, author information, plot summary, readability and interest level, literature extensions, alternative book report suggestions, and bookmarks with additional recommendations that could be reproduced. The appendixes list titles by interest and readability levels, genres, themes, authors, titles, and activities. This book is highly recommended as an aid for reading guidance, reference, and collection development for all libraries that serve young adults.

READING GUIDANCE; HIGH INTEREST–LOW VOCABULARY BOOKS

Y*

556. **Seniorplots: A Book Talk Guide for Use with Readers Ages 15–18**. By John T. Gillespie and Corinne J. Naden. Bowker, 1989. 386p. $43. 0-8352-2513-5.

This aid to booktalkers contains detailed notes on 80 books recommended for reading by senior-high-aged readers. For each book there are a general introduction, a detailed plot summary, a listing of thematic material, and a guide to ways of introducing the book. Of interest in collection building are the lists of 8–10 additional recommended titles after each book entry. Each title is briefly annotated and is on the same or a related theme as the main entry. The main titles are arranged by subject content (e.g., science fiction and fantasy, teenage concerns, historical fiction). There are author, title, and subject indexes. The introduction consists of a brief manual on how to booktalk. Recommended for senior high and young adult collections.

BOOKTALKS

Y

557. **Storytelling for Young Adults: Techniques and Treasury**. By Gail de Vos. Libraries Unlimited, 1991. 169p. $24.50. 0-87287-832-5.

This book on storytelling for young adults (ages 13–18) is divided into five sections that include a rationale for story telling at this level, a description of techniques, the types of tales that appeal, and sample stories. Of particular value in collection development is an annotated bibliography of 120 stories with appeal for young adults that supplies locational information. The stories are summarized and arranged by such subjects as folktales and fairy tales; myths and legends; ghost, horror, and suspense tales; and tales of love. This is the only book devoted entirely to storytelling at this age level; it should be of particular value in young adult collections and in junior and senior high schools.

STORYTELLING

Y

558. **Teenage Perspectives Reference Series**. ABC-Clio.

This series was designed for young people with personal questions. These bibliographies are helpful for teens working on research papers as well as for parents, teachers, and counselors who want additional information. Each work in the series includes chapter introductions to each broad topic; terms, definitions, and statistics; a fully annotated listing of organizations, hotlines, and print and nonprint resources; and listings of relevant young adult novels. Among the titles currently available at $39.95 each are:

558.1 **Focus on Addictions**. By Kay Porterfield. 1992. 250p. 0-87436-674-7.

558.2 **Focus on Eating Disorders**. By Sean O'Halloran. 1993. 297p. 0-87436-692-5.

558.3 **Focus on Fitness**. By Nicholas Karolides. 1993. 202p. 0-87436-662-3.

558.4 **Focus on Physical Impairments**. By Nicholas J. Karolides. 1990. 325p. 0-87436-428-0.

558.5 **Focus on Relationships**. By Elizabeth Poe. 1993. 257p. 0-87436-672-0.

558.6   **Focus on School**. By Beverly Haley. 1990. 250p. 0-87436-099-4.

558.7   **Focus on Sexuality**. By Elizabeth Poe. 1990. 225p. 0-87436-116-8.

558.8   **Focus on Teens in Trouble**. By Daryl Sander. 1991. 225p. 0-87436-207-5.

DISABILITIES; ADOLESCENCE; SUBSTANCE ABUSE;
SEX EDUCATION; EATING DISORDERS

Y*
559.   **What Do Young Adults Read Next? A Reader's Guide to Fiction for Young Adults**. Ed. by Pam Spencer. Gale, 1994. 816p. $39.95. 0-8103-8887-1.

Similar in purpose and format to Gale's *What Do I Read Next?* and *What Do Children Read Next?*, this reading guidance tool seeks to match the reading interests of sixth through twelfth graders to fiction, both classic and contemporary. There are about 1,500 entries in all genres popular with young adults. Each entry provides title, publisher, and publication date; series, if any; characters; setting; review citations; and a plot summary. Ten indexes permit access in a variety of ways: series, award, time period, locale, subject, character name, character description, age of readers, author, and title. This relatively inexpensive work is recommended for every middle, secondary school, and public library.

READING GUIDANCE

Reference Books

Y*; A*
560.   **Book Review Digest**. H. W. Wilson, 1905– . Cumulated annually. Sold on service basis.

This standard reference tool, which has been published continuously for almost 100 years, provides excerpts from and citations to reviews of current adult and juvenile fiction and nonfiction. Currently, it covers more than 6,000 English-language books each year. Concise, critical evaluations are culled from about 95 selected periodicals. Entries are arranged alphabetically. Each includes full bibliographic information, a descriptive note, age or grade level, and review excerpts. A subject and title index is provided. A subscription provides 10 monthly paperbound issues, including cumulations in May, August, and October, plus a permanent annual bound cumulation. This title is sold on a service basis, based on a library's annual book budget. *Book Review Digest* is also online and on CD-ROM (write to publisher for details). This guide is recommended for reference and collection evaluation and collection building for all but the smallest libraries.

BOOK REVIEWS

Y; A*
561.   **Book Review Index**. Ed. by Barbara Beach and Beverly Baer. Gale. Cumulated annually.

The average annual edition of this index, which began publication in 1963, reviews more than 73,000 books and periodicals covered in more than 131,000 reviews that appeared in more than 470 reviewing periodicals. Almost every conceivable area in the general social sciences, sciences, humanities, and fine arts are represented. Most annual cumulations are still available, and for convenience a master cumulation including the years 1965–1984 is available in 10 volumes ($1,250. 0-8103-0577-1). A 1985–1992 master cumulation is also available ($895. 0-8103-9626-2). BRI is useful for reference as well as collection development and is recommended for all libraries that can afford it.

BOOK REVIEWS

Y; A
562.   **The Grolier Guide to New Research Methods and Sources**. By Trudi Jacobson and Gary McClain. Grolier, 1994. 2 vols. plus CD-ROM. $149. 0-7172-7236-2.

This set can be used by advanced high school students as well as undergraduate and adult patrons. It consists of two print volumes and a CD-ROM that contains the complete printed text in both MS-DOS and Macintosh compatible formats. Volume 1 of the print format, *Methods*, discusses research techniques, general sources, and such specialized resources as online databases, CD-ROMs, and government publications. This text originally appeared as *State-of-the-Art Fact-Finding* (Dell, 1993), now out-of-print. Volume 2, *Sources*, is an unannotated list of publications, associations, government agencies, research organizations, foreign embassies, tourist boards, and other groups arranged by subjects. The arrangement and indexes provide access to all this information by subject, agency, author, and the like. The disc version is complicated to use (although a manual is supplied with the set). Some valuable tips on collection development can be garnered by browsing this work, particularly through the print version.

REFERENCE BOOKS

Y; A

563. **Guide to Reference Books**. 11th ed. By Robert Balay. American Library Association, 1996. 2,020p. $247.50. 0-8389-0669-9.

Although this guide is far too expensive and specialized for young adult collections, librarians should be aware of its existence and its importance in reference work. It is a guide to research works in all phases of knowledge, a selection guide for reference collections, and a useful tool for collection evaluation and weeding. The 16,000 entries are arranged first by broad subject areas, with many subdivisions by subcategory, and then by type of reference works and country of origin. A number of foreign titles are included. Each title has extensive bibliographic information and an annotation. Coverage ends with titles published early in 1995. There are author and subject indexes. A CD-ROM version is also available. Large public libraries and all academic libraries will want to have access to this basic reference source. For smaller libraries and schools, such titles as *Reference Sources for Small and Medium-Sized Libraries*, *Guide to Reference Books for School Media Centers*, and *Reference Books for Children* will be more valuable.

REFERENCE BOOKS

Y; A

564. **Guide to the Use of Libraries and Information Sources**. 7th ed. By Jean Key Gates. McGraw-Hill, 1994. 320p. $26.16 pap. 0-07-023000-5.

This basic guide to using libraries for the beginning researcher has been a mainstay in collections for many years. The first two sections give an introduction to libraries, their history, and how their collections are organized (DDC and LC). General reference sources like dictionaries and encyclopedias are introduced and annotated in the third section, followed by similar coverage for basic research sources in the sciences, social sciences, and humanities. Although primarily of use to students and patrons, the listings of resources can serve as a checklist for reference collection building in public and college libraries and in larger high school libraries with strong academic programs.

REFERENCE BOOKS

Y; A

565. **The Humanities: A Selective Guide to Information Sources**. 4th ed. By Ron Blazek and Elizabeth Aversa. Libraries Unlimited, 1994. 504p. (Library and Information Science Text Series). $42. pap. 0-56308-168-7.

The humanities are defined liberally in this bibliographic guide to include literature and language, the visual arts, applied and decorative arts, the performing arts, philosophy, religion, mythology, and folklore (no history). As in previous editions, each discipline has two-chapter coverage. The first chapter is an introduction to the subject, its subdivisions, a rundown on how its information is organized and used, details on computer use in the discipline, and the major organizations in the field. The second chapter consists of listings of principal information sources classified by types of material. Annotations are included for each work, many of them making comparisons with similar works. The choices are well made and cover each of the fields admirably. A total of 1,230 main titles are included. There are author, title, and subject indexes. This work is used as a library school text and also has value in public libraries for reference and collection development. Some high schools with advanced humanities programs might also find it of value.

HUMANITIES; REFERENCE BOOKS

Y; A*

566. **Introduction to Reference Work. Volume 1: Basic Information Sources**. 7th ed. By William Katz. McGraw-Hill, 1996. 512p. $30.25. 0-07-034227-6.

In addition to introducing the scope and nature of reference work in libraries, this volume introduces basic reference sources in a variety of formats. Most of the chapters deal with individual types of materials such as dictionaries, encyclopedias, indexes and abstracts, biographical dictionaries, and selected subject sources. This is an excellent beginning place for librarian-trainees to refresh their knowledge of basic sources. It can also be used as a guide to collection evaluation and a blueprint for future purchases in the reference section of public and high school libraries. A great deal of interesting background information is given on each type of reference book that also adds a new dimension to evaluating and using these materials.   *REFERENCE BOOKS*

Y; A

567.   The New, Completely Revised, Greatly Expanded, Madam Audrey's Mostly Cheap, All Good, Useful List of Books for Speedy Reference. 5th ed. By Audrey Lewis. White Pine Library Cooperative (1840 N. Michigan, Ste. 114, Saginaw, MI 48602), 1992. 83p. $10 pap.

The title says it all! Lewis has compiled about 500 relatively inexpensive titles organized in "loose Dewey arrangement." All entries are briefly and informally annotated. The emphasis throughout has been on securing the cheapest useful reference source when alternatives are available. As expected, the list is heavy on paperbound volumes. This popularly written, delightful short volume has a place in most public libraries, particularly small rural ones with limited funds.   *REFERENCE BOOKS*

Y; A

568.   The New York Public Library Book of How and Where to Look It Up. Ed. by Sherwood Harris. Macmillan, 1994. 400p. $14. 0-671-89264-9.

This convenient guide was designed for the lay researcher. The major divisions include reference books, government sources, picture sources, special collections, and electronic databases. These sources are arranged under very broad subject areas such as education, health, and ecology. There is very little that would be new here for most medium-size and large libraries; however, the list of more than 800 annotated databases carried by such vendors as DIALOG, BRS, and the like might be of interest. Also, the reference book chapter may prove useful to the high school or small public library as an evaluation and collection development guide.   *REFERENCE BOOKS; DATABASES*

Y; A

569.   Recommended Reference Books in Paperback. 2nd ed. By Andrew L. March. Libraries Unlimited, 1992. 263p. OP. 1-56308-067-2.

The nearly 900 in-print paperback reference books chosen for this edition have been selected on the basis of quality, availability, and economy. A variety of bibliographies, dictionaries, guides, and directories are included. The three dozen or more subject areas represented should appeal to a wide audience; they include botany, business and economics, ethnic studies, mythology, sports/recreation, and zoology. Each entry contains full bibliographic information and a brief descriptive and evaluative annotation. Hundreds of unannotated but recommended titles are also included. Use *Recommended Reference Books 98* (entry 196) in place of this out-of-print source.

                    REFERENCE BOOKS; PAPERBACK BOOKS

Y*; A*

570.   Reference and Information Services: An Introduction. 2nd ed. Ed. by Richard E. Bopp and Linda C. Smith. Libraries Unlimited, 1995. 626p. $47.50; $35.00 pap. 1-56308-130-X; 1-56308-129-6 pap.

This updated and revised text is designed for a basic course in information services and sources (reference). Part 1 deals with the essential principles and procedures of reference services in a variety of library settings. Part 2 covers selecting and evaluating reference sources in the process of building (and using) a basic collection of reference materials. A number of titles are described under each chapter dealing with specific types of reference and information sources, including electronic sources and reference services for special groups. This text is similar in purpose and coverage to Katz's *Introduction to Reference Work. Volume 1: Basic Information Sources*. Both are recommended for collection development in all school media centers and public libraries.   *REFERENCE BOOKS*

Y*; A*

571. **Reference Books Bulletin 1994–1995**. Ed. by Sandy Whiteley. American Library Association, 1996. 180p. $26. 0-8389-7816-9.

The annual compilation of RBB has been available for almost a quarter of a century and has become a basic selection guide for reference books for many libraries. This cumulation contains almost 500 reviews and omnibus reviews that were originally published in the "Reference Books Bulletin" section of *Booklist*. The quality of the reviewing is unquestionable. The advantage of this work is that it pulls together a year's worth of reviews in one convenient place. Entries are arranged alphabetically under major subject classes (e.g., literature, language, science, medicine, history). Subject, type of material, and title indexes are provided. Earlier annual compilations from 1988–1989 are still available at $25 each. Libraries Unlimited publishes a similar work: *Recommended Reference Books for Small and Medium-Sized Libraries and Media Centers*. While there may be some overlapping, many libraries would consider both guides to develop their reference collections. This guide is highly recommended for all libraries. *REFERENCE BOOKS*

Y; A

572. **Thematic Atlases for Public, Academic, and High School Libraries**. By Diane K. Podell. Scarecrow, 1994. 176p. $27.50. 0-8108-2866-9.

Based on a survey of the atlas holdings of 26 libraries and a thorough bibliographic search, Podell selected 100 atlases for inclusion in this bibliography (several other evaluative bibliographies of atlases are extremely out of date). All of the atlases chosen for inclusion are in English and meant to be used by the nonspecialist; most were published after 1985. Following a general overview of atlas collection organization and management, the reviews of the atlases are arranged alphabetically by title. Each detailed entry (many are two pages in length) contains complete bibliographic information and information on number and types of maps, illustrations, bibliographies, timelines, and indexes. The scope and purpose of the atlas and the table of contents are also included. To complete this useful tool are a glossary, bibliography, and name-title indexes. This much-needed selection/reference tool is recommended for all secondary school, public, and academic libraries as an aid in collection development. *ATLASES*

Science and Mathematics

General and Miscellaneous

Y; A

573. **Building a Popular Science Library Collection for High School to Adult Learners**. By Gregg Sapp. Greenwood, 1995. 329p. $45. 0-313-28936-0.

Sapp, a librarian at the University of Miami, examines popular science materials that he believes would be of interest to the nonscience-oriented student. Nearly 2,500 significant and well-written nonfiction science titles, most published since 1990 and written by well-known authors such as Isaac Asimov, Carl Sagan, and Annie Dillard, were selected for this excellent bibliography. The titles represent all fields of modern science and include books, periodicals, audiovisual materials, and CD-ROMs. The first part of the work presents an overview of science and includes such topics as scientific literacy, history of science, communication, and evaluation of popular science resources. The second and by far the largest part of the book includes the bibliography and is arranged by chapters of major science disciplines. The materials are listed under each topic; books are given the most emphasis. Each book title contains bibliographic data and a descriptive and evaluative note; however, the periodicals, AV materials, and CD-ROMs simply give full bibliographic data necessary for acquisition but little evaluative information. The index lists recommendations by title, author, and subject for quick reference. Hurt's *Information Sources in Science and Technology* would be an excellent complement to this bibliography; it lists more titles and is aimed at a more science-sophisticated and -motivated audience. Both titles are highly recommended for all public and secondary school libraries as an aid in reader's advisory as well as for collection evaluation and development. *SCIENCE*

Y; A

574. Dinosaurs: A Guide to Research. By Bruce Edward Fleury. Garland, 1992. 468p. $73. 0-8240-5344-3.

This guide to literature pertaining to dinosaurs is aimed at students in undergraduate and advanced high school courses. Each entry is annotated. The book begins with a chapter on 78 general and introductory works, followed by chapters on specific topics like extinction. The number of citations totals almost 1,200. This bibliography will be of use in college collections and large high schools with strong science programs. *DINOSAURS*

Y: A

575. Information Sources in Science and Technology. 3rd ed. By C. D. Hurt. Libraries Unlimited, 1998. (Library Science Text Series). In press. 1-56308-528-3; 1-56308-531-8 pap.

This text, formerly edited by Robert Malinowsky, begins with a chapter that defines science and technology and their areas of study. The body of the work is a series of chapters on such areas as astronomy, general biology, botany and agriculture, chemistry, geosciences, physics, mathematics, zoology, energy and environment, biomedical sciences, and various types of engineering. In each chapter is a subdivision by specialized areas plus a listing of informational sources by type. Each source is critically annotated. There is an emphasis on in-print titles and online and software sources. More than 2,000 reference sources are included. There are author/title and subject indexes. This valuable literature guide should be found in academic and public libraries and in high schools with advanced science programs. *TECHNOLOGY; SCIENCE*

Y*

576. Mathematics Books: Recommendations for High School and Public Libraries. Ed. by Lynn Arthur Steen. National Council of Teachers of Mathematics, 1992. 40p. $8.50. 0-88385-455-4.

Designed for secondary school media centers and mathematics departments, this handy and inexpensive list of trade books on mathematics provides enrichment and extensions beyond the commonly used textbook. The items are arranged by type of book and specific subject areas, such as reference, history, recreational mathematics, calculus, discrete mathematics, number theory, algebra and logic, geometry, and topology. A list of periodicals is appended. A companion list that lists works on the elementary school level and is still useful for secondary schools is Thiessen and Matthias's *The Wonderful World of Mathematics* by the same publisher. Both volumes are highly recommended for use by students and teachers, and for librarians for collection development in an area that is generally ignored. *MATHEMATICS*

Y; A

577. The Millennium Whole Earth Catalog: Access to Tools and Ideas for the Twenty-First Century. Ed. by Howard Reingold. HarperSanFrancisco, 1994. 381p. $50; $30 pap. 0-06-251141-5; 0-05-251059-2 pap.

The concept of this kind of catalog dates back to the countercultural movements of the sixties, when the original *Whole Earth Catalog* appeared, followed by about a half dozen similar works offering down-to-earth information on the environment, ecology, and the like. The current volume contains information related to the computer and to virtual reality. Included are evaluations of books, magazines, tools, software, video and audiotapes, organizations, services, and wild ideas. The general arrangement is by domain, which includes such topics as biodiversity, community health, sex, politics, and learning. Many book titles are listed within each section. Entries include lengthy annotations, excerpts, and a picture. An index is included; however, the format of the volume lends itself to browsing. A similar work that might serve as a companion volume is Richard Kadrey's *Covert Culture Sourcebook* (St. Martin's Press, 1993. $12.95 pap. 0-312-09776-X). *The Millennium* would appeal to young adults and be an interesting guide for the selection of offbeat and hard-to-find materials. Recommended for public and secondary school libraries. *SUBCULTURES*

Y; A

578.   **The Origin and Evolution of Life on Earth: An Annotated Bibliography**. By David W. Hollar. Salem Press, 1992. 235p. $40. 0-89356-683-7.

Hollar has provided a comprehensive bibliography of more than 800 books on evolution from the 1800s to the present. All of the entries contain full bibliographic data and lengthy descriptive annotations. A detailed table of contents facilitates subject access; an author index is also provided. The work is intended for the general reader as well as students of the subject and is recommended for academic, public, and secondary school libraries.   *EVOLUTION*

Y; A

579.   **Prominent Scientists: An Index to Collective Biographies**. 3rd ed. Ed. by Paul A. Pelletier. Neal-Schuman, 1994. 400p. $49.95. 1-55570-140-0.

More than 12,000 leaders in the field of science are included in this index to 262 collective biographies and other works that include biographical information. All of the works are published in English from 1960 to 1983. Current men and women as well as historical figures are included. The work is divided into two major parts: an alphabetical list of scientists by surname and lists of scientists by more than 100 scientific fields. The list of sources in the front of the volume includes complete bibliographic information. This excellent index is recommended for most secondary school and public libraries.   *SCIENTISTS*

Y; A

580.   **Reference Sources in Science, Engineering, Medicine, and Agriculture**. Ed. by H. Robert Malinowsky. Oryx, 1994. 355p. $39.95. 0-89774-745-3.

Malinowsky, a bibliographer and a noted authority on science and technology literature, has compiled a bibliography of almost 2,500 reference sources in science and related topics, including agriculture and medicine. The annotated bibliography is designed for use by a wide audience, including reference and collection development librarians, students, and researchers in these fields. The work is arranged in nine chapters. Early chapters contain a series of essays presenting an overview of the literature of science. From chapter 5 on, specific subjects are covered such as science, engineering, and technology. These are subdivided into more specific topics and then further subdivided by type of work such as abstracts and handbooks. Most works are in English, but important foreign titles are also included. Annotations for each work are brief, but they also indicate availability of various formats, such as print only, CD-ROM, and online. Also at the end of each subchapter is a list of periodicals in the field, without annotations. Author, title, and detailed subject indexes complete the work. This inexpensive work can serve most high school public and academic libraries as a reference and collection development resource. Libraries with strong science and technology collections may also want to consider another similar and worthwhile guide: Hurt's *Information Sources in Science and Technology* (see entry 575). Smaller libraries will not need both.   *SCIENCE; TECHNOLOGY; REFERENCE BOOKS*

Y; A*

581.   **Science and Technology [year]: A Purchase Guide for Branch and Public Libraries**. Carnegie Library of Pittsburgh, annual. 70p. $12 pap.

This annual annotated listing of outstanding new books in science and technology first appeared in 1960. At present, it consists of approximately 500 titles chosen both for their content and their suitability for the adult general reader. A few reference books and textbooks are included. Books are arranged by subjects according to Library of Congress classification. Annotations are brief but informative. Of particular interest to smaller libraries is a coding system that indicates books for libraries only purchasing 50 books and for those purchasing 100. Author and series indexes are included. This practical list emphasizes topics of current interest and importance. *Library Journal* also has an annual list of the 101 "Best Sci-Tech Books" of the year in the March 1 issue. Some high schools with advanced science programs might find the Carnegie list of value. Inquiries can be made to: Carnegie Library of Pittsburgh, 4400 Forbes Ave., Pittsburgh, PA 15213.   *SCIENCE; TECHNOLOGY*

C

582. **Science and Technology in Fact and Fiction: A Guide to Children's Books**. By DayAnn Kennedy et al. Bowker, 1990. 331p. $36. 0-8352-2708-1.

This bibliography lists more than 350 recommended juvenile titles suitable for children ages 3 through 12. Books are arranged in two principle sections—science and technology—with subdivisions for fiction and nonfiction titles. In each of these sections, books are arranged alphabetically by author. Picture books and easy readers are included in the fiction sections. The selections have been carefully and judiciously made. Each entry contains grade level suitability, full bibliographic citations, and a lengthy annotation that summarizes and evaluates the book's contents and usefulness. A few outstanding out-of-print titles are included. There are indexes by authors, illustrators, titles, subjects, and readability. This work will be useful in elementary schools and children's rooms in public libraries.

SCIENCE; TECHNOLOGY

Environment

Y*; A

583. **Earth Works: An Annotated Bibliography of Recommended Fiction and Nonfiction About Nature and the Environment for Adults and Young Adults**. By Jim Dwyer. Neal-Schuman, 1996. 507p. $39.95 pap. 1-55570-194-9.

Of the 2,601 titles included in this bibliography, two-thirds were published in the 1990s. The scope of the work is broad and includes materials on natural history, specific environments like deserts and forests, problems like waste disposal, environmental action, cultural factors (with an emphasis on Native Americans), philosophical questions, and literary nature writing. Arranged under 59 topics, the entries contain standard bibliographic materials and annotations. Most sections include books specifically for young adults, with grade levels indicated (some as low as fourth grade). Useful for readers' advisement and collection development, this bibliography is recommended for adult and young adult collections. For a younger audience, use *E for Environment*.

ENVIRONMENT; ECOLOGY; NATURE

Y; A

584. **The Environmental Sourcebook**. By Edith Carol Stein. Lyons and Burford, 1992. 264p. $16.95 pap. 1-55821-164-0.

This guidebook lists sources of information on 11 different major issues related to the environment and ecology: population, agriculture, energy, climate and atmosphere, biodiversity, water, oceans, solid wastes, hazardous substances and waste, endangered lands, and development. For each issue there are a general introduction to the problem, a bibliography of selected recent books and reports, an annotated list of periodicals, and directories of important organizations and grant-giving foundations. A comprehensive index is included. Two somewhat similar sources in content are the *Gale Environmental Sourcebook* (Gale, 1992. $75.00. 0-8103-8403-5) and *Your Research Guide to Environmental Organizations* (Smiling Dolphin Press, 1991. $15.95 pap. 1-879072-00-8). However, this work is outstanding in its ease of use and the details it supplies on foundations, periodicals, and organizations. Recommended for public and academic libraries and high schools that need this kind of information.

ENVIRONMENT; POLLUTION; CONSERVATION; ECOLOGY

Y; A

585. **Environmentalist's Bookshelf: A Guide to the Best Books**. By Robert Meredith. G. K. Hall, 1993. 272p. $45. 0-8161-7359-1.

This excellent "guide to the best books . . . on nature and the environment" is based on the recommendations of 200 leaders in the field who answered a questionnaire. The final list of about 500 books selected is divided into three major sections: a core list of the 100 most recommended; a second list of 250 titles that were recommended several times; and the third list of those only mentioned once, but still deemed important. These lists could be interpreted as priority lists for building a collection of environmental materials. Most of the annotations are in the form of selected quotes from the respondents. All entries contain full bibliographic data. Author, title, and subject indexes are provided, and a list of sources for further reference is appended. This bibliography is an excellent aid to collection development for all academic and public libraries and would also be useful in large high schools.

ENVIRONMENT; ECOLOGY

Y; A

586.   **Reading About the Environment: An Introductory Guide**. By Pamela Jansma. Libraries Unlimited, 1993. 252p. $27.50. 0-87287-985-2.

About 800 entries from books and popular magazine articles on important environmental issues as they relate to business, government, and personal decision-making policies are included in this bibliographic guide. Each citation lists full bibliographic data and a brief annotation that discusses the scope, organization, and slant of the work. This up-to-date and easy-to-use bibliography is intended for laypeople, students, and professionals in the field of environmental studies. Recommended for all libraries.   *ENVIRONMENT*

Health

Y; A

587.   **The Harvard Guide to Women's Health**. By Karen J. Carlson et al. Harvard, 1996. 678p. $39.95. 0-674-36768-5.

In 300 alphabetically arranged entries, this volume covers a wide spectrum of topics and issues involving women's health. Topics include mental health, sexual and reproductive health, domestic abuse, sleep disorders, and skin care. After each entry there is an extended bibliography that lists organizations, books, videos, and Internet addresses. There is also an extensive index. Though adult in scope and treatment, this work is simple enough to be read by high school students. The bibliographies can help collection development in this area.   *HEALTH*

Social Sciences

General and Miscellaneous

Y; A*

588.   **The Social Sciences: A Cross-Disciplinary Guide to Selected Sources**. 2nd ed. Ed. by Nancy Herron. Libraries Unlimited, 1996. 323p. (Library Science Text Series). $43; $32 pap. 1-56308-309-4; 1-56308-351-5 pap.

This highly selective bibliography includes entries for more than 1,000 reference sources in the social sciences. After a discussion of multidiscipline materials and the social sciences in general, there are separate chapters on anthropology, business and economics, communications, education, geography, history, law and legal studies, political science, psychology, sociology, and statistics and demographics. Each chapter begins with the structure of the reference literature in the subject, followed by lengthy descriptions of the best, most used resources in the field, including nonprint materials and online databases. High school libraries with advanced placement courses in the social sciences might consider this for purchase.   *SOCIAL SCIENCES; REFERENCE BOOKS*

History and Geography

Y; A

589.   **African Studies Companion: A Resource Guide & Directory**. 2nd ed. By Hans M. Zell. Bowker-Saur, 1997. 192p. $75. 1-873836-41-4.

In this updated and expanded guide to a large range of information sources on Africa, the almost 1,000 entries are arranged into 11 major sections by type of work, including reference works, bibliographies, and serials. Each entry includes a brief annotation and is indexed for fast retrieval. Recommended for all libraries having a special interest in or a growing collection of African materials.

AFRICA

Y; A

590.   **The American Presidents: An Annotated Bibliography**. By Norman S. Cohen. Salem Press, 1989. 202p. $40. (Magill Bibliographies). 0-89356-658-6.

This addition to the Magill Bibliographies is intended for the general reader. It continues the series' long-standing emphasis on quality and scholarship. The more than 750 books include biographies, autobiographies, and studies of the president's place in U.S. history. The works are divided into three sections: bibliographies about the presidents and the presidency, general studies on the presidency, and titles related to the individual presidents. The titles include an annotation of 50 to 100 words each and are arranged alphabetically by author within each section. This bibliography would be particularly useful for secondary school and undergraduate student reports. It is recommended for all libraries serving that audience as well as general readers.   *PRESIDENTS—UNITED STATES*

Y; A

591.   **Guide to Civil War Books**. By Domenica M. Barbuto and Martha Kreisel. American Library Association, 1995. 221p. $32. 0-8389-0672-9.

Although adult and somewhat scholarly in tone, this highly selective bibliography of 320 recent (1974–1994) books on the American Civil War will have value in some senior high school and most public libraries. Titles are organized under 32 subjects (e.g., art and war, battles, commerce and finance, literature and the war, personal narratives, race, slavery). Each entry contains full bibliographic information, a detailed annotation, and review citations. There are author, title, and subject indexes.
                                          UNITED STATES—HISTORY—CIVIL WAR, 1861–1865

Y; A

592.   **The Jewish Holocaust: An Annotated Guide to Books in English**. By Marty Bloomberg. Borgo Press, 1991. 248p. $29.95; $19.95 pap. 0-89370-160-2; 0-89370-260-9 pap.

This useful bibliography lists more than 800 books arranged by subjects that cover such areas as pre-war Jewish civilization, anti-Semitism, the Holocaust, and war-crime trials. All kinds of books are included, from reference sources to first-person accounts, though nothing after 1986 is listed. Each entry has full bibliographic information and a brief annotation. In an appendix, the editor chooses the contents of basic collections for public, academic, and high school libraries. This title will have value in general collections; however, an update would be helpful.   *HOLOCAUST; JEWS*

Y; A

593.   **Sources of Information for Historical Research**. By Thomas P. Slavens. Neal-Schuman, 1994. 577p. $45. 0-55570-093-4.

The items in this extensive bibliography are arranged by geography (continent and country), genre, and archival collections. Each is annotated. Imprints are chiefly in English and arranged by LC number. There are author, title, and subject indexes. This work would be of use in high schools with advanced programs in history and geography.   *HISTORY; GEOGRAPHY; REFERENCE*

Y

594.   **U.S. Government: A Resource Book for Secondary Schools**. By Mary Jane Turner and Sara Lake. ABC-Clio, 1989. 317p. $39. 0-87436-535-X.

This handy quick-reference book is loaded with excellent information resources on the U.S. government. For example, the beginning chapters include the purposes and principles of the U.S. government, the Constitution, political parties, a chronology of important documents, members of Congress, all the presidents, and more. The last third of the book contains a bibliography of reference works (including printed sources and online databases) related to the U.S. government and a list of classroom materials (including print, audio, video, and computer sources). Each entry gives complete bibliographic information and a brief annotation. A detailed index of subjects, titles, and authors is provided. Much of what is available here can be found in other readily accessible reference sources; however, the bibliographies are useful to students and teachers and can serve as a librarian's acquisition guide.
                                          U.S. POLITICS AND GOVERNMENT

Y

595.   **U.S. History: A Resource Book for Secondary Schools**. By James R. Giese and Laurel R. Singleton. ABC-Clio, 1989. 2 vols. Vol. 1, 1450–1865; vol. 2, 1865–Present. (Social Studies Resources for Secondary Schools). $39.00/vol. $66.50/set. 0-87436-525-2.

The two volumes cited above are designed to stand alone. While there is some duplication in the introductory pages, they include so much specifically suited to each volume's inclusive dates that both are necessary. They provide annotated listings of reference works on U.S. history, including atlases, dictionaries and encyclopedias, biographical sources, almanacs, periodicals, and online databases. AV materials, computer software, print material, and textbooks are listed by format with detailed descriptive annotations. This set is recommended for all secondary school library media centers and other libraries serving secondary school teachers and students.   *UNITED STATES HISTORY*

Y; A*

596.   **The Vietnam War: Handbook of the Literature and Research**. Ed. by James S. Olson. Greenwood, 1993. 500p. $65. 0-313-27422-3.

Fourteen contributors under the editorial leadership of Olson compiled this comprehensive review of the literature of the Vietnam War. It covers many facets of the conflict, including military, political, cultural, and social aspects. A large array of both popular and scholarly materials are included, such as nonfiction and fiction books, films and videos, and even comic books. Much of the material was published as recently as 1992. This volume is an excellent reference, research, and collection development handbook/guide that deserves to be in all academic and public libraries and in many senior high school libraries.   *VIETNAM WAR*

Y; A

597.   **Vietnam War Literature: An Annotated Bibliography of Imaginative Works About Americans Fighting in Vietnam**. 3rd ed. By John Newman. Scarecrow, 1996. 680p. $68. 0-8108-3184-8.

This updated and greatly expanded edition contains about 600 additional entries for a total of almost 1,400 entries published from 1964 to 1995. A chapter is devoted to each category of "imaginative" work, such as novels, short stories, poetry, drama, and miscellaneous. Entries are arranged chronologically under each category by publication date. Each entry includes complete bibliographical information and a descriptive annotation that is generally a plot summary. Author and title indexes are provided. This comprehensive bibliography of imaginative literature is recommended for most academic and many public and senior high school libraries for reference as well as for collection building.
                               VIETNAM WAR—FICTION

Social Issues

Y; A

598.   **Adolescent Pregnancy and Parenthood: An Annotated Guide**. By Ann Creighton-Zollar. Garland, 1990. 268p. (Reference Books on Family Issues, vol. 16). $46. 0-8240-4295-6.

This annotated guide to the serious problem of teenage pregnancy was sorely needed by social workers and people in health, education, and counseling, as well as students in these fields. The guide is arranged by broad topics relating to many aspects of the problem (e.g., adolescent sexuality, contraception, sex education, risk factors), as well as social, medical, and legal concerns. The entries from journals and books are well annotated and current. This title will be an important addition to all libraries serving interested professionals and students.
                               PREGNANCY, ADOLESCENT; PARENTS, ADOLESCENT; ADOLESCENCE

Y; A

599.   **American Homelessness: A Reference Handbook**. 2nd ed. By Mary Ellen Hombs. ABC-Clio, 1994. 272p. (Contemporary World Issues). $39.50. 0-87436-725-5.

This relatively brief handbook gives a great deal of background information on the problem of homelessness in America today, including a chronology of major events and a biographical sketch of individuals making major contributions in this area. Also included are documents, organizations, and important print and nonprint reference sources. The reference materials are listed under specific categories (e.g., children, alcohol, AIDS). Each entry provides adequate information for ordering. This handbook is recommended as a reference and selection guide to an important, timely topic for secondary school and public libraries. *HOMELESS PEOPLE*

Y*
600.   **The Best Years of Their Lives: A Resource Guide for Teenagers in Crisis**. 2nd ed. By Stephanie Zvirin. American Library Association, 1995. 210p. $25 pap. 0-8389-0686-9.

This excellent updated guide was compiled by the *Booklist* associate editor of "Books for Youth." The purpose is to give adolescents ages 10–18 a better understanding of what growing up in a rapidly changing world is all about. Today's youth are faced with problems and concerns such as drugs, AIDS, suicide, pregnancy, and abuse. This bibliography evaluates and analyzes about 400 nonfiction self-help titles, a highly selective number of fiction books, and 86 videos that deal with these subjects. All of the titles are relatively recent and in-print and will undoubtedly be of interest to today's teens. The work is organized by topic; each entry contains full bibliographic data and descriptive and evaluative information. This timely bibliography is highly recommended as both a reading guidance and selection aid for all school and public libraries serving today's adolescents. *ADOLESCENCE; BIBLIOTHERAPY*

Y; A
601.   **Contemporary Social Issues: A Bibliographic Series**. Reference and Research Services, 1986– . 4 issues/yr. 60p./issue. $15/issue ($55 for an annual subscription).

Each of the bibliographies in this series is devoted to a single social issue and contains about 500 citations to books, journal articles from both scholarly and popular works, government documents, and pamphlets. Each booklet covers various authoritative points of view on the subject and contains a separate list of bibliographies and directories, plus a list of organizations. There are now about 50 titles available. The four bibliographies released in 1996 were *Affirmative Action*, *Asian Americans*, *NAFTA and GATT*, and *Feminism Worldwide*. Some other titles currently available include *Investment and Social Responsibility* (1986), *Domestic Violence* (1986), *Current Central American–U.S. Relations* (1987), *The Feminization of Poverty* (1987), *Pornography and Censorship* (1987), *Biotechnology and Society* (1987), *Reproductive Rights* (1988), *AIDS: Political International Aspects* (1988), *Toxic Waste* (1988), *The Homeless in America* (1988), *International Debt and the Third World* (1989), *Eating Disorders* (1989), *Substance Abuse I: Drug Abuse* (1989), *Substance Abuse II: Alcohol Abuse* (1990), *The Greenhouse Effect* (1990), *Rape* (1990), *Food Pollution* (1990), *Animal Rights* (1991), *Environmental Issues in the Third World* (1991), *The Elderly in America* (1991), *The Feminist Movement* (1991), *Violence Against Women* (1992), *African Americans: Social and Economic Conditions* (1992), *The Environment I: Clean Air* (1992), *The African American Woman* (1993), *Latinos in the United States* (1994), *Violence in American Society* (1994), *Recent Immigration from Latin America* (1995), *Women in the United States: Economic Conditions* (1995), and *Violent Children* (1995). These bibliographies are timely, authoritative sources on current topics and will be of use in medium-size and large public libraries and some high schools. For more information write: Reference and Research Services, 511 Lincoln St., Santa Cruz, CA 95060. *SOCIAL PROBLEMS*

Y; A
602.   **Contemporary World Issues**. ABC-Clio, 1989– . $39.50/vol.

This extensive series contains separate volumes on timely world topics. Each is intended to provide a convenient one-stop reference that supplies a variety of information about its subject. Included in each volume are an introduction essay on the subject; a historical and chronological overview; biographies of prominent people; a directory of agencies and organizations; annotated surveys of important books, magazines, audiovisual products, and documents on the subject; and sources of information in databases and electronic bulletin boards. Some titles in this series are: *American Homelessness* (1990) by Mary Ellen Hombs; *World Hunger* (1991) by Patricia L. Kutzner; *Health Care Crisis in America* (1991) by Linda Brubaker Ropes; *Abortion* (1991) by Mary Costa; *Space Exploration* (1991) by Mrinal Bali; *Environmental Hazards: Toxic Waste and Hazardous Material* (1991) and *Environmental Hazards: Radioactive Material and Wastes* (1991) by E. Willard Miller and Ruby M. Miller; *Human Rights* (1990) by Lucille Whale; *Public Schooling in America* (1991) by Richard D. Van Scotter; *Nuclear Energy Policy*

(1990) by Earl R. Kruschke and Byron M. Jackson; *Adult Literacy/Illiteracy in the United States* (1989) by Mary Costa; *Child Care* (1992) by Diane Lindsey Reeves; *Oceans* (1992) by Martha Gorman; *The Global Economy* (1992) by James A. Lehman; *AIDS Crisis in America* (1992) by Mary Ellen Hombs; *Drug Abuse in Society* (1993) by Geraldine Woods; *American Homelessness* (1994) by Mary Ellen Hombs; *Violent Children* (1995) and *Childhood Sexual Abuse* (1995) by Karen L. Kinnear; *The Religious Right* (1995) by Glenn H. Utter and John W. Storey; *Violence and the Media* (1996) by David E. Newton; *Endangered Species* (1996) by Clifford J. Sherry; *Abortion* (1996) by Mary Costa; and *Gangs* (1996) by Karen L. Kinnear. Several of these titles have their own entries in this guide. These volumes have proven valuable in public and high school libraries. Another series of bibliographies that treats environmental problems is Vance Bibliographies (Box 229, Monticello, IL 61856). Also use *The Environment: Books by Small Presses* (Small Press Center, 1990. $5 pap. 0-9622769-2-8) available from the Small Press Center at 20 W. 44 St., New York, NY 10036.

SOCIAL PROBLEMS; ENVIRONMENT; ECOLOGY

Y; A

603.   **Focus on Families: A Reference Handbook**. By Ruth J. Cline. ABC-Clio, 1990. 233p. (Teenage Perspectives). $39. 0-87436-508-2.

Current information on a variety of family issues for teenagers and adults is given in this handbook. The work is divided into nine chapters covering such topics as family, stepfamilies, and divorce. Each chapter contains an introduction to the topic, with definitions and explanations of terms, followed by an annotated bibliography of nonfiction, fiction, and nonprint materials suitable for young adults. Most chapters also have listings of important organizations and hotlines. There is an author, title, and subject index. This work will be useful in high school and public libraries. For other titles, see entry under *Teenage Perspectives Reference Series*.

DIVORCE; FAMILY LIFE

Y; A

604.   **Focus on Teens in Trouble: A Reference Handbook**. By Daryl Sander. ABC-Clio, 1991. 225p. (Teenage Perspectives). $39. 0-87436-207-5.

Some of the teenage problems dealt with in this handbook are gangs, violence, substance abuse, runaways, and the juvenile justice system. Each chapter covers a different problem and, like other volumes in the series, contains an introduction to the topic with background information, definitions of terms, and important statistics. This introduction is followed by annotated lists of fiction, nonfiction, and nonprint sources for further study. All are suitable for young adults. There is a single index for authors, titles, and subjects. This book is a useful addition to young adult collections in schools and public libraries. For other titles in this series, see the entry under *Teenage Perspectives Reference Series*.

ADOLESCENCE

Y; A

605.   **The Information Please Women's Sourcebook**. By Lisa DiMona and Constance Herndon. Houghton Mifflin, 1994. 568p. $13.95. 0-395-70067-1.

Intended as an annual publication, this is a valuable source of information on issues important to women today. It is divided into 12 major sections on such topics as education, work, child care, health, and activism. Each section is subdivided and contains almanac-like information, important speeches, graphs, statistics, charts, a number of background bibliographies, and lists of sources used. Many of these sources will be useful in collection development. After several appendixes (e.g., important legal decisions, resources used to compile the book), there are indexes by organization and subject.

WOMEN STUDIES

Y; A

606.   **Intellectual Freedom: A Reference Handbook**. By John B. Harer. ABC-Clio, 1992. 328p. $39.50. 0-87436-669-0.

After introductory sections that give an overview on intellectual freedom, the First Amendment, citizen rights, censorship, and current issues, the author outlines important court cases and provides biographies of people involved in intellectual freedom issues. Of particular use to librarians are the listings that follow. After a directory of organizations that includes a mention of their publications, there are annotated bibliographies of print materials, including such reference works as indexes, bibliographies, yearbooks, directories. Following are important monographs and periodicals. The nonprint section lists films, videos, filmstrips, online databases, CD-ROMs, educational software, and games. The book has great overall value, and these bibliographies will be particularly useful in public and academic libraries as well as high schools that need material on this subject.

INTELLECTUAL FREEDOM; CENSORSHIP

Y; A

607.   **Millennialism: An International Bibliography**. By Ted Daniels. Garland, 1992. 657p. $90. 0-8240-7102-6.

This interesting bibliography deals with millennialism, a philosophy that says the world will end and be replaced with a heaven (or a hell for the evil). Daniels has compiled a bibliography on the subject culled from many disciplines, including sociology, religion, and psychology. The work is divided into two major parts. Part 1 lists almost 800 fully annotated entries; part 2 contains almost 3,000 numbered items without annotations. The entries are alphabetical by title, with an author and subject index for the first part and an author and group subject index for the second part. Despite some confusing organization of the material, the amount of information collected here is noteworthy. The volume is recommended for those libraries with a particular interest in this field. *MILLENNIUM*

Y; A

608.   **Violent Children: A Reference Handbook**. By Karen L. Kinnear. ABC-Clio, 1995. 251p. (Contemporary World Issues). $39.50. 0-87436-786-7.

Crimes committed by teens and even younger children are reported in the news almost daily. In several beginning chapters, this handbook presents an overview of the problem, highlighting concerns and issues relating to prevention and treatment. However, the most useful chapters are the listings of organizations concerned with the subject and the extensive bibliographic lists of print and nonprint resources; these deal with crimes committed by youth generally as well as violent crimes. Sources that help youth in the resolution of conflict are especially useful. A title index of these sources complete the work, which is an important addition to the series. Recommended as a reference and as a selection aid for all secondary school and public libraries. *ADOLESCENCE; CHILDREN; CRIMINAL JUSTICE*

Sports, Hobbies, and Recreation

Y; A

609.   **Baseball: A Comprehensive Bibliography**. Comp. by Myron J. Smith, Jr. McFarland, 1986. 915p. $55. 0-89950-222-9.

Along with its supplement (see next entry), this is the most exhaustive bibliography on baseball currently in print. More than 21,000 entries for books and articles in 365 journals are arranged by subject categories that include every imaginable aspect of the subject, such as the World Series, baseball cards, minor leagues, individual teams, players, and others involved with this "All-American pastime." There are also author and title indexes. Despite the fact that it may have to be updated periodically, this ambitious work will serve as the basic bibliography on baseball for years to come. Recommended for most libraries. *BASEBALL*

Y; A

610.   **Baseball: A Comprehensive Bibliography. Supplement 1 (1985–May 1992)**. Comp. by Myron J. Smith, Jr. McFarland, 1993. 437p. $68.50. 0-89950-799-9.

Intended for both the baseball scholar and those just interested as fans, this bibliography of more than 8,000 sources about baseball updates the author's earlier work, which was published in 1986. However, this supplement can be used independently. Subject and author indexes are included. See the previous entry for complete details. *BASEBALL*

Y; A

611.   **Hobbyist Sourcebook**. 2nd ed. By Denise M. Allard. Gale, 1995. 459p. $55. 0-8103-7614-8.

This unique reference work collects a variety of useful information about 50 popular hobbies, including amateur radio operation, antique dolls, crafts, painting, sports card collecting, and woodworking. After an introduction to each hobby, there are 15 subcategories of information that cover such things as associations, learning opportunities, catalogs and sources of supplies, basic guides and reference books, periodicals and magazines, juvenile literature, nonprint materials, conventions, special libraries, databases, and other information sources. Most entries have brief annotations. There is an extensive index. This is a useful reference book as well as one that can be used to evaluate and develop collections in high school and public libraries.   *HOBBIES; HANDICRAFTS*

V

SOURCES FOR PROFESSIONALS

A

612.   **AV Market Place, 1995: The Complete Business Directory of Audio, Audio Visual, Computer Systems, Film, Video, Programming, with Industry Yellow Pages**. Bowker, 1995. 1,500p. $144.95 pap. 0-8352-3579-3.

As the subtitle states, this work is intended to be the complete directory of the audiovisual/computer field. It has achieved its stated purpose beyond a doubt and is an important aid to purchasing materials and equipment in most libraries. Also pertinent to collection building are the excellent annotated lists of periodicals and reference books related to the audiovisual field. This is a recommended guide for most libraries, including school district-wide systems building a professional collection that answers questions involving who, what, when, and where in the AV industry.   *AUDIOVISUAL MATERIALS*

A

613.   **Complete Directory for People with Disabilities**. 1996–97 ed. Ed. by Leslie Mackenzie and Amy Lignor. Grey House, 1996. 650p. $145. 0-939300-73-7.

This directory is arranged in several sections that cover associations and organizations involved with the disabled, construction considerations, government agencies, independent living centers, the law, support groups and hot lines, veterans' topics, and programs. Subdivisions in the latter section deal with the arts, camps, education, exchange programs, foundations, music, sports, travel, vocations, and consultants. The two sections of most interest to librarians are "Media for the Disabled," which lists books, conferences, newsletters, magazines, videos, and films, and "Products for the Disabled," which includes computers, special devices, clothing, and toys and games. There are indexes by name, state, and specific needs or disabilities. This title will be of value in public libraries serving a substantial population of disabled people or in large professional collections in education.   *DISABILITIES*

A

614.   **A Consumer's Guide to Tests in Print**. 2nd ed. By Donald D. Hammill et al. Pro-Ed, 1992. 202p. $29. 0-89079-548-7.

More than 250 tests intended for use with K–12 students are reviewed by using a standardized evaluation form that makes the potential user's task less difficult. Group tests such as the SAT are not included; rather, there is "a focus on tests that are individually administered for diagnostic, screening, or identification purposes." The norm-referenced tests evaluated are given an A to F rating: highly recommended to not recommended. The tests are cited under 86 content areas and classified under four general types: achievement, aptitude, effect, and general intelligence. This guide is recommended for all academic libraries with education and psychology departments, as well as school and public libraries that need material on testing.   *EDUCATIONAL TESTS AND MEASUREMENTS*

A

615.   **Core List of Books and Journals in Education**. By Nancy Patricia O'Brian and Emily Fabiano. Oryx, 1991. 125p. $39.95. 0-89774-559-0.

This highly selective guide to the current literature in the field of education contains about 1,000 entries for books and journals. The book section is organized into 18 subject areas like special education and measurement. For each title, bibliographic information and a detailed evaluative annotation are given. There are also a list of basic periodicals and author, title, and subject indexes. This book is recommended for large public libraries and others needing a guide to collection development in education. *EDUCATION; PERIODICALS*

A

616. Directory of National Information on Sources on Disabilities. 6th ed. National Rehabilitation Information Center, 1995. 2 vols. $15 pap.

As well as descriptions of 700 organizations representing more than 70 types of disabilities, this directory includes material on more than 100 resource directories and 42 databases. Each entry includes information on disabilities served, users served, and aims and programs, and a section called "Information Services." The latter lists publications, film and video resources, and databases. There are several indexes, including an extensive one that covers all types of disabilities. Professional collections will find this excellent directory useful in locating all sorts of resources involving disabilities. The Center's address is 8455 Colesville Rd., Silver Spring, MD 20910-3319. See also *Complete Directory for People with Disabilities*. *DISABILITIES*

A*

617. Education: A Guide to Reference and Information Sources. By Lois Buttlar. Libraries Unlimited, 1989. 258p. (Reference Sources in the Social Sciences Series, 2). OP. 0-87287-619-5.

Both general and special reference sources are listed in this bibliography, which includes almost 900 selected titles on education and related fields from the elementary school through college levels. The contents are arranged in 20 chapters covering such subjects as educational administration, career and vocational education, art education, bilingual and multicultural education, women's studies, special education, and higher education. Each chapter contains critically annotated entries for major guides to the literature, bibliographies, indexes, abstracts, online databases, and other reference sources. Fifty major periodical titles are listed. Most of the sources in the book date from 1980 through 1988.

There is a comprehensive index. This volume will be of value in school professional collections and in some public and academic libraries. *EDUCATION; REFERENCE BOOKS*

A

618. Educational Media and Technology Yearbook, 1998. Volume 23. By Robert M. Branch and Mary A. Fitzgerald. Libraries Unlimited, 1998. 308p. $65. 1-56308-591-7.

This yearbook is intended to give educators involved with educational technology up-to-date information on trends, research, and issues in the field. There are articles by specialists in educational media and technology, plus lists of media-related organizations in Canada and the United States and educational programs in colleges and universities. For collection development, there is a section called "Mediagraphy," a comprehensive, annotated guide to reference sources, books, articles, and ERIC documents arranged by subjects. There are directories of publishers, distributors, and producers plus a general index. Back issues are also available from the publishers. This yearbook will be of value in large district-wide media collections and perhaps in some academic and large public libraries. *EDUCATION; EDUCATIONAL TECHNOLOGY; INSTRUCTIONAL MATERIALS*

A*

619. The Educator's Desk Reference: A Sourcebook of Educational Information and Research By Melvyn N. Freed et al. American Council on Education/Macmillan, 1989. 536p. $49.95. 0-02-910740-7.

This handbook, intended for educational professionals (particularly at the administrative level), is a combination of research manual, directory, and bibliography. There are six major sections. The first is useful for collection development and consists of an annotated list of important reference sources in education arranged by such types as encyclopedias, bibliographies, and statistical digests. There are also directories of leading publishers of books, journals, and software arranged by field; profiles of important standardized tests; lists of professional organizations; and a great deal of material for researchers and authors, including information on various types of research design and on where to submit manuscripts. Though in need of updating, this is a fine basic volume for professional collections in schools and colleges. It will also be useful in any collection serving educators. *EDUCATION; REFERENCE BOOKS*

A

620. Encyclopedia of Education Information: For Elementary and Secondary School Professionals. Ed. by Leslie Mackenzie. Grey House, 1994. 563p. $125 pap. 0-939300-59-1.

Though expensive, this comprehensive one-volume source contains information otherwise scattered throughout a number of other books. The 5,387 resources are divided into these categories: associations, organizations and government agencies, conference and trade shows, databases, directories and centers, employment resources, grants and fundraising, publications, education publications, and suppliers. Each entry has a short annotation. Librarians building a professional collection will find many of the sections helpful, including a subdivision of "Publications" that lists materials for professional development. *EDUCATION*

A

621. Encyclopedia of Educational Research. 6th ed. Ed. by Marvin C. Alkin. Macmillan, 1992. 4 vols. $330. 0-02-900431-4.

This massive work is an important contribution to education literature. In volume 1, all of the entries are grouped under large subjects such as curriculum and organizational structure, but in the body of the work these entries are arranged alphabetically. Each subject entry contains a summary of pertinent research in the area plus an extensive bibliography listing materials for each of these studies. There are many cross-references and comprehensive indexes. An interesting section called "Doing Library Research in Education" has an annotated listing of the standard basic reference works in education both in print and nonprint formats. The bibliographies in the body of the work and this special research section contain valuable items for collection development. Recommended for public and education libraries. *EDUCATION*

A

622. The Equipment Directory of Audio-Visual, Computer, and Video Products. 1997–98 ed. International Communications Industries Association, 1997. $89. 0-935144-21-3.

The products of more than 400 manufacturers are listed and pictured in this catalog that contains information on about 3,000 pieces of equipment, technological hardware, and furniture. There are also lists of the members of the association plus addresses and a glossary of terms. The directory can be ordered directly from the publishers for $89, plus $5 for postage. The address is: International Communications Industries Association, Box 100, Shawnee Mission, KS 66201. *LIBRARY FURNITURE AND EQUIPMENT; COMPUTERS*

A

623. ERIC (Educational Resources Information Center) Database. U. S. Department of Education, 1966– . Various formats and publications.

The ERIC database, begun in 1966, now has close to a million citations. It is kept up-to-date in two formats. The print version is *Current Index to Journals in Education* or CIJE (which indexes more than 700 periodicals and continuations), and the machine-readable format is *Resources in Education* or RIE. Searching in these complex databases is simplified by the use of the *Thesaurus of ERIC Descriptors*. These titles are not selection tools, but they act as clearinghouses for all sorts of educational materials, including those in library science. For more information, write: ERIC, Office of Educational Research and Improvement, U. S. Department of Education, 555 New Jersey Ave., NW, Washington, DC 20001. *EDUCATION*

A

624. From Cover to Cover: Evaluating and Reviewing Books for Children. By Kathleen T. Horning. HarperCollins, 1997. 160p. $24.95. 0-06-024519-0.

Written as a beginning guide for anyone who wishes to enter the field of children's book reviewing, this clear and interesting manual gives excellent tips on analyzing literature in various genres (e.g., informational books, beginning readers, folklore, poetry, picture books). Many examples are given, and references are made to important books in the field. An appended source notes section gives a list of all the books and magazines mentioned. Though not specifically a collection-building tool, this work supplies good information on how to find out about children's literature and on key critical guides.

LITERATURE—STUDY AND TEACHING; BOOK REVIEWING

A

625. Guide to American Educational Directories. 7th ed. By Barry T. Klein. Todd Publications, 1993. 350p. $60. 0-915344-29-7.

This spinoff from the author's *Guide to American Directories* contains entries for about 5,000 directories arranged under such broad subjects as art, communications, medical science, and travel. The word "educational" is defined broadly so that peripheral material is also included. Entries include title, name and address of publisher, content notes, and price. There is a title index. Large professional collections might consider this work for purchase. *DIRECTORIES; EDUCATION*

A

626. Library Service to Children: A Guide to the Research, Planning, and Policy Literature. By Phyllis Van Orden. American Library Association, 1992. 160p. $27 pap. 0-8389-0584-6.

Van Orden has pulled together a wealth of information relating to library service to children. Included are "policy literature, historical works, research studies, reports, and conference proceedings." The items date from the early 1900s to the present. Types of materials included are periodical articles, books, governmental and private reports, and theses. Each entry includes complete bibliographic information, a descriptive annotation and notes on funding source, type of literature, and research method. This list should prove useful to library school students, children's librarians doing library planning, and elementary school librarians. *LIBRARY PROGRAMS*

A

627. The Professional Collection for Elementary School Educators. By Patricia Potter Wilson. H. W. Wilson, 1996. 356p. $50. 0-8242-0874-9.

The subtitle on the cover of the book says it all: "A Selection Aid Focusing on Professional Materials for Library Media Specialists and Elementary Teachers." One of the major responsibilities of school library media specialists is the maintenance of a professional collection of materials for the faculty of that school or district. Based on a survey of 1,000 media specialists on professional collection in their elementary schools, Wilson has developed this practical selection aid. The first chapter presents an overview of the status of professional collections and their role in curriculum development. This is followed by an extensive, annotated list of books, journals, nonprint media, and professional organizations. This valuable guide is recommended for all elementary school or districtwide libraries.

EDUCATION

A

628. Resources for Early Childhood: A Handbook. By Hannah Nuba et al. Garland, 1994. 555p. $80. 0-8240-7395-9.

The authors of this work have compiled a series of essays written by authorities on various aspects of early childhood. This work is really an updated and expanded edition of a 1983 work. Some of the same essays appear; however, most of the work has been revised and many new topics are included, such as AIDS, computers, and databases. Each essay is followed by an extensive list of resources that were personally examined and found in the Early Childhood Resources and Information Center of the New York Public Library. Many of the essays also include bibliographies of other sources. The final chapter includes relevant organizations, periodicals, and databases. Author, title, and subject indexes complete this interesting handbook. This handy work is recommended for every elementary school and most public libraries as an aid to parents, teachers, and other professionals working with young children. It should also prove useful to librarians in collection development. *CHILD DEVELOPMENT*

A

629. Resources in Education (RIE) Annual Cumulation. Volume 30. Oryx, 1995. 4 vols. $415 (subscription rate).

RIE indexes educational research findings, speeches, unpublished manuscripts, and books identified by the ERIC (Educational Resources Information Centers) clearinghouses. RIE serves as a companion volume to CIJE, which indexes current periodicals in education and is also under the auspices of ERIC. The annual four-volume sets of RIE cumulations include two volumes of abstracts and a one-volume index. Entries in the abstracts contain author, source, date, price, and similar information and a 200-word description of the contents. The index permits searching of the abstracts by subject, author, or publication type. Back volumes are also available at $415/yr. This valuable index, which identifies thousands of documents that might otherwise go unused, is recommended for school district professional libraries as well as academic and other libraries supporting programs in education. See also entry under ERIC. *EDUCATION*

A

630.　**School Library Media Annual. Volume 13: 1995.** By Betty J. Morris. Libraries Unlimited, 1995. 400p. $45. 1-56308-388-4.

No longer published, this annual volume summarized for school library media specialists developments in the profession. Part 1 consists of articles on topics of current importance in education, curriculum materials, and school library media centers. Part 2 reports on the year's happenings in international and national organizations, government affairs at state and national levels, library education, and awards to people, and has an almanac of general information. The third part is of direct value in collection development because it lists current professional tools and award-winners in media, including software plus tools in children's and young adult literature. This work supplies excellent background information in one handy source. Some back issues are still available. For school libraries at all levels. SLMA is being replaced by a series, under development, of current trends and themes in libraries. The first book in the new series will be on Information Literacy. *SCHOOL LIBRARIES*

A

631.　**Serving the Disabled: A How-to-Do-It Manual for Librarians.** By Kieth C. Wright and Judith F. Davie. Neal-Schuman, 1991. 159p. (How-to-Do-It Manuals for Libraries, 13). $39.95. 0-55570-085-3.

This book is essentially a practical manual on how to accommodate and serve disabled people in the library. It contains many background bibliographies and sources of information that will be helpful to librarians at all levels. *DISABLED*

A

632.　**Sourcebook on Parenting and Child Care.** By Kathryn Hammell Carpenter. Oryx, 1995. 269p. $35 pap. 0-89774-780-1.

About 940 books, journals, and agencies that deal with parenting and child care are listed and annotated in this work. The dates covered by the entries run through 1993. The items are arranged by seven major parenting concerns, such as motherhood, fatherhood, adoptive parents, and homosexual parents. A special section on reference tools lists Internet resources, commercial online networks, videotapes, and discussion groups. In each part of the other sections, popular and professional books are discussed, along with various journals. National agencies are also listed. Asterisks indicate highly recommended resources. This resource will be useful in building professional collections.

PARENTING; CHILD CARE

A

633.　**The Special Education Sourcebook: A Teacher's Guide to Programs, Materials, and Information Sources.** By Michael S. Rosenberg and Irene Edmond-Rosenberg. Woodbine House, 1994. 325p. $21.95 pap. 0-933149-52-2.

Parents, teachers, librarians, and specialists can use this sourcebook of materials on special education. After a section on general works, there are chapters on specific disabilities (e.g., sensory disabilities, autism), early childhood special education, assessment, specific academic skills, and lifelong partnership. Technology in special education has a separate section. Resources include texts, general books, multimedia products, periodicals, agencies, and organizations. Brief annotations are supplied, and, in addition to a list of publishers and producers, there are author, title, and subject indexes. A similar work is *The Complete Directory of People with Learning Disabilities*.

SPECIAL EDUCATION; DISABILITIES

Author-Title Index

Note: Reference is to entry number.

Subject Index

Note: Reference is to entry number.

ADOLESCENCE

Adolescent Pregnancy and Parenthood: An Annotated Guide, 598

Adolescents at Risk: A Guide to Fiction and Nonfiction for Young Adults, Parents, and Professionals, A, 545

Best Years of Their Lives: A Resource Guide for Teenagers in Crisis, 600

Focus on Addictions, 558.1

Focus on Eating Disorders, 558.2

Focus on Fitness, 558.3

Focus on Physical Impairments, 558.4

Focus on Relationships, 558.5

Focus on School, 558.6

Focus on Sexuality, 558.7

Focus on Teens in Trouble: A Reference Handbook, 604

Teenage Perspectives Reference Series, 558

Violent Children: A Reference Handbook, 608

ADOLESCENCE—AFRICAN AMERICAN

Black Adolescence: Current Issues and Annotated Bibliography, 535

ADULT BOOKS AND READING

Booklist, 7

Choice: Current Reviews for Academic Libraries, 15

Kirkus Reviews, 26

Library Journal, 29

New York Times Book Review, The, 34

AEROSPACE SCIENCE

Integrating Aerospace Science into the Curriculum: K–1, 200

AFRICA

Africa in Literature for Children and Young Adults: An Annotated Bibliography of English-Language Books, 215

African Studies Companion: A Resource Guide & Directory, 589

AFRICAN AMERICAN LITERATURE.
See also LITERATURE

Masterpieces of African-American Literature, 437

Schomburg Center Guide to Black Literature: From the Eighteenth Century to the Present, The, 538

Telling Tales: The Pedagogy & Promise of African American Literature for Youth, 168

Young Adult Fiction by African American Writers, 1968–1993, 487

AFRICAN AMERICANS

African American Resource Guide, The, 533

African-American Voices in Young Adult Literature, 534

African American Writers, 425

American Ethnic Literatures: Native American, African American, Chicano/Latino, and Asian American Writers and Their Backgrounds, 525

Black Adolescence: Current Issues and Annotated Bibliography, 535

Black Americans Information Directory: A Guide to Approximately 4,500 Organizations, Agencies, Institutions, Programs, and Publications, 536

Black Experience in Children's Literature— 1994, The, 167

Black History Month Resource Book, 217

Black Literature Criticism: Excerpts from Criticism of the Most Significant Works of Black Authors over the Past 200 Years, 527

Rap Music in the 1980's: A Reference Guide, 400

Voices of the Spirit: Sources for Interpreting the African American Experience, 539

ALPHABET BOOKS

ABC Books and Activities: From Preschool to High School, 301

AMERICAN LITERATURE. See also
LITERATURE

Chelsea House Library of Literary Criticism, 493

Concise Dictionary of American Literary Biography, 427

Facts on File Bibliography of American Fiction Series, 494

GEOGRAPHY
Exploring the United States Through Literature, 220
Great Lakes States, 220.1
Mountain States, 220.2
Northeast States, 220.3
Pacific States, 220.4
Plains States, 220.5
Sources of Information for Historical Research, 593
Southeast States, 220.6
Southwest States, 220.7

GRAPHIC NOVELS. *See also* COMICS
Graphic Novels: A Bibliographic Guide to Book-Length Comics, 479

GREEK LITERATURE. *See also* LITERATURE
Classic Epic: An Annotated Bibliography, The, 474
Classical Greek and Roman Drama: An Annotated Bibliography, 489

GUIDANCE
Educators Guide to Free Films, Filmstrips and Slides, 128.2
Educators Guide to Free Guidance Materials, 128.8
Educators Guide to Free Health, Physical Education and Recreation Materials, 128.11
Educators Guide to Free Home Economics and Consumer Education Materials, 128.9
Educators Guide to Free Materials, 128
Educators Guide to Free Science Materials, 128.7
Educators Guide to Free Social Studies Materials, 128.10
Educators Guide to Free Teaching Aids, 128.5
Educators Guide to Free Videotapes, 128.1
Educators Index of Free Materials, 128.4
Elementary Teachers Guide, 128.3
Guide to Free Computer Materials, 128.6

HANDICRAFTS
Crafts Index for Young People, 233
Crafts Supply Sourcebook: A Comprehensive Shop-by-Mail Guide, The, 234
Fun for Kids II: An Index to Children's Craft Books, 235
Hobbyist Sourcebook, 611
Multicultural Projects Index: Things to Make and Do to Celebrate Festivals, Cultures, and Holidays Around the World, 293

HEALTH
Children's Literature for Health Awareness, 348
Educators Guide to Free Films, Filmstrips and Slides, 128.2
Educators Guide to Free Guidance Materials, 128.8
Educators Guide to Free Health, Physical Education and Recreation Materials, 128.11
Educators Guide to Free Home Economics and Consumer Education Materials, 128.9
Educators Guide to Free Materials, 128
Educators Guide to Free Science Materials, 128.7
Educators Guide to Free Social Studies Materials, 128.10
Educators Guide to Free Teaching Aids, 128.5
Educators Guide to Free Videotapes, 128.1
Educators Index of Free Materials, 128.4
Elementary Teachers Guide, 128.3
Guide to Free Computer Materials, 128.6
Harvard Guide to Women's Health, The, 587

HIGH INTEREST–LOW VOCABULARY BOOKS
Best: High/Low Books for Reluctant Readers, The, 177
Choices: A Core Collection for Young Reluctant Readers, Volume 3, 336
High Interest–Easy Reading: An Annotated Booklist for Middle School and Senior High School, 548
High-Interest Books for Teens: A Guide to Book Reviews and Biographical Sources, 547
High/Low Handbook: Encouraging Literacy in the 1990s, 549
Light 'n Lively Reads for ESL, Adult, and Teen Readers, 551
Quick Picks for Great Reading [year], 553
Rip-Roaring Reads for Reluctant Teen Readers, 555

HISPANIC AMERICANS
American Ethnic Literatures: Native American, African American, Chicano/Latino, and Asian American Writers and Their Backgrounds, 525
Best of the Latino Heritage: A Guide to the Best Juvenile Books About Latino People and Cultures, 169
Culturally Diverse Library Collections for Children, 152
Culturally Diverse Library Collections for Youth, 153
Dictionary of Hispanic Biography, 540
Latino Heritage, Series V: A Guide to Juvenile Books About Latino People and Cultures, A, 171
U.S. Latino Literature: An Essay and Annotated Bibliography, 541

HISTORICAL FICTION
America as Story: Historical Fiction for Secondary Schools, 508
Historical Figures in Fiction, 150

PARENTS, ADOLESCENT
Adolescent Pregnancy and Parenthood: An Annotated Guide, 598

PEACE. *See also* **NUCLEAR WAR, WAR**
Nuclear Age Literature for Youth: The Quest for a Life-Affirming Ethic, 222
War and Peace Literature for Children and Young Adults: A Resource Guide to Significant Issues, 224

PERIODICALS
Children's Magazine Guide, 14
Core List of Books and Journals in Education, 615
El-Hi Textbooks and Serials in Print 1997, 66
Free Magazines for Libraries, 471
Magazines for Children: A Guide for Parents, Teachers, and Librarians, 297
Magazines for Kids and Teens: A Resource for Parents, Teachers, Librarians, and Kids!, 298
Magazines for Young People: A Children's Magazine Guide Companion Volume, 71
Parent's Choice: A Sourcebook of the Very Best Products to Educate, Inform, and Entertain Children of All Ages, 83
Primary Search, 299
U.S. Government Subscriptions, 43

PHONORECORDINGS
All Ears: How to Use and Choose Recorded Music for Children, 264
All-Music Guide: The Best CDs, Albums & Tapes, 403
Mother Goose Comes First: An Annotated Guide to the Best Books and Recordings for Your Preschool Child, 307

PHYSICAL EDUCATION
Educators Guide to Free Films, Filmstrips and Slides, 128.2
Educators Guide to Free Guidance Materials, 128.8
Educators Guide to Free Health, Physical Education and Recreation Materials, 128.11
Educators Guide to Free Home Economics and Consumer Education Materials, 128.9
Educators Guide to Free Materials, 128
Educators Guide to Free Science Materials, 128.7
Educators Guide to Free Social Studies Materials, 128.10
Educators Guide to Free Teaching Aids, 128.5
Educators Guide to Free Videotapes, 128.1
Educators Index of Free Materials, 128.4
Elementary Teachers Guide, 128.3
Guide to Free Computer Materials, 128.6

PHYSICAL HANDICAPS. *See also* **DISABILITIES**
Reader's Guide for Parents of Children with Mental, Physical, or Emotional Disabilities, A, 231
Understanding Abilities, Disabilities, and Capabilities: A Guide to Children's Literature, 232

PICTURE BOOKS
A to Zoo: Subject Access to Children's Picture Books, 300
Adventuring with Books: A Booklist for Pre-K–Grade 6, 237
Art of Children's Picture Books: A Selective Reference Guide, The, 302
Bringing the World Alive, 347
Counting Your Way Through 1-2-3: Books and Activities, 349
450 More Story S-t-r-e-t-c-h-e-r-s for the Primary Grades: Activities to Expand Children's Favorite Books, 306
How to Use Children's Literature to Teach Mathematics, 351
Multicultural Picture Books: Art for Understanding Others, 292
Picture Books for Children, 308
Picture Books for Looking and Learning: Awakening Visual Perceptions Through the Art of Children's Books, 309
Picture Books to Enhance the Curriculum, 310
Play, Learn, and Grow: An Annotated Guide to the Best Books and Materials for Very Young Children, 311
Primaryplots 2: A Book Talk Guide for Use with Readers Ages 4–8, 339
Using Picture Storybooks to Teach Literary Devices: Recommended Books for Children and Young Adults. Vol. 2, 284
Wordless–Almost Wordless Picture Books: A Guide, 315
Worth a Thousand Words: An Annotated Guide to Picture Books for Older Readers, 76

POETRY. *See also* **AMERICAN POETRY, LITERATURE**
Columbia Granger's Index to Poetry, The, 500
Index to Poetry for Children and Young People, 1988–1992, 139
Poetry Criticism, 502

POETS
Contemporary Poets, 431
Speaking for Ourselves: Autobiographical Sketches by Notable Authors of Books for Young Adults, 442

POLLUTION. *See also* **ECOLOGY, CONSERVATION, ENVIRONMENT**
Environmental Sourcebook, The, 584